AT THE SPEED
OF LIFE

By Gay Hendricks

The Centering Book (with Russell Wills)
Learning to Love Yourself
The Learning to Love Yourself Workbook

By Gay Hendricks and Kathlyn Hendricks

Centering and the Art of Intimacy
Conscious Loving
*Radiance! Breathwork, Movement and
  Body-Centered Psychotherapy*

AT THE SPEED OF LIFE

OF LIFE

A NEW APPROACH TO PERSONAL
CHANGE THROUGH
BODY-CENTERED THERAPY

GAY HENDRICKS, PH.D.
KATHLYN HENDRICKS, PH.D.

BANTAM
NEW YORK   TORONTO   LONDON   SYDNEY   AUCKLAND

AT THE SPEED OF LIFE
A Bantam Book / September 1993

Copyright © 1993 by Gay Hendricks and Kathlyn Hendricks.
Book design by Glen M. Edelstein.
Illustrations by Myles Pinkney.

Library of Congress Cataloging-in-Publication Data

Hendricks, Gay.
　At the speed of life : a new approach to personal change through
body-centered therapy / Gay Hendricks, Kathlyn Hendricks.
　　　p.　　cm.
　　ISBN 0-553-07322-2 : $21.95
　　1. Mind and body therapies.　I. Hendricks, Kathlyn.　II. Title.
RC489.M53H46　　1993
158′.1—dc20　　　　　　　　　　　　　　　　　　93-6990
　　　　　　　　　　　　　　　　　　　　　　　　CIP

Published simultaneously in the United States and Canada

Bantam Books are published by Bantam Books, a division of Bantam Doubleday Dell Publishing
Group, Inc. Its trademark, consisting of the words "Bantam Books" and the portrayal of a rooster,
is Registered in U.S. Patent and Trademark Office and in other countries. Marca Registrada.
Bantam Books, 1540 Broadway, New York, New York 10036.

PRINTED IN THE UNITED STATES OF AMERICA

RRH　　0 9 8 7 6 5 4 3 2 1

DEDICATION

We dedicate this work to the memory of William Blake. Two hundred years ago Blake understood and predicted the body-centered revolution that would come to flower in our time.

Thirty years ago the following passage from *The Marriage of Heaven and Hell* mystified us. What on earth could it mean? Now, after decades of resonating with the energies of our own bodies and being with others as they uncovered their own streaming wisdom, we feel the truth of it in our cells.

All Bibles or sacred codes have been the causes of the following Errors:

1. **That Man has two real existing principles Viz: a Body & a Soul.**
2. **That Energy, call'd Evil, is alone from the Body, & that Reason, call'd Good, is alone from the Soul.**
3. **That God will torment Man in Eternity for following his Energies.**

But the following Contraries to these are True:

1. **Man has no Body distinct from his Soul for that call'd Body is a portion of the Soul discern'd by the five Senses, the chief inlets of Soul in this age.**
2. **Energy is the only life and is from the Body, and Reason is the bound or outward circumference of Energy.**
3. **Energy is Eternal Delight.**

We are proud to have our book see the light on the two hundredth anniversary of the appearance of these prophetic words.

CONTENTS

ACKNOWLEDGMENTS

In developing our method of body-centered therapy over the past twenty-five years, we have been privileged to be in conversation with some of the most remarkable human beings on the planet. In traveling in the realm of mind/body healers, we have been deeply moved not only by the qualities of the minds we have encountered but also by the amount of heart. To the hearts and minds of the following people, some now no longer among the living, we owe much gratitude: Mary Whitehouse, Jack Downing, Moshe Feldenkrais, John Pierrakos, Thomas Hanna, Alexander Lowen, Fritz Perls, and Ida Rolf. We owe a particular debt to the written work of Wilhelm Reich, who first pointed us along the mind/body path by sensitizing us to the power of breath and movement.

We would like to thank Dr. Loic Jassy for his invaluable help over the years. A salute also goes to Amy Glovin, Sandra Hill, Haven Thomas, and Helen and Chris Hendricks, for their good works and assistance at dozens of trainings. To the several hundred graduates of our professional training programs, our gratitude is absolute. We can only say that we could not have developed our method without your participation and feedback.

We are extremely grateful to the executive director of our institute,

Kathy Allen, for the loving light she brings to our lives each day. As authors we are blessed with the guidance of Sandy Dijkstra, agent and miracle worker, and Toni Burbank, whose gifted editorial vision makes writing books a pure pleasure.

We are grateful beyond words to the loving support of our family. To our parents—Polly and Bob Swift and Norma Hendricks—and to our children—Chris and Amanda—we owe deep appreciation for the love and space you have given us throughout our lives. To have a happy family and to be doing the work that we love is life at its best, and we are grateful for it every day.

A REVOLUTION IN HEALING

Human beings are losing their feelings. I know at first hand that people today cannot tell where in their bodies they experience the core emotions of human existence. The body awareness of feeling—the feeling of emotion—is missing. And in the absence of this skill a host of ills comes into being.

For over twenty years Gay and Kathlyn Hendricks have been helping human beings to feel, and to feel better. They are so gifted at this process that they are widely known as the therapists' therapists. Now they have written a wonderful book—an essential book—about their approach to healing. I consider *At the Speed of Life* a turning point in the profession: It lays the foundation for where I believe psychotherapy needs to go in the twenty-first century. It represents the first leap forward in therapy in many, many years.

There is no question that such a leap forward is deeply needed. As a neurologist specializing in headache and pain, I am witness to the suffering that occurs when people lose their feelings. Week in and week out, patients come to me with bewildering and frightening sensations in their bodies. To discover how to help them, I must ask them not only about the pain but about the other sensations that precede and surround the pain. People find this process very difficult. Many have so lost touch with their bodies that pain is the only sensation they recognize.

My patients are afraid they have a tumor or multiple sclerosis. They are frustrated with how little their medications have helped, or with side effects or risks of addiction. They are saddened by the loss of life's satisfaction. But they speak of these emotions vaguely, with suspicion and outright distaste. They suspect that I will tell them that these emotions are only in their minds. They have become so alienated from themselves that they do not consider their feelings real or valid.

Fortunately, feelings can be rediscovered. When they are, human beings get healthier, both mentally and physically. The great value of Gay and Kathlyn's book is that they show us exactly how to do this. With boundless care and encouragement, they walk us step by step through the process of becoming reacquainted with our bodies. They have invented a new term, *presencing,* to make the old but forgotten act of feeling new for us again.

WHY HAVE WE LOST TOUCH WITH OUR BODIES?

To understand the importance of this book requires an understanding of the importance of feelings in the history of healing. In modern times many forces—social, cultural, even scientific—have shifted our attention away from the feelings that live in our bodies. Science has typically examined only those things that are objective, publicly observable, measurable, and quantifiable. Thoughts, feelings, and sensations have been relegated to the backseat because they are subjective and hard to measure. In fact, many scientists today would say that feelings do not exist.

In psychology, feelings have been particularly ignored. While one would think that psychology would be the study of thoughts and feelings, the field abandoned these subjects in the late nineteenth century. For more than half a century only behavior—that which could be observed and measured— was the major focus of psychology. In the latter part of the twentieth century, cognitive theories and therapies reappeared and are attempting to restore thinking to its rightful place in psychology.

Even psychologists who study emotions have ignored the feeling component—how human beings experience those emotions in their bodies. A major split occurred in the mid-1920s when the famous Harvard physiologist Walter Cannon rejected the James-Lange theory of emotions, described in all basic psychology texts. The James-Lange theory held that sensations from our muscles and our viscera (internal organs) are the source of our emotions. Cannon rejected this view and sought to confirm his view with a famous experiment. He injected adrenaline into the veins of a number of Harvard undergraduates and asked them if they felt anything. The students described various sensations but did not mention any specific emotions like fear or anger. According to Cannon, this proved that body sensations are not the source of emotions. He invented the famous phrase *fight or flight* to mean that the body experiences only a general arousal that is the same whether we are fighting or fleeing. Modern theorists have largely sided with Cannon, ignoring the feeling component of emotion in favor of a focus on behavior and cognitions.

There are exceptions, of course. In the 1960s the humanistic psychology revolution of Carl Rogers, Fritz Perls, Abraham Maslow, and others popularized the notions of getting in touch with and expressing feelings. The purpose of therapy, they thought, was to free people from their social taboos so that authentic underlying feelings could emerge. These theorists also clarified a key distinction between feeling and thinking. They would point out that saying "I feel that . . ." is often equivalent to saying "I think that. . . ." An important therapeutic maneuver became to shift the client's focus from beliefs to feelings. If people said that their bosses were unfair, for example, the therapist would ask clients to focus on how that unfairness made them feel. These therapists were inclined in the right direction but were guilty of a major oversight. They thought that their clients knew how they felt but were simply too socially conditioned to acknowledge those feelings. They assumed that their clients needed only support and encouragement to express their feelings. This assumes too much: You cannot express a feeling if you do not know you are having it.

We physicians have contributed to the problem in a myriad of ways. Our general tendency is to look for a disease to explain every dysfunction. We look for infection, tumor, or inherited chemical abnormality. If we cannot find one of these, we all too often dismiss it as a nervous condition or blame it on that current catch-all, stress. To the extent that feelings are acknowledged at all, they are often considered *symptoms* of a disease. Thus, feeling depressed becomes a symptom of a disease caused by inherited abnormalities of brain chemistry. When patients come in with symptoms of tachycardia, sweating and tremor, we order extensive tests looking for hormone or metabolic disease. We run EKGs and treadmill tests looking for heart disease. If all these tests are negative, we raise the possibility that the person is suffering from the anxiety disease. The physician is most unlikely to consider that the patient's symptom is actually a feeling. It usually does not occur to us to inquire about the circumstances—such as giving a speech—that trigger the feelings.

While psychology and medicine have been ignoring feelings, society has done so as well. Feelings represent our animal side, to be opposed and resisted by reason. As a result, we do not teach our children much of value about feelings. In fact, the only feelings that are formally taught are bladder pressure and urge to defecate. Every child is carefully taught to recognize the sensation of a full bladder and what to do about it. We call it toilet training, but this is a misnomer: No child has difficulty knowing where the toilet is or what it is for. The problem is teaching them when to use it. The key to successful toilet training is teaching the child to recognize an internal sensation. Unfortunately we do not teach our children how to feel and deal with any of the other crucial human feelings. In fact, we often teach them the opposite.

HOW DO WE GET OUR FEELINGS BACK?

Until recently there have been no systematic methods of therapy that specifically train us to regain our feelings, to learn again how to pay attention to visceral sensations. At our clinic in La Jolla we have worked with more than five thousand headache and pain patients over the past ten years. The backbone of our treatment procedures is to teach these patients how to feel again. As they learn to discriminate feelings such as anger and fear, they are able to reawaken to lives without drugs and without pain. Our staff, along with graduate students at University of California at San Diego, is also engaged in a line of research that is mapping out scientifically the unfamiliar world of feelings. Our intention is to place feelings squarely in the center of mainstream medicine.

Gay and Kathlyn Hendricks are pioneers in this new territory. At their institute in Colorado Springs they are quietly doing some of the most innovative work in the field of psychology. Their two central interests are the realms of close relationships and body-centered psychotherapy. They have gained the reputation of being on the leading edge of both fields. Now they have trained enough professionals that their work is entering the mainstream. This news could not be better for all of us. At the Speed of Life is the first book to describe in detail how to employ the body and its feelings as a path of healing and a means of psychospiritual growth. Gay and Kathlyn make it fun, too. That is their special gift.

David R. Hubbard, Jr., M.D.,
Medical Director, Neurologic Centre for Headache and Pain,
and Assistant Clinical Professor of Neurology,
University of California, San Diego

PART I

BODY-CENTERED THERAPY

AT THE SPEED OF LIFE: BODY-CENTERED THERAPY AS A PATH OF AWAKENING

Mr. Dufy lived a short distance from his body.
—James Joyce

This is a book about a form of healing that is also a way of life. We feel so deeply privileged to be sharing it with you that the operator of the keyboard is feeling a sweet ache in the chest at the moment these lines are being written. The ideas and processes we will explore in this book have made such a profound difference in our own lives that if we did not communicate them, we would consider our lives to have stopped short of full expression. We offer them to two main audiences: therapists on the leading edge of their profession, and growth-oriented lay persons who want powerful tools for healing in their own hands. We have done our best to describe the philosophy and the techniques in sufficient detail to allow both the lay reader and the professional to put them to work immediately.

The book appears at a time of unprecedented disenchantment with therapy. Across our desks recently have come magazines with headlines like "Is Therapy Turning Us Into Children?" and "Does Therapy Really Work?" Some of the criticisms of therapy that they make are easy to dismiss, particularly those in the popular media that attempt to shame or belittle people who are doing therapy, inner child work, men's movement activities, and other growth techniques. The cynical tone of many of these critics belies their psychological immaturity: They simply have not done enough work on themselves to be taken seriously.

But there is another stream of criticism that warrants thoughtful consideration. Some of these critics are participant-observers in the field—writers and therapists who have done a great deal of work on themselves. They must be heeded when they cite statistics that therapy is hardly better as a healer than time itself. They remind us that no inquiry on the inner plane is useful unless it translates to improved action, even social action, in the outer world. They point to clients who become articulate at spouting the favored jargon of their therapies without any discernible change in their happiness or productivity. These criticisms are all valid, perceptive, and helpful. They force those of us in the field to ask ourselves powerful questions. We have asked ourselves those questions, and the answers have inspired us to develop a new approach to growth and change; the body-centered approach we describe in this book.

The most relevant critics, the ones to whom we must pay the most careful attention, are the clients we see every day in our practices. In fact, we have learned more from our own clients about the flaws of therapy and how to correct them than we have from professionals in the field. In our first session we always ask people what their past experiences have been in therapy, and why they are interested in our body-centered approach. Since our approach and the body-centered tradition from which it comes are relatively new, almost all our clients come to us after trying traditional verbal therapies as well as newer approaches such as Neuro-Linguistic Programming (NLP) and hypnotherapy. We are interested in finding out why they are no longer choosing those paths of growth. Here is the criticism that almost all of them mention: Talk therapy gave them insight and understanding but did not lead to any immediate or noticeable changes in their daily lives. In the words of one of our new clients, "It took a long time, and nothing much happened." We have heard this complaint hundreds of times, and we feel that it represents a genuine problem. Body-centered therapy offers a genuine solution.

The skilled practitioner of body-centered therapy will rarely hear anybody complain that it takes too long. The great advantage of body-centered therapy is that it goes immediately to where people live: the reality of their somatic experience. People feel actual shifts in their inner experience as the work proceeds from moment to moment. And it works with a speed that is often astonishing. In fact, people sometimes tell us that the changes were so immediate that they were hard to keep up with. Why this approach works so quickly will become clear as we lay out its strategies.

Another important criticism our clients mention is that therapy promotes a one-up, one-down power imbalance between the client and therapist. If we as healers place ourselves above our clients in any way, this inequality will come back to haunt us. There is something very seductive about the power of being a therapist. It feels good to be so highly regarded, in charge of such powerful magic. The fact that people are often hurting when they come in makes them ripe for becoming overly dependent on the therapist. But woe to the therapist who steps into the trap of accepting too much responsibility for his or her client's well-being. This is the era of mushrooming malpractice litigation, all of which is based on perceived abuse of clients by the professionals in whom they have placed their trust.

Our approach to body-centered therapy addresses the power problem in two radical ways. First, we place the technology of healing directly into our clients' hands. We teach them the nine strategies presented in this book and expect them to practice them on their own. The therapist is as much teacher as healer. Giving away the means of healing lessens the possibility that clients will become addicted to the therapist as the source of it. Second, we carefully discuss the issue of responsibility from the first session. Specifically, we teach that each of us can claim one hundred percent responsibility for everything that happens to us. We expect our clients to demonstrate mastery of this principle by overcoming their tendency toward victimhood in every area of their lives.

Another common question about therapy is whether it is even necessary. Some people find that some problems eventually go away by themselves, much as even untreated wounds often heal over time. It is true that many of the most troublesome problems can eventually clear up simply through the process of living. All the techniques we present in this book are things people may eventually get around to doing by themselves. Body-centered therapy takes these fundamental life-processes and focuses them consciously and intensively, speeding up the process of healing. For example, you may eventually figure out on your own how to breathe through your fear of flying, but it may take you quite a while to do it. A body-centered therapist can help you condense the natural process of healing. One of our clients avoided flying until she was fifty-seven, then was able to get on an airplane after only one session of intensive work. In talking with her, it became clear that for years, life itself had been attempting to get her to sit down, focus on the problem, and learn to handle it. But she had avoided doing that simple thing: Her resistance had kept her from moving at the speed of life. Finally, she presented the issue, breathed through it, and got up to speed. Then she could fly.

THE CENTRAL PROBLEM

Body-centered therapy works because it solves a fundamental problem of living. In describing this central problem, keep in mind that our perspective is close-up, clinical, and practical, not purely philosophical. We have worked personally with about twenty thousand individuals and approximately fifteen hundred couples as they have wrestled with this problem. We have spent the better part of our own lives clearing up our own difficulties that relate to the problem. The central problem is this: Early in life human beings develop a split between feeling and thinking, which can also be thought of as a split between body and mind. Messages from the body (such as what we are feeling and what we want) become ignored or denied by the mind. There are powerful reasons why we mentally tune out these body messages: for approval, for control, and even for survival. But ignoring or denying messages from the body does not make them go away; it simply makes them come out crooked. They are expressed through too-tightly held parts of the body, through pain, through distortions in the breathing mechanism, through gestures and other movements, as well as through the more commonly acknowledged vehicles of dream, fantasy, and communication patterns. They are expressed most painfully in actions that do not work and that bring more pain to ourselves and to others. Relationships suffer, becoming entanglements of lost souls wearing masks rather than dances of whole beings celebrating each other.

A clinical story may help illustrate the problem. We worked intensively with a young woman whom we will call Jenny, age twenty-four. Jenny suffered from severe headaches. She had been to a range of healing professionals, from neurologists to chiropractors, but her headaches continued. In exploring this issue with her, it became clear that she was a living example of what we are calling the central problem. Her father and mother had suffered through a painful divorce when Jenny was in kindergarten, and the father left for a different part of the country. She had missed him deeply, but she found that if she expressed this feeling, her mother would get very upset. Her mother was angry at him, and any mention of his name, particularly in a benign or tender way, would send her into a rage. So Jenny hid her sadness and longing. The act of hiding these tender feelings put her mind and body at odds with each other. The body said, "Here's what I'm feeling," while her mind said, "Better not." If Jenny had been blessed with a guardian angel, the angel would have counseled her, "It's okay to feel it and express it—but not around your mother."

The stress of hiding her feelings made Jenny's body hurt. Her headaches began, and they continued off and on until she was twenty-four. In addition to causing headaches, the fundamental split deep inside her affected the quality of her relationships. She tended to seek out men who were unavailable, then got angry at them when they were not there for her. She was replaying her relationship with her father but using her mother's anger as her response to her loneliness. Her authentic feelings of longing were buried under anger that was not even really her own.

What finally freed her from her headaches was the courageous act of reconnecting with her somatic experience, the body-sense of her feelings, in therapy. Over several months, she learned to notice what she was feeling just before a headache began. At first, she usually noticed it was anger. Later she found that the anger was usually preceded by a feeling of sadness or longing. She had no idea how to express this deeper feeling, but she did have a lot of practice (and a lot of modeling by her mother) on how to be angry. Part of her work involved learning how to express anger cleanly, in a way that took responsibility for it and did not blame anyone. What eventually ended her headaches was learning to contact the longing in her body, to feel it and love it. As she did this, she reestablished contact with her father. She began to relate to him as herself rather than through the filter of her mother's feelings about him. Her relationships with men became more satisfying because she was no longer trying to connect with them as father figures. After a detour through a torturous path of pain, she had found the straight road again.

Unless splits like Jenny's are healed, they result in the fundamental loss of contact with being—what in this book we call *essence*. Essence is the part of us that makes us truly us. It is the body-space in which our "I" resides. Take it away, and we don't know who we are. Fail to contact essence, and nothing satisfies us. Human beings must be in moment-by-moment contact with the body-sense of essence to feel satisfied. If we lose touch with essence—our authentic somatic experience of ourselves—we are likely to seek to restore our wholeness by a host of methods that absolutely do not work. There is no substitute for the body-sense of essence, although people have gone to ends of the earth attempting to find them.

One tragic path that has been trod by millions is the use of substances: food, drink, and drugs. In one way or another, all addictions and eating disorders are toxic attempts to produce a good feeling in our bodies—the restoration of essence—through artificial means. Essence is the open, spacious feeling in your body in which all the other phenomena rest. When you are in touch with essence, you can feel unpleasant sensations such as fatigue, fear, or toothache—*and still feel good*. Essence is bigger than these other phenomena, and one can feel the distinction between essence and everything else as one's contact with essence grows. This paradox—feeling good even when you feel bad—is a hallmark of essence.

A second dead-end path is the pursuit of things, the attempt to connect with essence by acquiring symbols of it. A survey of people who were entering a megamall found that almost none of them had any idea of what they wanted to buy there. In other words, they were engaged in the process of consuming, with no specific object in mind! The advertising industry knows this territory very well and has sophisticated ways of making use of it.

As relationship therapists, we have become very familiar with a third futile path to the restoration of essence: the attempt to find oneself through close relationships. A healthy relationship is one in which each partner celebrates essence in the self and in the other. But such relationships are rare. Instead, we find that many people use relationships like alcohol: The relationship dulls them and takes them farther away from themselves, rather than helping them engage in a mutual awakening of creativity. Couples do this in many ways: They ignore their own feelings and needs so that they can please the other. They put aside their own creative powers in favor of supporting the other. They put their energies into power struggles and attempts to control the other, sacrificing their own relationship with themselves. Their embroilment in relationship or family dramas gradually takes them away from an authentic sense of who they are.

On CNN awhile back, we saw a group of Madonna imitators, young women standing outside a Madonna concert waiting to go in. They were all dressed alike, in the style of their heroine, complete with bleached hair, garish makeup, and lacy undergarments. The perceptive interviewer asked one girl whether her Madonna imitation was keeping her from finding out who she really was: "Shouldn't this be a time in your life where you are discovering your own unique contribution to the world?" The young lady shook her head with irritation. "Look, you don't seem to be getting it," she said. "I actually *am* Madonna. That's who I really am." This example is extreme, perhaps, but it reminds us that any of us can fall prey to the acts we adopt and then forget that they are simply acts.

At the most practical level, the central problem is that human beings are losing their ability to know their authentic somatic experience and how to tell the truth about it. Verbal therapy can actually make the central problem worse. Jenny had tried talking about her problems, but her headaches did not go away. In fact, they got worse. She was trapped in the world of concepts, out of touch with the sensations in her body. She found that her conversations with her therapist, whom she experienced as an empathic and caring person, kept her at the level of concepts and did not reconnect her with her body. What made the pain go away was learning to be with her body feelings in a new way.

THE SOLUTION

Body-centered therapy offers a powerful and direct solution to the central problem. By working skillfully with movement, breathing, and tension patterns, the body-centered therapist assists clients in healing the mind/body split. The immediate reward is a greater feeling of aliveness and well-being in the body. A perceptible feeling of oneness replaces the uncomfortable fragmentation. This sense of unity comes from a somatic source and so is experienced most pleasurably in the body. From the therapist's point of view, there is no need to ask whether the process is working: He or she can see it on the client's face.

It is important to help clients walk out of each session feeling better than when they came in, but that is only the initial advantage of a body-centered approach. As body-centered therapy works, most people experience a renewed relationship with creativity. As a child, Gay had a small stream running through his side yard. He would sometimes dam it up with rocks and watch how the stream would try to solve the problem. Sometimes the stream would disappear into the ground; at other times it would reroute itself in a roundabout way. So it is with creativity. If our basic contact with essence is dammed up, our creativity often goes underground or is misdirected, even squandered, through other activities. When the flow is restored, our creativity comes back. We have watched with awe as clients rediscovered their creativity in later life after decades of blockage.

THE BODY-CENTERED APPROACH IN BRIEF

Early in life most of us lose touch with *essence*—the part of us that is pure being, the clear space in which all of our thoughts and feelings rest— because *something happens* that triggers *overwhelming feelings* in us. The "something that happens" is often a loss or an intolerable bind that results in fear, grief, or anger. To deal with these feelings we put on one or more *personas* (from the Latin *persona*, meaning "mask"). The purpose of any persona is twofold: to gain recognition from those around us, and to protect us from the pain of our overwhelming feelings. Through the filters of our personas, we see the world differently. Instead of seeing things as they actually are, we see our *projections*. Now, here is where a body-centered approach becomes crucial: These personas are false selves, and they call forth the false selves of others. Our personas mask essence, causing a fundamental split in ourselves. *When this split is in force, it shows up in the breathing pattern, in body language, in physical symptoms, in psychological disturbance, and in distortions in our relationships with others.* The therapist who can read the language of the body and the breath is in a unique position to help people rapidly and effectively recover their birthright; a deeply felt connection with essence.

Any deep form of therapy is really a study of relationship. Certainly the relationship between therapist and client is paramount—nothing can happen without it. But when people succeed in therapy, it is because of a shift in the quality of their relationship within themselves. A headache disappears when its bearer stops fighting the pain and starts listening to the pain's message. A fear dissolves when the scared person embraces it rather than denying its existence. In both cases we see a new face of pain. The headache may originally have sprung from the person's pretending that she was not angry, and her anger may likely persist as long as she keeps pretending it is not there. As soon as her relationship within herself shifts, to embrace life the way it is rather than cling to how she would like it to be, her pain and troublesome emotions begin to transform.

What then is the essence of good relationship and good therapy? In a word, the secret is *attention*. The feelings inside must be heard, and must not be told to shut up. The meaning of a tense neck must be received, not ignored or denied. The shy inner self must be drawn out by paying careful attention. This inner self has been regarded as the Other for so long that most of us are no longer in friendly contact with it. For some of us, the inner self takes on the persona of a rebellious two-year-old, causing havoc and demanding attention in the form of pain. For others, the inner self retreats in sullen silence, sentencing us to a numbness and a void inside where there should be celebration.

Early in life we abandon the world of how we feel inside for the largely visual world of how we appear from outside. The gap that opens may have pernicious consequences and may result in profound relief when healed. One of our clients, in a burst of poetic language that sent chills up our spines, calls this gap "the primordial pain of duality." He had split himself in two as a child—caught in the conflict between how he really was and how he had to appear in order to succeed in his family—and he still felt the pain of this split in his body decades later.

THE RESEARCH METHOD

The research method by which we derived the principles presented in the book is twofold. First, we took notes on several thousand body-centered therapy sessions that had yielded positive results. We looked for the common elements that seemed to be connected to breakthroughs on the part of our clients. Second, we did something that may sound tedious but that actually is endlessly fascinating: We watched hundreds of hours of videotaped sessions, looking for the tiny moments that resulted in the relief of symptoms or an increase in aliveness. Then we spent about three years sifting, sorting, and boiling off the inessentials. What is left is what we feel to be the absolute essentials. Most of the data were collected from sessions in which we were the therapists. In addition, however, we drew upon sessions conducted by our students and supervisees. We have been privileged to train and supervise approximately five hundred therapists over the past twenty years, so we have been afforded a rich opportunity to observe therapy not only from the driver's seat but from the backseat as well.

THE LIMITS AND THE POTENTIAL
OF BODY-CENTERED THERAPY

Not all difficulties will resolve themselves through the principles and techniques we offer. Some ills can be traced to the absorption of a specific microbe, and some problems are passed through the gene structure, only to show up in the hapless third or fourth generation. These problems are the province of traditional allopathic medicine. The approach described in this book will not cure malaria or a depression due to biochemical imbalance.

But more often than not, the fields of traditional medicine and psychology overlap. This is an era when the profound linkage of mind and body is being rediscovered. In the history of healing, only recently have mind and body been thought of as separate. The upsurge in power of allopathic medicine in the late nineteenth and early twentieth centuries caused a split to develop in the field. Allopathic medicine made so many miraculous leaps forward—defeating such scourges as polio, tuberculosis, and smallpox—that it seemed only a matter of time before it would bring all of humankind's ills under control. Of course, it did not. What happened instead was that the mind and the emotions were restored to their powerful place in medicine. Every week seems to bring across our desks more reports of how even the most subtle body systems respond to changes in attitudes and emotions.

Consider this example: A woman came in for a first appointment with us. She is one of the beautiful people, a star. She said, "People keep telling me I've got to get in touch with my feelings, but I don't see why. I've gotten by just fine for thirty years without messing around with my feelings." Then, we asked, why are you here? "Oh," she said, suddenly glazing over, "I've got this incapacitating tightness across my chest. My chest hurts so much, I thought something was wrong with my heart. The cardiologist says nothing is wrong with it, though he did say my diaphragm was the tightest he'd ever seen." Through careful and courageous inquiry on her part, she soon learned that the tightness was the wall she had constructed against her feelings. Her grief over incidents in her life was so great that she had shut it out with tension. Tension had become her focus, diverting her attention away from the real issue. Now as she headed into her thirties, her facade, built up to wall off a lifetime of hidden feeling, was beginning to crumble. Her body was finally having its say, using the unsubtle language of tension and pain to communicate with the stubborn, proud conscious mind. When she listened to what it had to say, the new relationship was celebrated by renewal of health. As she succeeded in embracing her feelings again, her average heart rate dropped by ten beats a minute.

Based on the direct experience of several decades of work with people, we feel that an important healing message of our time is this: Be present to the truth within yourself, and problems disappear. See the truth the way it is, say the truth the way it is, and life gains a remarkable integrity. Withdraw your attention from the truth, swallow the expression of it, and a parade of pains, heartaches, and lost opportunities will march through your living room. We are not saying it is easy. In one sense it is simple, but to develop an intimate relationship with the truth in ourselves is the most radical thing we know of. The payoff is priceless, but earning it requires a leap of consciousness the likes of which we seldom encounter in life.

Martin, a fifty-year-old stockbroker, came for his first appointment with us with two major complaints. He had felt burdened by a sluggish, depressed mood for the previous few months, and with this mood had come occasional pain between the shoulder blades. His medical doctor could find nothing organically wrong and had written him prescriptions for a muscle-relaxing tranquilizer, Valium, and an antidepressant, Prozac. Martin took them for a few days but did not like the way they made him feel. His wife, a health-conscious aerobics instructor, gave him a hard time about taking pills for what she thought was a psychological problem. He came for his first session voluntarily but with the skepticism frequently encountered in those who are not accustomed to approaching their body problems through psychological work.

If a therapist sensitively observes them, the first few moments of contact with a client usually reveal much of the information that is necessary to understand and treat a problem. With Martin, we noticed several key elements of his makeup within the first minute. First, he was somewhat apologetic in his manner, saying that he appreciated our taking the time to see him. This could be contrasted with a diametrically opposite type of patient, the one who opens with a hostile comment ("So you're a shrink, huh?") or expresses an attitude of "Okay, pal, let's see what you can do for me" toward treatment and therapist. Was Martin apologetic in all areas of his life, even toward his feelings? What was the cost of this apologetic facade? These questions were in the backs of our minds as we pressed on. His tone of voice was quiet, his overall appearance unassuming. His every gesture broadcast a message of modesty, restraint, and blandness. But then there was the matter of his left jaw. Within moments after meeting Martin, our attention was drawn to the asymmetry of his jaws. The right side was quite normal, but on the left side was a major distortion of his modest persona. The jaw muscles bulged with tension, as if he were holding a wad of bubble gum in his cheek. We think of such things as "feeling leaks," places where unexpressed emotion bursts through from the unconscious. Modest guys are not supposed to have bulging jaw muscles, especially on only one side. If you took an isolated picture of just that area, cropping out the rest of his persona, it would look like rage being portrayed by a not-very-subtle character actor.

The actor analogy is a particularly valuable one to keep in mind. We are all actors, having learned our act in order to survive and to get recognition (even if only negative recognition) in the sometimes brutal and always challenging play of life. Fortunately for us and for the world, our acts are benign in the main. Without question, though, our acts always mask our realness beneath. And for all of us at times, our acts bring us pain. In some cases, our acts harm others as well as ourselves. Then we have to remove ourselves from the stage, or else be removed by the justice mechanisms of society.

The challenge for the therapist is this: The people in pain do not know that they are playing an act. They do not *have* an act; they have *become* their act. No separation remains between person and persona. There is no essence beneath the mask, no realness. The problem for the therapist is to help the client open up to essence—the space in which all our acts are held but not taken seriously—often after much of a lifetime has gone by, during which the client has confused his act with who he or she actually is.

Martin woke up in time. His act was running out, as it nearly always does in midlife, if not before. At midlife the forces of realness are gaining; it becomes quite obvious that the messages of the body must be heeded. As Martin apologetically described his sluggishness and back pain to us, he quite unconsciously rubbed his lumpy left jaw. We didn't stop to ask him why he was stroking his jaw. Our first task is to help a client—asking *why* is for later. We interrupted him in midrub and asked him to do it more.

We said: "The way you're touching your jaw, Martin—just let yourself make that gesture a little bigger." This was our first therapeutic move to heal his mind/body split. Asking a person to bring consciousness to bear on an unconscious action changes the whole pattern. There are several ways to do this seemingly small thing, but asking the person to magnify the action is one of the best. It is a bold thing to do, for client and therapist alike. There is no other place in society where one can have this experience but the therapist's office. In ordinary life, Mom may say "Martin, quit rubbing your jaw!" but where else but therapy can one focus attention on a symptom like jaw-rubbing in a nonjudgmental spirit of genuine inquiry?

How a person reacts to this moment is powerfully revealing. Would Martin try to hide his hand, as if he had been caught doing something wrong? Would he deny that his jaw had anything to do with anything? In fact, what Martin did was apologize: "Oh, I'm sorry," he said. "I didn't realize I was doing that." Now it was time for our second major therapeutic move: "That manner of apologizing, Martin—tune in to the feeling under that," we said. This offered Martin his second opportunity within seconds to bridge the mind/body gap. As you can see, this gambit was very similar to the first one, in which we brought consciousness to his jaw-rubbing. Here, though, the focus was broader. An entire way of being was brought under scrutiny.

Such moments have an electric quality to them. Sometimes people explode in rage at being seen in this way. The thing they thought they were hiding turns out to be visible in neon. In Martin's case it worked—or rather, Martin was courageous enough to take the opportunity to bridge his mind/body gap. Suddenly he burst into tears. As he sobbed, he even apologized for the tears. We wondered to whom he had felt apologetic in his early life. Some tone in his voice made it sound to us as if he were apologizing to his father. We took a guess: "It sounds like you might be apologizing to your father, Martin." His crying intensified. "I always had to apologize to my father," he said.

Our third request: "Recall the first time you can remember doing that." He recalled an event that had a great deal of significance to him. He was standing at his father's bedside, where the father lay wasting away with cancer. Martin tried to conceal his sadness, but his nine-year-old body would not let him. His act, his mask, was not yet in place. He broke into tears. His father asked him not to cry, then got angry when the tears could not be brought under control. Finally Martin reined in his grief with a series of thoughts: "How can I feel this way? It's Daddy that's hurting, not me. I need to show I'm strong so he won't hurt. Maybe if I'm strong enough he won't die. If I hide my feelings well enough, he'll be happy. Maybe if I hide who I am, my father will live."

Here we are viewing the birth of a mask. Little Martin thinks: "I have no right to feel how I feel. Excuse me for being. My realness has no place in this world." From now on he must consider every inner experience through that filter. His authentic experience must be shifted and sorted before it's presented to the world. The split second it takes him to do all this cogitation is enough to remove him from the present. His body and its feelings are left behind; his mind is now in charge. He has found a way to live split in two, and he will get away with it for forty years. His aliveness has been reduced, but at least he will survive.

In therapy, Martin was able to build a bridge back to his body, using techniques we will describe later. He did it fairly quickly, too. Within six sessions his sluggish depression lightened and his back pain disappeared. Life felt good to him again.

We began with Martin's simple example because it illustrates the possibilities succinctly. Don't think for a moment, though, that body-centered therapy is always so easy. It happened to work quickly in Martin's case because everything went right: The client was willing (the fundamental requirement), and a host of other variables fell into place without a hitch. Usually, however, there is some complication—more often a dozen of them—that keeps the work from unfolding in such textbook fashion. In time we will explore those complications, but for now let's move on to a thorough understanding of the fine-grained detail of the problem.

THE FLIGHT FROM EXPERIENCE

Simply being present with *what is* has so much power that we often do not give ourselves more than a split second of it. Here are some of the major ways human beings avoid becoming present to what is:

- SOMATICIZING. We generate a body pain or problem to take our attention (and others' attention) from our feelings.
- FAULTY ATTRIBUTION. We blame something Out There for something that is actually In Here. We attribute our headache to our boss's tirade rather than see that we are tensing our neck muscles in response to the tirade.

- EXPLANATION. Some people get caught up in lengthy explanations for their feelings. Whether or not the explanations are helpful or accurate—and often they are not—they serve to take attention away from the actual experience of the feeling. After twenty-plus years as therapists we have coined a slogan that fits the typical finding—"You are never upset for the reason you think you are."

- JUSTIFICATION. Instead of simply being present with the sensations of anger, some people often become righteous about their anger, thinking that it is the correct response to life. They often try to justify their point of view instead of simply noting that their shoulders are tight and they feel angry. Justifying is a defense against finding out what our feelings are actually about. If we can be righteous about them, we do not have to look any deeper into ourselves.

- CONCEPTS. Any conceptual thought can remove us from the immediacy of our feelings. The person who is lonely may escape from that loneliness by picturing the various contents of a refrigerator. Concepts are symbolic pictures of things or ideas about them. Directing attention to a feeling, such as the tight-throated sensation of sadness, gets beneath the concept level and deals with something that is not symbolic in the least.

- SOAP OPERA. Many of us create recycling dramas in our lives that are as predictable as the buttons on a jukebox. Punch B-13, and out comes Wronged Victim; C-12 dials up Concerned Rescuer. These acts are ways to avoid discovering the authentic feelings that lie buried beneath the act. In other words, if we stay in the repetitive drama—which usually involves making ourselves right and somebody else wrong—we never get to find out what is real underneath.

- LOGIC. Reason is wonderful and has its rightful place in life, but superreasonableness can be a formidable barrier to being with feelings. Instead of simply feeling them, we stop to figure it all out.

- JUDGMENTALNESS. Many of us approach every moment with a question: Is this the right experience, the one I'm supposed to be having? Many of us get so judgmental about our own feelings and the feelings of others that we don't give ourselves any room to be with them.

To illustrate how these flights from experience work, here is more detail on the story of Gay's early life:

"Anger was the big unacceptable feeling in my household growing up. Of course, I did not see it that way at the time; it was only after a lot of work on myself that I had any accurate view at all of what was going on around me as a child. When anger would arise, different people had their strategies for dealing with it. My mother would light a cigarette, while my brother might go to sleep. I ate. By the time I was in the eighth grade, I weighed close to three hundred pounds. I used large doses of ice cream, chips, and cola to silence the anguish of my stunted inner life. This is somaticizing, the turning of an emotional problem into a body problem. The body problem then takes precedence, keeping the attention away from the painful underlying issue. Soon I had somaticized so successfully I had no inkling I was so angry, but I knew I was fat. It was on my mind every waking moment, and on my family's mind, too. By focusing on my fat, my family also got to avoid the seething emotional turmoil beneath the icy glaze on the surface.

"I wanted to deal with concepts, explanation, justification, and logic all in one swoop, since they all represented ways my mind dealt with the problem of my emotions. When the pain of feelings is too great, where else can we go but up into the mind? The cool world of concepts gives us some relief, a place to hide while the body carries out its program of destruction or, if we're lucky, regeneration. I took my refuge in knowing. I would know it all, or if not I would pretend to know it. I took on an air of supercilious disdain for the world, a quality that would be laughable in an eighth grader if it were not so obnoxious. I also somaticized in my eyes; I wore big, thick Buddy Holly glasses to correct my 20/400 vision. I know I was somaticizing because later, when I embraced my feelings as an adult, my vision cleared up.

"The soap opera was that I recycled the issue for years. The dominant quality of soap opera is that the problem recycles over and over, with no real breakthroughs to a new way of being. That's how my life became. I would lose some weight, then gain it right back. Even when I got relatively slender, I would still obsess about food and my weight.

"It was not until well into my twenties that I finally got in touch with the real issues and feelings that my weight obsession was masking. I learned to feel anger without judging it or escaping it or expressing it in hurtful ways. I learned to be with loneliness—both the primal loneliness of childhood and lonely feelings in my current life—without running away from it into the open arms of the refrigerator."

To claim our full birthright as human *beings*, we need to claim our full ability to *be* with whatever is there. Otherwise we are humans *fleeing*. There is no unity in flight from ourselves—we split in two and then have to undergo some remedial procedure to become whole again. Making the transition from human fleeing to human being requires a major act of courage. In our personal experience, however, and in our work with many people over the years, we have found nothing else in human life that matches the exhilaration of the journey. Along the way are trials, for certain, but the rewards of the journey are to be found in love, energy, clarity, and creativity. If you are a certain type of person, nothing will satisfy you but the full expression of your creativity and the full empowerment of those around you.

BEING PRESENT

The deeper we worked on ourselves and with others on the journey, the more we were surprised and heartened by the simplicity of the journey. Twenty years ago, if a client was stuck, we attempted to pull him out of the mud, but now we invite him to be with the experience of stuckness. And as if by magic, the stuckness disappears and creativity floods in. From the outside it looks as if what speeded up the process was the act of doing nothing. How rare it is to do nothing, to be with something with no agenda attached to it!

Many of us think of "nothing" as something negative: depression, void, darkness, loss of hope. But true "nothing" has none of this baggage attached. It is open space—pure consciousness—and has absolute potential in it, the potential for everything. Hark back to the James Joyce epigram that opens this chapter: "Mr. Dufy lived a short distance from his body." When our consciousness is one step removed from ourselves, we are split in half—not here, not there. When we let ourselves *be with* whatever is there, the gap is healed and we are one. This is the promise and potential of body-centered therapy. From the opening provided by pure being— nothing more and nothing less—comes a glimpse of everything. As the poet Kabir said: "All know that the drop merges into the ocean; few know that the ocean merges into the drop."

People flee experience as if it were the plague, when what they are really fleeing is their own creative power and divinity. Early in our work we discovered a happy surprise. Often a courageous person would open up to a powerfully negative feeling like rage or grief, sometimes about an event so ancient that it was buried beneath many layers of life's debris. Inevitably, if the person was willing to *be with* the feeling long enough without flinching, it would turn into an equally powerful positive opposite. Rage would transform into forgiveness, grief into joy, alienation into oneness with all creation. We have come to feel that there is nothing separating us from the divine element of life but the flimsiest of screens, and the screen is our own beliefs and concepts.

Everything is connected together in one universe; only a twitch of the mind produces separation. We are not saying that there is anything wrong with separation. There is great value, survival value, in separation under key circumstances. The human mind early on had to learn to separate the poison mushroom from the tasty, the hungry beast from the potential pet. Only the hardiest mystic would advocate blissful union with a freezing downpour. But in the great human tradition of overdoing it, we have become so skilled at separation that we are no longer in union with ourselves, others, and the universe itself. The cost is awesome: We avoid a little pain through separation, but we also miss out on our organic creativity and our natural connection to the divine.

In this book we are particularly interested in what brings about integration. In therapy, integration means the organization of fragmented aspects of ourselves into one harmonious personality. In the original Latin (*integrare*), the idea of integration meant not only to bring together fragmented parts, but also to renew, to restore and bring forth the untouched part of ourselves. This untouched part of ourselves, which we call essence, is the outcome of the journey. To experience an unshakable, moment-to-moment sense of one's personal essence is the purpose of our method of body-centered therapy.

A comprehensive approach to therapy must embrace the full range of human experience, from the practical to the mystical. Most people who seek change have fairly modest goals. They want to feel better from moment to moment, to lessen the pain they feel. They want to end the random sweeps of anxiety through their bodies. They want to lighten the leaden sense of depression that weighs upon their chests. They want to bring some order and peace to their minds while they are going through the confusion of a life change such as divorce. They want to know what they want, or whether it is all right even to want. First and foremost, the body-centered approach can bring immediate relief to these real-life concerns. Based on our files and notes from more than twenty thousand sessions, we can tell you that 95 percent of the time our clients leave sessions feeling better emotionally and physically than when they came in an hour before. A great advantage of body-centered therapy is that you can actually feel the positive shifts occur in your moment-to-moment body sensations.

Yet one of the happiest discoveries in our work is that the very same processes that relieve a seemingly mundane problem like depression can result in spiritual growth, as well. After a deep session, a decidedly unmystical dentist had this to say: "The strange thing was what happened later, when I was parking my car back at my office. I was thinking of the anger we had been working on. You had been trying to get me to be with it and breathe into it, to breathe through it so I could come to terms with it. I just sat there in my car doing that, breathing deeply into my belly and focusing on where I still felt the anger in my arms and shoulders. Suddenly I felt a shift in my body, and at the same time a thought occurred to me. I could forgive Jane [his ex-wife]! I had never seen that possibility before! I could just forgive her! How did I get from feeling anger to forgiving her in a flash like that? I still don't know. But I sat there in my car and this peace descended on me, like nothing I'd ever really felt before."

A LOOK AHEAD

As you read this book, you will see that nine strategies are presented: presencing, breathing, moving, magnification, communication, grounding, manifestation, love, and responsibility. They are presented in this order because they unfold in that order in body-centered therapy. In a recent example, we were working with a woman on her grief over her son's death. First we asked Susan to be with her sadness—simply to feel it. She had not done this—busy-ness and taking care of others had been her defenses—and so the few moments she gave her sadness full attention proved liberating for her. This act is what we call *presencing*. To enhance her ability to be with her grief, we invited Susan to *breathe* into it, filling her body with it, then breathing it out. As she did this unusual procedure, her fists began clenching, a *movement* that often signals the presence of anger. We invited her to be with anger, if indeed it was there. It was, and she breathed with that, too. We urged her to *magnify* the movements and the breathing, to exaggerate them so that she could bring them fully into her awareness. Next, a number of *communications* burst forth spontaneously. There were people to whom she needed to say "I'm angry" and "I'm sad," and there were a number of other communications she needed to make as well. By now, we were nearing the end of Susan's session, and we spent some time helping her get *grounded*, turning the insights into a plan of action. We had her set goals and plan some actions to help her *manifest* what she had learned. She had learned to *love* and take *responsibility* for a part of herself that she had previously disowned.

As the Upanishads put it thousands of years ago: What you cannot find in your own body, you will not find elsewhere. The body-centered approach makes this philosophy completely practical and accessible. We will offer a theoretical explanation of principles and a set of very practical techniques, as well as examples of how the principles and techniques have been applied to the common problems that every healer sees daily. Our style will be an amalgam of discussion, metaphor, example, and technical detail. We invite you—even urge you—to try everything out as you go. Breathe the book as you read it. Dance it as you think it over. Be with it in your belly as well as in your brain.

The moment of experience—when the magnificent human power of attention is focused on the reality of what the person is feeling—is the healing process in miniature. When it happens, miracles happen. Body-centered therapy is one of the few places where miracles can and do happen on a regular basis. In fact, sometimes they happen with such regularity that we come to take them for granted.

We once did a private session with a woman who was experiencing nerve deafness. During the course of the session, she uncovered a sexual moles-tation incident in her past and came to a degree of resolution with it. We have frequently found that hearing problems result from sexual abuse, so it came as no surprise to us when a sexual incident came to light. A year later when we were on a seminar tour of the West Coast, the same woman came up to us during a break. She told us that within two weeks after the session, her hearing had fully returned. We smiled and nodded.

She appeared slightly agitated at our response. "Maybe you don't under-stand," she said. "My hearing came back!"

We indicated that we got the message and were pleased.

"Oh," she said. "I thought you'd be a lot more excited."

She went on to say that she had been so excited by this seeming miracle that she was disappointed that we didn't jump up and down. As we talked to the young woman, we realized that the practice of body-centered therapy has given us such a steady diet of miracles that perhaps we had become blasé about them. At first we felt some guilt about that, then we realized that this is the ultimate potential of body-centered therapy. It allows the practitio-ner and the beneficiary to experience the miraculous as quite ordinary. When therapy proceeds at the speed of life, one sees every day what an absolute miracle it is, and what miraculous things human beings can attain.

THE THEORY AND PRACTICE OF BODY-CENTERED THERAPY: A NEW PARADIGM FOR HEALING THE MIND/BODY

All things come out of the one, and the one out of all things.
—Heraclitus

A new paradigm must be employed to describe what happens in body-centered therapy. As we studied tapes and notes from hundreds of hours of therapy sessions, we saw that the kinds of breakthroughs people had could be explained only with a paradigm more inclusive than the one we had been using. Specifically, we will use a quantum paradigm to explain our method. Just what this new paradigm entails, and how body-centered therapy is the practical expression of it, is the subject of this chapter.

QUANTUM SHIFTS

In therapy, quantum shifts occur in at least two major situations. The first is when a person (or couple or family) jumps from one level of functioning to another. Some years ago, for example, we worked with a writer who had been stuck in a writer's block for nearly two years. After a breathwork session in which he reexperienced a sexual molestation incident from his childhood, he exploded into a creative outpouring that enabled him to complete the book with which he had been wrestling. The second type of quantum shift is when the client discovers a fundamental unity underlying a conflict. For example, we frequently see couples who are locked in a power struggle over some issue. One couple had been struggling over whether to have a child. On the surface it looked like complete polarization—he emphatically did not wish to have a child, and she desperately wanted to. As they looked beneath the polarized positions, they each had a realization that ended their struggle. Both of them found that they had been abandoned in different ways as children. This common feeling had been driving the argument. When they both dropped into the shared feeling that underlay their polarized positions, they experienced an organic resolution of the problem. She felt a lessened urgency to have a child, while he made a complete about-face. As he dealt with his own abandonment as a child, he discovered that he very much wanted to be a father. He had resisted becoming a father because of his fears of thirty years before. This was a quantum shift. A year later, they were the parents of a healthy little boy.

Two major definitions of *quantum* correspond to these two types of quantum shifts. First, a jump in the level of functioning from one state to a different one; second, the presence of an irreducible and indivisible state that contains previously conflicting substates. Both types of quantum events occur readily and observably when the strategies described in this book are used. It is for this reason that we talk about changes that occur "at the speed of life." Over the twenty-five years we have been in the psychotherapy field, we have seen the field move from a Newtonian-based model to an Einsteinian paradigm. Now a quantum view is emerging that has ramifications for every area of human life. Understanding how these paradigms interlock—and at times clash—can be of considerable benefit to the therapist.

FROM NEWTONIAN TO EINSTEINIAN

At the heart of the Newtonian paradigm is the idea that for every action there is an equal and opposite reaction. A Newtonian observation might be something like this: "When I get near an elevator, I feel queasy. Therefore

I am afraid of elevators. I need to eliminate the fear or stop getting near elevators." The Newtonian view is at the heart of behavior therapy, which seeks to change the stimulus (the elevator) or the response to it (the queasiness). This view is useful to a point, but it can also be the source of a great deal of misery. To use a concrete example; a couple with a problem may come in to therapy with a Newtonian understanding of that problem. He says: "She is always criticizing me, so of course I never want to hang around the house." His Newtonian view is that her criticism is the *action* that triggers his *reaction* of leaving the house. She says: "He doesn't spend any time with me, and he doesn't pick up his underwear, so of course I criticize him." Her Newtonian view is that his actions trigger her criticism. Both perceive themselves as victims, each perceives the other as the perpetrator, and every action on one's part leads to a corresponding reaction on the other's. It is a neatly organized view of the situation, and we have seen people defend this misguided view all the way to court. But a novice psychotherapist quickly learns to see beyond the Newtonian view, even though the client may not see it so quickly. Part of the reason clients are stuck, after all, is that their paradigms have not kept up with their situations. They are experiencing the paradigm shift as a crunch, often in the pit of their stomach.

The solution is to apply an Einsteinian or a quantum paradigm to the situation. Using an Einsteinian view is a major improvement, but ultimately a quantum view offers the broadest possibilities for change. The Einsteinian interpretation gives a radically new view of the situation, but it does not offer an immediate solution to getting out of it. The quantum paradigm, because it takes us to a level in which the conflict is held in a new way, offers a rapid means of change.

The richest bit of wisdom that Einstein left us, the one that is urgent for all of us to understand, can be expressed like this: What you see and experience in a given situation depends largely on what you bring to the situation. People trapped in the Newtonian paradigm will focus instead on what others are doing to them and their reactions to it. In the Einsteinian paradigm, they instead focus on the qualities, intentions, and requirements they are bringing to the situation. The husband we have described needs to see that he creates a world of people around him to criticize him, based on his own inner relationship with criticism. As his relationship with his Inner Critic shifts, so will his wife's behavior. He will see that he brought his pattern of leaving the house with him to the relationship, based on his early strategies for avoiding his overbearing mother. For her part, she will need to see how her background and unconscious requirements make it inevitable that her husband won't pick up his underwear. The Einsteinian question is: How are my present unconscious intentions and my past conditioning contributing to creating my present situation?

  ✓ The Newtonian question leads us to look for the trigger in the current situation in order to develop an accurate model of the chain of events. A Newtonian paradigm in psychotherapy is only useful up to a point and has several severe limitations thereafter. When the Newtonian paradigm works, it enables us to make an accurate attribution. A Newtonian break-through in therapy might be a client's realization that he or she feels anger and tightens the muscles of the abdomen when the boss comes in the office and that a stomachache tends to follow. But this paradigm is fraught with potential for faulty attributions. If we are inclined toward self-pity and victimhood, it may look as if the boss has caused the stomachache. Carried further, we might tend to adopt a primally misery-making strategy: Trying to get others to change their behavior so we'll feel better, or waiting around for them to do so. In addition, the Newtonian paradigm does not encourage us to consider the expectations, based on our past conditioning history, that we are bringing to a situation.

The shift from a Newtonian to Einsteinian paradigm often has life-changing and relationship-saving consequences. Here is an example of how just such a shift transformed one couple's relationship. Bruce and Joan, both forty years old and married for ten years, came in for therapy, saying they were considering divorce after many months of struggle. He was big, angry, and blustering. She cowered at his side in a tucked-in crouch. Bruce's complaint: Joan had initiated a brief affair with a co-worker while on a visit to a neighboring state. Her complaint: "I've been begging him to forgive me, but he won't." She saw his anger as entirely justifiable, and she wanted only to be forgiven for her transgression. He had been unable or unwilling to forgive her or release his anger in the six months since the affair. On the surface, it might look like a clear-cut case of Victim (him) and Persecutor (her). That is certainly the way it looked to them, from their Newtonian perspective. But holding this view had done nothing to change the situation for the better. Instead, the preceding six months had been a hell of verbal abuse on his part and cowed but unsuccessful attempts to placate on hers. No matter how many times Joan apologized and promised never to do it again, Bruce never budged from his position.

In the first of three hours we worked with them, we listened carefully to their respective stories; then we asked them if they were both willing to solve the problem. This question is essential, because people come to therapy for many reasons other than to solve a problem. Some are there to get justification for a position, others to prove that nothing they do will work. We like to make sure both partners are committed to solving a problem before we approach it. After some initial resistance ("Would I be here if I weren't willing to solve the problem?" and "Maybe, but I don't think it's possible") we were able to secure a clear yes from both of them.

We then asked Bruce and Joan if the problem situation was like any other situation they had ever experienced. They both automatically shook their heads in denial. We persisted. Interestingly, it was Joan who suddenly remembered that the situation had some similarities for her husband. "Oh, yes," she finally said. "Both of his former wives left him for other men." So he *had* experienced a similar situation on at least two prior occasions. Here was the beginning of the meltdown of their Newtonian understanding of the situation. And did their situation remind Joan of anything in her own life? After some reflection, she volunteered that she had had an affair in her previous marriage. "I didn't know that" was his reply. "Oh, yes," she said. "I figured I'd show him for abusing me." The marriage had eventually dissolved without the affair becoming known. We asked them about any earlier events that resembled the present situation. Neither could recall anything else.

By that time, the first hour was over. We gave them a communication assignment and made arrangements to get together the next day.

When they arrived, we asked them again about other earlier situations that involved betrayal or abandonment. "The only thing I can remember is that situation with my mother," Bruce said. And what was that? "My mother left my father when I was six months old and ran off with another man. I never saw her again." He went on to say that his father had spent the rest of his life in bitter denunciation of women and their treachery, never remarrying or even dating another woman.

Joan came from a background in which she witnessed a great deal of verbal abuse and some physical abuse directed toward her mother by two different husbands. She had developed a belief that she was always wrong, that if a problem occurred, she was somehow at fault. So naturally, but quite unconsciously, she had set up her first marriage so that she got physically abused, and the present one so that she was harangued verbally.

We were amazed. Here were two very bright people, both well-employed and equipped with Ph.D.s, and it had not occurred to either of them that they both were playing out an unconscious role in each other's dramas. We pointed out what we saw: He had based his life on an event that had occurred before he could even walk. His fear of abandonment was so extreme that it was exceeded only by his requirement that it happen over and over again. When he entered a relationship, he was abandonment waiting to happen. Once he caught on to his role in perpetuating this script, he quickly saw that he had set up a series of betrayals in every significant relationship in his life. They both saw that underneath their warring personas they both had the same feelings: the fear, loneliness, hurt, and anger of two children who had both loved and lost long ago.

These learnings signaled a shift from the Newtonian to the Einsteinian. They had been stuck when they came in because each of them was convinced the problem was the other's fault. He knew beyond a shadow of a doubt that his upset was caused by her infidelity. She was convinced that if she tried hard enough, he would forgive her. What got them unstuck was making a breakthrough to the Einsteinian view. They needed to focus on the expectations and requirements they were bringing to the situation, not on how the other person had wronged them. He realized that he was bringing the expectation of abandonment to their relationship, so it was only a matter of time until it manifested. She was bringing the expectation of being wrong to the relationship, so it was only a matter of time until she messed up.

The next great shift, from the Einsteinian to the quantum level, came when they saw that underneath all their projections and personas they

shared the same feelings. They were both scared, but they both concealed
their fears, each in a different way. Bruce hid his fear under accusatory
bluster; Joan hid hers under quivering placation. They were unified by
virtue of their shared fear. Once they got below their diametrically opposed
personas to the level at which they were connected, each could perceive
the other as an ally rather than an enemy.

Their case had a very positive outcome. Not only did their relationship
transform before our eyes (the quantum shift), but subsequent changes
continued to unfold over the following months. They both recognized that
their essences adored each other but that their personas required constant
conflict. We had them practice some of the techniques of body-centered
therapy, and to date the presenting problem has not resurfaced. To see people
go from victim positions to accepting responsibility for powerful life scripts
is one of the most moving experiences we have had. Although we have
witnessed it thousands of times in therapy, it never fails to move us.

A QUANTUM PARADIGM FOR THERAPY:
THE FOUR-PART MODEL IN BRIEF

In our training workshops we identify four components of the human
psyche that are the key areas of the new paradigm. These components are
essence, feelings, persona, and projection. When a person moves from one
of these elements to another, a quantum shift occurs in his or her experience of the world. The model is depicted by the diagram in figure 1.

When a person shifts toward the right in the diagram—toward
projections—they experience less freedom, clarity, and happiness. When
the shift is to the left—toward essence—greater freedom, clarity, and
happiness are the results. In relationships, any such quantum shift *stops
conflict*. When we are trapped inside a projection, for example, seeing the
world a certain way, there is a high likelihood of our getting stuck there.
Bruce was stuck because he was convinced that Joan was going to leave
him. This was his projection onto her, and all his interactions with her
sprang from this context. The conflict effectively stopped when he shifted
from his projection to the persona underneath it. When he saw that his sure

knowledge that she was going to leave him was based on a persona
developed out of early childhood abandonment, everything changed for
him. When he got under the persona to the feelings upon which it was
based, he made another major step toward resolution of the issue. When
we can get to the feeling level, we lose our death-grip on the persona,
because we see that it is only one of many that we could have adopted. But
before this moment, the persona feels real and necessary.

Let's explore the four components of the model briefly. The deepest level
that we have been able to access in ourselves and in our clients is what we
call *essence*. The dictionary tells us that essence (derived from the Latin
word for "to be") is the fundamental nature or being of a thing. It is the most
intrinsic part of ourselves. Further, the dictionary defines essence as the
substance that maintains in concentrated form the flavor or other property
of the entity from which it is derived. In our work we have experienced two
flavors of essence. The first and seemingly deeper is what we call *universal
essence*. It is a clear, open spacious feeling that feels connected to the same
open space in others and to the universe itself. It has no personal flavor.

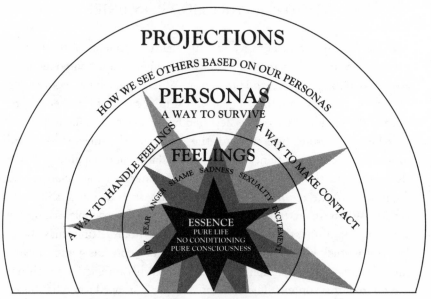

FIGURE 1. The Four Components of the Psyche

From our clinical experience we have discovered that when a Christian feels universal essence, he or she feels the clear space that holds all religions. There is no flavor of Christianity to universal essence. The Buddhist experiences the same clear space, with no Buddhism attached. The second type of essence is what we call *personal essence*. Here one feels the most fundamental, irreducible thing that makes one who he or she is. When Sara feels personal essence, she is in touch with the thing that most fundamentally makes her Sara. When Jim feels personal essence, he feels his basic Jim-ness. However, when they are in universal essence, there is no Jim or Sara flavor to it.

Most babies are living examples of essence. They are deeply resonant with their body sensations, in touch with the wholeness of themselves. They express their feelings readily in the ways nature has given them. When they are hugged, they snuggle. When they are tired, they go to sleep. In addition, the perceptive observer can see personal essence in the baby, the flavor that makes this particular baby different from other babies. Recently one of us had the opportunity to observe quadruplets closely over several days. Although at first they all looked alike, after an hour or so it was very clear which one was which; although the physical attributes were very similar, the personality flavors were as distinct as strawberry and vanilla.

Of course, babies do not know they are in essence in the same sense that adults do. They have not developed the self-observing feedback loop that will come with their later development. The philosopher of consciousness Ken Wilber makes a distinction between the prepersonal state of transcendence that the baby feels, prior to the development of the ego, and the transpersonal state of reconnection with essence from the vantage point of adult development. The adult can be enjoying a deep contact with essence and still cross a busy street safely. There may be a direct connection between the prepersonal and the transpersonal, the latter containing resonant elements of the former. Gay, for example, has a characteristic way of holding his arms skyward during states of deep essence-connection. Frequently at the end of meditation or a breathwork session, it just "feels right" to him to hold his arms this way. On a trip to Florida to clean out his mother's house after her death, he discovered a baby photo of him in this same position, arms aloft, looking like a fat, diapered little Buddha.

Some babies are not blessed with as clear an early connection with essence. Perhaps they had it for a fleeting time, but early trauma intervened. We have seen babies born to drug-addicted mothers enter the world in a screaming frenzy and stay that way, inconsolable, for months. It is likely that loss of essence happens prenatally in these unfortunate infants. It has been demonstrated that a fetus kicks and appears agitated for hours after the mother has smoked crack cocaine.

Most of us do not have our individual essences assaulted with such strong blasts of toxicity, but almost all of us experience events early in life that trigger feelings that we subsequently do not know how to integrate. Early in life some event may happen that triggers emotions in us, something that is too strong for us to handle. We have seen babies just after they lost a parent. Although they were too young to know exactly what happened, they knew that something had happened. Fear, anger, shame, and grief are strong feelings that the events of life can trigger. These feelings are often so strong that they overshadow our underlying *essence*, the part of us that is free, clear, and intrinsically connected to self and others.

Deep feelings have two main qualities that make them overwhelming. They feel as if they will endure forever, and if we open up to them, they will make us die or fly apart. When we explore with our clients what they most dread about their deepest fears, angers, or griefs, they always tell us the same thing: If they allow themselves to experience them, they will die or go crazy. It does not take sharp traumas to trigger these kinds of deep feelings. They can be absorbed slowly over time, too.

Of the three main feelings with which human beings struggle—anger, sadness, and fear—fear is the deepest and most pervasive. At the physical level, most people even experience fear deeper in their bodies than the other feelings. People tend to feel anger up toward the top of their bodies, in the neck, shoulders, and forehead. Sadness tends to be felt in the throat and higher chest. Fear is usually experienced in the lower chest and belly, in the form of antsy and queasy feelings. In our work with people we have found that when they are angry, they are also scared. Many people defend against their deeper fears by getting angry; the anger keeps them from contacting the underlying feeling. The same is often true with sadness. There is often a hidden component of fear underneath sadness. The fear needs to be addressed as well as the surface feeling of sadness.

Fear makes human beings hide or attack. When we are scared, we hide our feelings from ourselves and from others. A glance at any biology text will show clearly that living organisms tend to contract under stress to protect the soft parts. If a threat continues, some of us bite back. Others withhold the "bite-back" impulse. In the extreme, the "bite-backers" go to jail, while the "withholders" get ulcers.

To deal with these feelings, we develop *personas*, from a Latin word meaning "mask." A secondary meaning sheds further light on the problem: The Latin word *personare* means "to sound through." Our personas, then, are the masks we make our sounds through, so that we will be recognized by the world around us. Personas serve two main functions. First, they help us hide and seal off confusing feelings. Second, they give us a means to get attention from those on whom we depend for survival. We may develop several different personas to deal with different people and situations. We even may adopt a variety of personas to relate to the same person. The child may find that Sick Kid and Accident Prone are personas that resonate with Mom, while Rebel works with Dad. Here are some common personas that our workshop participants have identified:

Little Professor	Get Sick
Hard Worker/Supercompetent	Have Accidents
Jock	Space Out
Delinquent	Withdraw/Loner
Devoted	Get Tough, Get Tight
Drama Queen/King	Victim
Ramblin' Man/Gal	Peter Pan
Vigilant	Stoic
Emotional Roller Coaster	Caretaker
Dependent/Clingy	

Based on these personas, we begin to see the world and other people in a distorted way. Here is where *projection* enters. From within the confines of a certain persona, we project upon the screen of the world what we want to see there. We begin to project upon others the requirements of the persona rather than the true self or essence. For example, the world looks very different to someone with a Dependent persona than it does to someone who wears a Ramblin' Man persona. To Dependent personas, the world is made up of people to whom they can cling and people to whom they cannot. To Ramblin' Men, the world is full of people who are potentially going to limit their freedom or not.

These projections interlock with the projections of others, making communication between the essences of people difficult or impossible. Our projections require other people to act in ways that actually make us upset. For example, a woman with a Dependent/Clingy persona may initiate a relationship with a Ramblin' Man because her persona requires such a partner to play out its script. She may have developed her persona through trying to make contact with a standoffish father. Now her persona clings, while her unconscious requirement is for a distant man. The Ramblin' Man, on the other hand, may require a Dependent/Clingy partner because he learned his Ramblin' Man act in reaction to a smothering mother early in his life. The louder she sings "Stand by Your Man," the louder he sings "Don't Fence Me In." When their personas interlock, people often engage in power struggles instead of learning from each other. The opportunity, when two people interact, is that they may learn from each other, becoming more whole. When a power struggle develops between two personas, this opportunity is lost.

By the time we get to adult life, the web of our personas and projections is very complex. It obscures who we really are inside and who we think others are. As Eugene O'Neill put it, speaking of the things life does to us;

> They're done before you realize it, and once they're done they
> make you do other things until at last everything comes
> between you and what you'd like to be, and you have lost your
> true self forever.

In contrast to his bleak view, though, we have seen so many people wake up and restore their connection to essence that our faith in the resilience of human beings is very strong.

Why do we form personas? Ultimately, the answer is always the same: survival—not simply physical survival, but survival of our identity. In a painful or confusing situation we use a certain persona, and it works. So later in life we continue to create situations that resemble the early moments when we successfully controlled our feelings and got recognition from those around us by using that persona.

But human beings have evolved beyond survival. At this stage of evolution we have access to essence. The quest to establish ourselves in essence is strong. Essence is focused on unity. While the persona is bent on simple survival, essence seeks its own expression: to make us whole, and to give all of our actions a sense of authenticity. So it, too, propels us toward situations that resemble the early events in which it was snuffed and when fragmentation replaced our organic sense of unity. The essence part of us wants us to feel whole, and it sends us into situation after situation in which we might reconnect with it. With these two powerful motivations—the drive for survival and the quest for unity—we create one opportunity after another in which we get to choose between wholeness and fragmentation, truth and withholding, love and pain. Essence seeks to get us to the light, while persona seeks only to get us through the night. Both are important, and both gain momentum as the years roll by, so that by the time we are in our thirties and forties, the pressure is enormous.

ESSENCE

Although essence is a concept that goes far back past Aristotle, modern psychology has not addressed it. It is a concept that is absolutely unprovable except by direct experience and personal observation. For this reason it does not lend itself to the research methods of contemporary "hard-nosed" psychology. One of our professors at Stanford, Ernest Hilgard, broke modern psychology into two main camps: hard-nosed and warm-hearted. Essence is definitely a product of the warm-hearted school. But essence is much more than a concept. When skillfully approached, it has great clinical relevance and healing power.

In our use of the term, essence is the part of human beings that is clear, spacious, and free of conditioning. Essence, as distinct from personality, is intrinsically connected to the universe and to others. It is pure consciousness. As such, it has no striving built into it. We have found that our work has grown in both power and speed as we have personally become more grounded in essence. Essence is not hard to contact. It requires you to willingly place your attention on whatever you are feeling, without doing anything else with it. For many of us, this is easier said than done. As Blaise Pascal said, "All man's miseries derive from not being able to sit quietly in a room alone."

In our own relationship as husband and wife, we have had over a decade's rich opportunity to observe our projections onto each other, and to discover the personas on which those projections were based. Exploring the feelings underneath our respective personas has given our relationship a deep base of shared emotional experience. As we have explored these feelings, we have discovered to our great surprise and pleasure that we share many of the same basic feelings. Although the personas we chose long ago were very different, our feelings are the same. For example, we both experience at times a fear of being alone. Kathlyn's persona is to deal with this fear by being very busy and surrounding herself with friends, while Gay's persona leads him to isolate himself and overeat. But underneath, we are both responding to the same feeling.

In addition, we have both found it extremely helpful to practice daily meditation and body-centering techniques such as breathwork and movement activities. Exploring our feelings and practicing these techniques has given us daily access to essence. We have learned to place the highest priority on practicing the principles and techniques because we have learned to place the highest priority on essence. If our daily connection with essence in ourselves is strong and clear, all of life seems to proceed smoothly. When life drifts toward the rough and rocky, as it does from time to time, we make sure we meditate and do breathwork more. Inevitably, enhancing our connection with essence smooths things out again.

As we have rested more in essence, we have grown in our ability to perceive essence in each other and in others in general. Essence is one of those rare human experiences that becomes observable in others the more one feels it inside. The therapists whom we have trained over the years tell us that as their own sense of themselves becomes more deeply grounded in essence, the process of helping people heal themselves and their relationships is speeded up significantly. We think this result is because when people perceive essence in themselves and in others, they know cellularly that there is a unifying principle at the bottom of all conflict. There is *a place to come home to.*

What we all desperately need to learn is that this place to come home to is inside ourselves, at the core and center of ourselves. You cannot get there by going outward, only by going inward. We have seen people do everything else to find essence except opening up to their inner world. They try to find unity through building dream houses, sharing hobbies, buying things, having children, and serving on committees together, but none of these can work without the inner essence connection. Many people in this culture are secretly sick at heart because they have everything but the essence connection.

If we work on ourselves deeply enough with the appropriate tools, we discover that there is part of all of us that is true consciousness, that has no conditioning. It simply is. Mystics have spoken of it in various terms for millennia, but it was not until it became a surprise byproduct of effective therapy that we began to appreciate its significance. We want to make it clear that we are not speaking of anything that needs to be believed in. In fact, we have found that believing in essence is a strong barrier to actively experiencing it. Rather, we are talking about the living, palpable feeling of essence, the perception of an all-pervading clear space that is at the center of ourselves. It is also in others and throughout the universe. Our evidence that it exists is based on direct experience in ourselves and in watching and listening to our clients. When therapy is truly effective, client and therapist alike experience essence directly. In our work, essence is an active experience, not a discussion item. There is no question ever about its presence or absence.

What does essence feel like? One day toward the end of a session, a client gave us a clear description of a body-sensation of essence. He had opened up to a deep sense of sadness in himself about the loss of his connection with his father. We invited him to presence the sadness, to feel the sensations of it, and to breathe his way through it. After he shed a great many tears, his face took on a radiant look. We asked him what he was feeling, and he replied that he was feeling a warm and golden open space throughout his chest and up into his throat. We invited him to breathe into that, too, and he experienced radiant waves of this spacious feeling throughout his upper body. We happened to capture the moment on video, enabling him to use it for inspiration in subsequent life.

In relationships, essence may be experienced somewhat differently. As one woman described it, essence "felt like a sudden seeing of myself and my husband as we actually are. There was no artifice between us, and all our 'issues' dropped away. We were joined together by the same energy of connection that connects everything else in the world. I could feel the layers of feelings that we had about each other and see the stacks of thoughts and beliefs that often separated us, but at the center there was only the clarity of pure connection. This was what our relationship was really about, not all the feelings and problems and goals and such." This is essence.

The power of such moments in healing cannot be overestimated. When people come in for relationship therapy, they often have not experienced a second of essence in years. A momentary flash of it can rekindle even long-moribund relationships. We have come strongly to feel that at the center of every psychological or relationship problem is an experience of essence waiting to happen. For this reason we have become a great deal more hopeful about the healing of human difficulty than we were even five or ten years ago. Granted, not every exploration of a problem resolves in essence, but the potential is there at all times.

FEELINGS

Why, then, is essence not perceived more often? If it is such a strong force, how does it come to be lost so easily? Paradoxically, the way it is lost is also the key to its recovery. Early in life, sometimes very early indeed, feelings occur that overshadow essence. The feelings engender a catastrophe of contraction in us, reducing or eliminating our experience of essence. It is clear that whatever triggers these feelings can occur very early. Either suddenly or gradually, an event or series of events in childhood triggers feelings that are powerful enough to overwhelm essence. The events may take place in the bonding phase of the first year or in later phases such as exploration, self-regulation, or sexual development. Regardless of when essence is lost, the problem is the same. If we are in touch with essence, we may *have* feelings, but we experience them in the larger context of essence. Grounded in essence, we know that we are more than our feelings. When we are out of touch with essence, the feelings have us.

If we are grounded in essence, a feeling will arise (such as anger or fear) and we can accept it as part of ourselves. If we are out of touch with essence, the same feeling will seem to dominate us. To control it, we withhold it and remove ourselves from the situation. This action leads to projection. One client, David, gave us this example: "I was at a junior high school dance. I wanted to ask a certain girl to dance. I stood on the edge of the floor for minutes, trying to overcome my fear. Then suddenly it was bigger than I was, and I sat back down. Immediately my mind began manufacturing meanings: Girls are scary, girls are awful, I didn't want to dance with her anyway, she probably wouldn't dance with me if I asked her, et cetera. My gym teacher, Coach Mac, wandered over just then, having seen my indecision. 'Heck, son, a little fear ain't gonna kill you. Go ahead and do it anyhow.' I squirmed with embarrassment at having been 'caught' by him, but I jumped up and went across the dance floor. Fortunately, she accepted, and I didn't have to make the long trek back to the boys' side."

This example tells us a lot. David's fear became greater than his identity—it overwhelmed his essence—and he withdrew. The moment he withdrew, the projections started. They did not end until David faced the fear and acted in spite of it. This action established that his identity was bigger than the fear: It lived in him, but he didn't live in it. His coach knew something intuitively that Nietzsche had said long ago: "Anything that doesn't kill you makes you stronger."

A classic illustration of what we are talking about emerged in the course of therapy with a young couple named Ellen and Mike, both health professionals. Mike was exploring a tendency to obsess over Ellen leaving him, in the face of absolutely no real-life evidence that she had any interest in doing so. Sometimes the feeling would sweep over him, for example, if she drove off to the store, or sometimes even if she left the room to go to the bathroom. We asked Mike to be present with the underlying feeling of abandonment as he experienced it in his body. He described a queasy feeling and a tight knot behind his navel. Being a medical doctor, he would often reach for the Tagamet or the Pepto-Bismol when this sensation gripped him. We asked him to feel these sensations and to find out if they reminded him of any other time in his life. A flood of tears broke forth as Mike recalled an incident that had happened one day when he was five years old. His parents had called him in from play and subjected him to a grilling. Specifically, they asked him to choose which of them he would rather live with if they split up. He was shocked and stunned as each of his parents came into the room singly and presented an individual case of why he or she would be the better parent. His terror and confusion were utter. This bind is an intolerable one for the child, and it is nearly guaranteed to produce overwhelming feelings.

If we were accompanied by guardian angels during traumatic events, we might hear a message that sounds like this: "You are having an awful experience right now. You are feeling scared and confused and angry. You had to leave the timeless world of essence to submit to an experience over which you have no control. These kinds of feelings you are experiencing right now are like thunderstorms. They have a beginning, a middle, and an end. The best you can do at this moment is to feel the feelings you have until they move on through. Breathe with them, participate with them until they pass on through."

If Mike had been accompanied by a wise guardian angel, he might have come through the experience with less emotional baggage attached, because he would have participated with the feelings at the time. But instead, he was alone with his parents who were in their own state of emotional overwhelm, so caught up in their own pain that they could not see what a burden they were placing on their five-year-old. The stressful situation continued for the next year. During this time, Mike found that he could escape from his terror by living in a mental fantasy world or by immersing himself in sports. Both of these strategies took him out of the painful and confusing world of his feelings. The bottom-line issue for him was his fear of abandonment: Who will take care of me if Mom and Dad split up? Quite rightly, he perceived that both of them were too deeply concerned with their own pain to be of much help to him (and indeed, he had to live with his grandparents while his parents unraveled their marriage). While his mental fantasies and sports offered him a way of temporarily transcending the feelings that lived in his body, neither of these strategies really ever made the feelings go away.

This example illustrates how we develop personas to deal with feelings that are too confusing or overwhelming for us to handle. Mike put on one persona to relate to his father (sports) and one to deal with his mother (fantasy). He could talk to his father about sports and to his mother about ideas and his dreams of a better world. But as an adult, these strategies did not work very well. When he argued with Ellen, he would often retreat into his mental fantasies of other women who would treat him better. These fantasies distanced him from the very feelings that, if expressed, would have generated intimacy with his wife. In addition, he would often withdraw from conflict to go shoot baskets in the back yard, an action that would never fail to stimulate his wife to criticize him. The very personas that had helped him survive his childhood pain were now the barriers to intimacy that he had to overcome. As one of our clients ruefully put it, "I spent the first half of my life assembling all these personas, and now I'm spending the second half dismantling them."

The world of feeling is unpredictable, confusing, and hard to control. That is the nature of feeling. At the very best, learning to deal with feelings is a complex art. Some people are fortunate enough to grow up in families that teach that it is all right to experience feelings and tell the truth about them. Many families—perhaps most—teach their children strategies that become problems for us later. But we are given virtually no training in our schooling in how to deal with feelings in ways that are effective. It is left to life itself—often the harshest of teachers—to administer the curriculum on how to handle feelings. No wonder, then, that we often choose to remain in the false security of personas.

PERSONAS

When a persona is in charge, the world must be shaped to fit it. The Dependent/Clingy persona, as we mentioned earlier, sees the world as full of people to whom he or she can either cling or not cling. Such a perception overlooks richer possibilities the world has to offer. To the Ramblin' Man, the world consists of people who are trying to fence him in or who will give him plenty of space. We see what we believe, and that our beliefs shape our perceptions is beyond argument. For example, in laboratory studies using a tachistoscope (a visual device that flashes a picture for a split second, long enough to be unconsciously but not consciously perceived), people who are hungry think they have seen a banana flashed at them, whereas in fact they were shown a pencil. People who have not been allowed to go to the bathroom see the pencil as a fire hydrant. How we see reality is determined by how we are inside.

History gives even more vivid examples. Several hundred years ago, according to the captain's log, a sailing ship was moored three hundred yards offshore in a bay along the African coast. No Europeans had visited there before, and the captain wished to assess the potential friendliness of the natives. He expected the ship's presence to cause an uproar among the natives, but he thought that the distance to shore would prevent any unpleasant encounters. To the crew's amazement, the villagers went about life as usual *for three days*, not seeming even to notice the ship in the harbor. Finally, a child playing in the water comprehended the strange sight and alerted the others. The only plausible theory that we can think of to explain this event is this: The villagers did not see it because it did not fit into their belief system. It took a child's awareness, not yet dulled by lengthy participation in the group's belief structure, to create an opening for the new perception.

The Ramblin' Man may walk into a room and end up with the one person there who fits the requirements of his persona. All would be well if he wanted only someone to give him space. However, the hidden requirements of the persona are more troublesome. The Ramblin' Man may not know it consciously, but what he really wants is someone who will challenge his persona. He may select the one person in the room who will initially give him space but who will turn Clingy on him as the relationship deepens. Will he learn from this occurrence? Perhaps, if his awareness is well-tuned, he may think: "Out of my fear of closeness I have created a relationship with someone who will crowd my space. What a wonderful opportunity to learn to be whole!" More likely he will think: "Women! You get close to 'em, and all they wanna do is own you. I've had it. I'm outa here." The wheel turns, and he has molded one more situation to fit his script.

It is important to understand that every persona has its useful side and its troublesome side. The negative side emerges under stress. For example, an associate of ours works for the welfare department. One of his personas, formed during an abused childhood, allows him to have empathy for underdogs. This persona, used effectively, has enabled him to be very helpful in empowering people from helplessness out into useful roles in society. But under stress he often lapses into self-pity and helpless victimhood himself. He berates his wife for keeping him from a better life. Here is a chart of positive and negative sides of common personas. By *positive*, we simply mean that it tends to create results that produce happiness and satisfaction rather than pain.

POSITIVE	NEGATIVE
Devoted	Clingy
Independent	Loner
Assertive	Pushy
Conscientious	Obsessive-Compulsive
Empathetic	Victim
Vivacious	Drama Queen/King
Reliable	Killjoy
Healer	Placater
Ethereal	Space Case
Freedom-seeker	Ramblin' Man

It's all in how the persona is used. Most of us get in trouble when we use our personas as a way of hiding feelings and getting attention in crooked ways. We often use our personas as tools of concealment and as ways to manipulate. To make matters worse, when a persona does not work, we often run it more forcefully instead of discarding it. As life proceeds, this strategy gradually gets less tenable. But where do we go from here? Unless we are lucky enough to find some useful psychological information, through therapy or otherwise, we are likely not to discover that the only way we can get out from under our personas is to find the authentic feelings on which they were originally based.

Two Categories of Persona

In our work, we have found it useful to separate personas into two general categories. The first, which we call the #1 Personas, are positive in nature. They are designed to get recognition in ways that have generally pleasant consequences for us and others around us. Some #1 Personas are Mother's Helper, Smart Kid, and Jock. They are certainly learned acts, but they are relatively straightforward and lead to largely positive consequences. These are winning personas, designed to get recognition and approval. Then there are the #2 Personas, learned to avoid pain and control our feelings. Examples of #2 Personas are Sick Kid, Delinquent, or Hysteric.

Often people will first try a #1 Persona, and if that does not work, they will run a #2. In the aisles of a supermarket one day we saw a vivid example of this process in action. A harried mother was pushing a heavily laden cart with her three-year-old aboard. Passing the cookies, the child asked politely, "Can I have a cookie?" Caught up in her shopping, the mother didn't seem to hear. A few seconds later, he said more loudly, this time with a whine in his voice, "I want a cookie!" This time she snapped her head around irritatedly and said, "You be quiet!" He then let out an anguished howl and began kicking the cart, saying "I want a cookie, I want a cookie, I want a cookie!" With a sigh of exasperation she grabbed a pack of cookies off the shelf and ripped it open. "Here," she said. "If you don't shut up, you'll never get another one out of me!" Then she put one in her own mouth.

The little boy had started with a #1 Persona but quickly escalated to #2 when the first one failed. Which one will he start with next time? It is interesting to note that his #2 triggered his mother's #2, sending both of them into a spiral of negative energy. It is sobering to see how many human interactions end up this way. Two people may begin to communicate from their #1 Personas, but the communication often quickly devolves into the deeply dug-in defensive positions of #2.

Feelings and wants are sometimes expressed authentically, but unfortunately they are more often expressed through the filters of personas. For example, one of our clients wanted to make sure his father did not leave his mother. Sid was afraid that the parents would split (which they eventually did), and he covertly took on the responsibility of keeping his father at home by adopting the personas of Good Boy and Jock. If he had been able to express his true feelings authentically, he would have said, "Dad, I'm really afraid you are going to leave. I want you here. I want your love. Will you stay?" But as we all know, simple, straightforward feelings are often the most difficult to express. Sid said none of these things to his father but went to great lengths to do things that pleased his father and that he knew would get his father's attention. Although he was not a particularly talented athlete, he worked long hours to make the Little League Team. The harder he worked, though, the more his father seemed to criticize him. Finally the father, caught up in his own pain, left his mother and moved into a little apartment. He even quit coming to the baseball games. So Sid gave up Good Boy and Jock, defending himself against the pain of loss by moving into Sullen Adolescent and Druggie. He continued this way until a sensitive counselor at his high school helped him get under his personas back to his authentic feelings.

This chart depicts the relationships among the two levels of personas and the authentic level on which they are based.

AUTHENTIC	#1 PERSONA	#2 PERSONA
Feelings and needs clearly expressed (I'm scared, I'm angry, I need help)	Seeks approval	Controls feelings and others, blames others, justifies self (I'm right/you're wrong, my reality is the correct one)

One couple we worked with some years ago had many battles about what kind of food they would eat and which restaurants they would patronize. John would invite Martha to go out for dinner, or vice versa, and soon their discussion would degenerate into a shouting match. One time we video-taped them as they attempted to decide during a therapy session where they would eat that night. The session was taking place in the late afternoon, so both of them were actually hungry. Here are some excerpts, along with our comments after the fact.

We opened the discussion with a specific, carefully chosen question: "What kind of food would taste especially good to you tonight?" Notice that this question can be answered only by turning the attention inward, getting the information, then bringing an answer forth. As it happened, neither Martha nor John did this simple thing. What they did was very revealing of their troublesome interaction pattern.

MARTHA: We always end up going where he wants to go.

Instead of answering our question, Martha answered a different one. The response she gave would have been appropriate if the question were "Where, from your point of view, do you always go?" Clearly her response expressed anger, but not authentically. Instead it was filtered through a #2 Persona. She was saying, "I'm right and you're wrong."

JOHN: Well, maybe we could just forget all that and just get something to eat. How about the little Italian place up on Oak? They've got that clam sauce you really like.

After only seconds, their personas were already emerging. Martha had jumped straight into one of her #2 Personas, the vengeful victim of past injustice and oppression. John had brought forth one of his favorite #1 Personas, the people-pleasing appeaser. But through the filter of her #2, she heard his placation only as further oppression.

MARTHA: See! You always have to be in charge, don't you? Just because I liked that clam sauce one time doesn't mean I've got to live with it for the rest of my life. Can't I eat what I want just once!

JOHN: Aw, Jesus. I give up. I'd rather not eat than do this again.

He crossed his arms and retreated, actually going out of the range of the video camera. Now he was in #2, his Withdrawn Loner persona, the guy who tries and tries but nobody understands him. No wonder they had so much difficulty; within two or three interactions they were both toe-to-toe in the defensive postures of their #2 Personas.

All personas are tied to a specific relationship in the past and in fact are rooted in a specific moment in time. Not everyone can access that moment, but nearly everyone can remember the relationship that triggered the adoption of the persona. Our next move with John and Martha, then, was to get to the original past relationship that each of them was replaying in the present. Let's fast-forward to a few minutes later in the session, after they had gone a few more rounds with their personas.

US: Martha and John, we have a question for each of you. Martha, who was it that oppressed you way back there when you were a kid? And John, who was it you could never please?

This question triggered a breakthrough. First, as we had hoped, it stopped the argument dead in its tracks. It is hard to take an argument in the present seriously when you realize it is really based on something that happened decades ago.

Martha surprised all of us by immediately reliving and describing her awful relationship with her bossy and narcissistic parents. For her own survival she had gradually let them define her experience, what she wanted, and how she felt. But she had collected a lifetime of resentment, which she now was cashing in with John.

From John's viewpoint, Martha was an extension of the stepmother he could never please. She had entered his life at age nine, and he had finally given up in sullen retreat when he was thirteen. He was plastering her face all over Martha's, still bent on pleasing and still totally convinced he could never win.

Let's move forward again, to the point in the session in which both of them were free of their personas, speaking authentic truth.

MARTHA: I'm afraid of never being myself. I so want to know who I am and what I want. Every time we do this restaurant thing, I'm totally terrified I'm going to lose everything I've gained.

JOHN: I never saw it that way before. I get that you're scared. The funny thing is, I'm scared too. I'm scared you're going to withdraw your love. No, more than that—I'm scared I'm not going to ever get the kind of love I want.

Underneath the battling #2s and the approval-seeking #1s, two authentic people have emerged, both scared. Before, their fears were being played out crookedly through their personas instead of through authentic contact with their true needs and feelings. Now their exhilaration and sense of liberation was very palpable as they slipped free of these burdens from the past.

Anytime blame, control, or approval is present, people are locked in personas. From within personas there is no possibility of genuine freedom: We are simply rearranging the deck chairs on the *Titanic*. Only by being courageous enough to jump free of personas can the genuine nurturance of authenticity be tasted. Underneath all the personas there is the big prize waiting to be claimed.

THE BENEFITS AND COSTS OF PERSONAS

One thing we usually have our clients do when they are beginning to identify and explore their personas is to calculate the payoff and the cost of maintaining them. What was the purpose, or payoff, for the persona originally? What is the cost now? If you were in the grip of a Loner persona, for example, you might find that the original payoff was that it got you some freedom and space in a difficult time. One of our clients who wears this persona grew up in a large family where the only way he could get some privacy was to wander in the woods for hours at a time. He also withdrew into himself as a coping strategy amidst the family maelstrom around him. In this case the original payoff of the Loner persona was escape from pain and confusion, along with the attainment of a temporary state of peace. But in his life now, the cost of it is high. He wears his persona like an overcoat indoors. In times where emotional transparency and intimacy are appropriate, such as when his wife asks him "How are you feeling right now?" he cannot access the information.

You may wonder, as you read the following list of the benefits of personas, if they are really very beneficial. The answer is: No, they are not. Even when they work, personas conceal authenticity. The real positivity in life comes from loosening our identification with our personas, so that we can operate more authentically. From within the personas, though, there are certain payoffs for keeping them in place.

The major benefits of personas are:

- While we are operating from within a persona, we do not have to think creatively. We are on automatic pilot, run by our past programming. Just as a trolley car cannot jump the track and drive around town freely, the persona keeps us locked into familiar patterns of interaction.

- We do not have to feel. One of the main purposes of a persona is to keep us from having to experience feelings that we find very unpleasant. A young person running a Juvenile Delinquent persona may prefer the ugliness of clashes with judges, police, and jail personnel to the painful reality of the authentic emotions that lie underneath that persona.

- We get to make other people wrong. There is a temporary satisfaction in pointing the finger of blame at someone else, chiefly because it keeps us from having to look inside ourselves and do the sometimes difficult work of taking responsibility for a given issue. Judging others is easy, compared with understanding them or relating to them as equals, and it is more socially acceptable in many quarters.

- We get to justify our own position or invalidate someone else's position. Justification and invalidation have short-term satisfactions that are very sweet to people who have acquired the taste for them. Justifying a position is much easier than doing the inner exploration of the authentic feelings that underlie the position.

Gary, a client of ours, wore a Wronged Victim persona. He had the position that his mother was cold and indifferent to him, and that this behavior on her part contrasted with the warmth she showed his brother. Gary justified this position in numerous ways; among them, he showed us a watch his mother had given him that was of less value than one she had given his brother. We confronted him on this justification and invited him to look underneath the position for the authentic feelings that his persona of Wronged Victim was concealing. After some initial reluctance he dropped his position and came face to face with the realization that he had withdrawn his love and compassion from both his mother and his brother when he was a teenager. As a teen he had been scared and confused, whereas his mother and brother seemed to have their lives well organized. He reached out to them from his authentic feelings rather than through his persona, and soon they were communicating as equals again.

While we are running personas, we are also running up a debt in the authenticity account. There are long- and short-term costs to staying locked in personas. The main costs of a persona are:

- We do not get to think. There is no possibility of fresh, creative action when we are running personas. They are part of a script, often one written long ago, and so they have a repetitive predetermined pattern to them.

- We do not get to feel. Personas mask authentic feelings, so there is a decrease in our aliveness. All feelings, both positive and unpleasant, come out of the same faucet. To turn down the faucet on pain is to slow the flow of pleasant feeling as well.

- We do not get to experience genuine love. When we are operating from within a persona, we cannot give or receive the authentic experience of love.

The major problem with personas, though, is that they force us into a view of the world that is unreal. Recall the tachistoscope experiment in which the hungry person sees a banana and the full person sees a pencil. The hunger was real, but the banana was a projection of the imagination based on the unacknowledged reality of the hunger. The concept that we are discussing is crucial to an understanding of human behavior. It is called projection.

PROJECTION

When we are in touch with essence, we know that we have feelings and personas, but we are not in their grip. When we lose touch with the clear space at the center of us, it is easy to give too much weight to feelings. If you are scared, for example, a deep connection with essence can allow you to feel that feeling of fear instead of running away from it. This is possible because you know that the fear will not overwhelm you, that you have a space or context in which to hold it. Essence gives us a sense of calm even when there are disturbances at the periphery.

A deep connection with essence also gives us a larger context in which to hold our personas. If our contact with essence is strong enough, we can make use of a persona without its using us. When we are running a persona but are not aware that it *is* a persona, we lose touch not only with essence but with the authentic feelings that underlie the persona. When we form projections out of the persona, we lose touch with the crucial fact that the persona is the only reason we are seeing the world that way after all! Then we often defend our projections vigorously, instead of recognizing that they are simply our distortions of the world. No wonder human interaction is so fraught with difficulty. As someone at one of our seminars plaintively asked, "Is everyone just projecting on each other all the time?" Maybe not all the time, but it sure looks like it to people when they first begin to wake up to the pervasiveness of projection.

In our trainings, we like to call projection the Lasso Principle, drawing the image of the cowboy with his rope. When in the grip of a persona, we have to lasso someone to play the other parts in the drama. If one person escapes the lasso, we have to rope in another one or pursue the escapee more vigorously.

The projections that give people the most trouble are those that do not seem like projections at all. The truly life-damaging projections are those that make us think, "That's the way the world actually *is*." Every week in our practices we witness the meltdown of projection. People go from projections such as "Women are fickle" and "Men are dullards" to realizing that those generalizations were based on specific personas in themselves. The projection of "Women are fickle" might be based on a persona of Abandoned Man, while a female Little Professor might judge men as dullards. These personas were originally adopted to deal with feelings from specific times of life. Then they were generalized to deal with the future at the sacrifice of spontaneity.

Once in Gay's days as a Stanford graduate student, he was swimming laps in the pool, the kind that has the lanes painted on the bottom. As he was swimming along, a man suddenly crashed into him. Both sputtered to a stop, and the man bellowed, "Why doncha watch where you're going?" Gay looked down, befuddled, to see if he had veered over into the man's lane. In fact, the man had veered into Gay's lane. The man, looking down, saw that he was the transgressor. Recovering his poise, he said, "They make these lanes too narrow."

Not very many projections are so amusing, however. Locked into projections, human beings visit great misery on each other. A successful attorney we worked with, for example, had complained for much of his adult life that people always lied to him. For him the world had two types of people: those who lie to him, and those (rare ones) who don't. After some self-exploration he began to discover that this projection was based on a persona of his. In other words, he was attracting into his life people who fit that projection. This projection had even influenced his career choice. As he explored the issue, it dawned on him that there had been a specific event in his young life where his father had lied to him. He had felt betrayed and lost by this event. Out of it he had crafted a persona of hypervigilance to lying. "Call me paranoid," he would say righteously during his college years, "but sometimes paranoia is justified." While his persona was running him, "if someone had told me that my attitude was just a persona I had adopted, I would have howled in scorn." Only with courageous work on his part was he able to revisit the feelings that he had felt in this initial betrayal. The feelings still lived in his body, even though they were covered by the lacquered layers of his persona. Ultimately, by opening up to them he was able to reconnect with essence.

PUTTING THE NEW PARADIGM TO WORK

In the next chapter we will begin to explore how you can put this new view of the psyche into practice. Our body-centered approach integrates readily into verbal therapy. The strategies in the book are not substitutes for traditional clinical skills like careful listening, insight, and empathy. Both of us are the grateful beneficiaries of a classical training in clinical skills, and we could not have developed our body-centered approach without an immersion in these skills. Rather, our strategies represent a new dimension—a deepening—that can make the traditional skills work much more rapidly. Some bodywork approaches, such as rolfing, are focused on getting the mechanics of the body's structure into greater harmony. If the psyche benefits from this physiological integration, so much the better. We approach the problem from a different perspective. Our approach begins where most people begin; with a verbal description of the issues that are troubling them. We listen as keenly as possible to how people describe their problems verbally, and we watch the reactions of their body language and breathing patterns as they do so.

In the next two chapters we show how to bring body-centered therapy into action at the perfect place: exactly where the person is.

THE QUANTUM QUESTIONS: THE KEY QUESTIONS TO PRODUCE RAPID TRANSFORMATION

Several key questions allow people to move from one level of being to another. We call these the Quantum Questions because the person has to make a quantum shift in order to answer them. We teach people to ask these questions as often as needed in their lives, in any situation where change is desired. Although we have tested them most thoroughly in therapy, we have also taught them to medical doctors, lawyers, teachers, and even young children.

The Quantum Questions have the power to keep people from getting stuck at one level—say, the level of projection—and going around in circles with the same interpretations based on this projection. It is a quantum breakthrough when a client learns that a lifelong pattern is a projection, simply a way of seeing the world. For example, Gay's Loner persona was firmly in charge of him for many years. One of the projections that grew out of that persona was that people could not be trusted. Sure enough, this perception brought him into contact with plenty of people and situations who confirmed this view of the world. Prior to the breakthrough in which he realized that this was a projection, he thought that the world actually *was* that way. He remained trapped within this projection for a number of years.

It was also a breakthrough when he realized that this projection was based on a persona, an act he had adopted to survive in a difficult time. The next breakthrough that awaited him was the discovery that beneath this persona were a number of feelings that were still alive in his body, although he sealed them off a lifetime ago. This awareness opened the door to the ultimate awareness; that he was more than his feelings, that he was grounded in a connection to the universe that is pure essence, pure being. When essence opens up, not as a concept but as a living reality, everything changes. The Quantum Questions are designed to produce this result reliably rather than at random.

Although a question is verbal, the Quantum Questions quickly lead people beyond the verbal. In body-centered therapy a Quantum Question produces a singular result: When a therapist asks a client a powerful question, one that causes the client to shift levels, *the client's body reacts in a way that reveals crucial data that the therapist can use to help the client.* Breathing patterns and body language shift unconsciously simply in the act of considering the question.

Consider this moment from Sherry's first session of body-centered therapy with Kathlyn. It is about twenty minutes into the session, and Sherry had been describing how men do not seem to treat her as an equal.

KATHLYN: When did you start experiencing men this way?
SHERRY (*wrinkles her forehead in thought, as if she were straining to remember; her right hand unconsciously reaches up and strokes her upper sternum*): I'm not sure.
KATHLYN: I notice that as you were thinking about it, your hand was stroking your chest. Maybe your body knows something about it that your mind doesn't. Tune in to what you're feeling in your chest.
SHERRY (*her breath catches suddenly and she starts to cry*): I was thinking of all the times I've been hurt.

The Quantum Question—When did you start experiencing men this way?—shifted her from the projection to the experience beneath it. It confused the mind, but the body went right to the heart of the problem, where the issue lived in the flesh.

The most important Quantum Question is:

What are you experiencing right now?

This question always yields a crucial piece of information. It may actually reveal what the person is experiencing, if the person says something like "I'm angry." In our experience, however, this type of response is in the minority, especially in the early stages of personal growth. More likely a different crucial piece of information will be revealed: the person's habitual defensive strategy. If the person defends against his or her pain by intellectualizing, for example, the response will be intellectualized. A person who tends toward a paranoid approach to life may greet the question with suspicion or hostility. In any case, the question never fails to yield something of value.

The following Quantum Questions are more specific, designed to reveal information about each of the four elements discussed in chapter 2: projection, persona, feeling, and essence. Note that sessions often unfold without our ever mentioning concepts like projection by name. In our work we use our understanding of the concepts constantly, but we teach people an intellectual understanding of the concepts only if they are interested. Often it helps clients to understand the concepts in order to apply the principles beyond the therapy office. Sometimes, though, people are not interested in anything more than breaking through specific problems in the office. We do not force our concepts on them; instead, we do our best to translate them into whatever language a particular client understands.

THE PROJECTION QUESTION

First, a client's projections must be accessed and clarified. Because most of us think that our projections are the way things actually are, the therapist cannot simply ask "What are your projections?" If people can answer that question, they probably have already stopped projecting. The quickest way to find out the client's projections is to ask:

What are your complaints?

Listen to a bit of dialogue from our initial session with Tim and Louise.

US: What exactly are your complaints with each other—the ones that are making you consider divorce?

LOUISE (*exasperated sigh*): Where do I start? Everything from not picking up his clothes to leaving the toilet seat up to forgetting to pay the credit cards on time. Just basic irresponsibility, pure and simple.

TIM (*fists clenching*): Listen to that! One time I forgot to pay the Visa bill on time! But what you're hearing is the way it is. Always! I can't do anything right. Absolutely nothing.

What is playing out here is the eternal battle to prove I'm Right and You're Wrong. But in the real world of therapy and relationships, there are never such simple divisions. No one is all right or all wrong: There are simply interlocking personas who are projecting all over each other. Usually there is some reality to a projection. Tim may not have paid the credit card bills on time. But problems in relationships are not solved quite so simply. As their story unfolded, it became clear that Louise's personality tended toward the obsessive-compulsive end of the spectrum, while Tim's tended toward the sloppy. We have seen this combination hundreds of times in our therapy experience. Frequently a sloppy person will seek out a relationship with a tidy partner, and vice versa. Ideally, they learn some valuable things from each other: One learns better organizational skills, while the other learns to loosen up and lighten up. But instead of using their differences as an opportunity to learn, many couples simply complain about each other.

Listen in on a subsequent session, where Louise was beginning to explore her persona:

US: So how did you learn to be such a policeman for responsibility?

LOUISE: From my mother! She was a librarian. If you think I'm concerned about Tim being a slob, you should have heard her with my father. I don't think a day went by when she didn't scream at him for something he did to mess up the house.

US: How did you feel about all that?

LOUISE: I hated it.

US: How would you like it to be now?

LOUISE: I'd like to just have everything be nice all the time without me having to worry about it.

US: Can you see, though, that you're treating Tim the same way your mom treated your dad, the way you hated back then?

LOUISE: Yeah, I'm doing the same old thing that didn't even work thirty years ago.

The issue was similar for Tim. His mother had been the policeman for responsibility while he was growing up. She had bailed him out when he was broke, paid his traffic fines for him, and made calls to his part-time job for him when he was too tired to go in. He never developed a sense of responsibility and the healthy self-respect that goes with it. When he married, his mother even held a lengthy meeting with Louise to explain how he liked his eggs and shirts done.

Both Tim and Louise have learned that the very things they most complained about—lack of responsibility on his part and uptight pickiness on hers—were the very things they required in the other. Such insights are where the great leaps forward are made in personal growth. Rather than focusing on the reality of the problem—who's right or who's wrong, whether he actually is irresponsible or not—a quantum shift is under way. Both of them will eventually discover why they have dreamed up this particular problem upon which to focus (or squander) their energies.

The reality of a situation is best determined when both parties are willing to take one hundred percent of the responsibility for creating it. Anything less is a power struggle over who's responsible. The reality will reveal itself much more clearly once both people have taken complete responsibility for it.

Whenever we use examples like this one in front of a live audience, as on a television talk show, it always amuses us to watch the crowd instantly identify with one or the other of the personas. On several occasions big arguments have broken out in the audience as to which of the personas is right and which is wrong. This speaks to the deeply ingrained tendency to take refuge in and defend the personas, and to how difficult it is for any of us to break free of them.

Years ago, when we were beginning to explore our own personal projections, it became clear to us that projections are easy to discover: *They are simply all the things we complain about.* It was awful at first to see that most of our complaints are projections. After all, our complaints seemed so *right*, so perfectly accurate and justified. It was at first humbling, then liberating as we came to see that our complaints, even some of our most cherished ones, were based on our own personas. In fact, it was the complaints that seemed most accurate that were our biggest projections.

For simplicity's sake, we have devised the Rule of Three. When we find ourselves complaining about something three or more times without taking effective action, we assume it's a projection. One of Gay's cherished complaints, for example, was that people got angry at him "for no reason" and were always trying to control him. As we worked on ourselves, it became clear that *he* got angry at people and tried to control his anger at other people, but was so skillful at concealing it that even he didn't know he was doing it. Deeper exploration revealed that fear of abandonment was actually at the source of his complaint. He was afraid of being left and having people distance themselves from him, so he distanced himself from them first. At first, this awareness was difficult to accept, partly because he had put so much energy into the complaint over the years that he didn't want to cut his losses now. Ultimately, though, the awareness brought an exhilarating sense of freedom. Soon, after accepting the complaint as something he was creating, it simply disappeared.

THE PERSONA QUESTIONS

These Quantum Questions are designed to allow clients to recognize that their projections are based on their personas. The first basic question a therapist can ask is:

Exactly what was happening when you started seeing the world this way?

Another way we sometimes ask this question is:

When did the version of you emerge that experiences the world this way?

(In Gay's example, the question would be "When did the version of yourself emerge that experiences abandonment?")

A second Quantum Question is:

How is this situation familiar?

Another way to ask this question is:

What does this situation remind you of?

This question is best asked when the person's fullest senses are engaged in the projection. For example, we often have the person exaggerate the projection through voice, posture, and gesture, so that he or she gets the deepest sense of how the projection feels. If the person understands the theory, we simply ask, "What persona of yours requires that these events happen to you?" A corollary question is: "How is this present life inevitable, given your background and beliefs?"

One of the profound characteristics of asking Quantum Questions is that they often elicit resistance. In fact, a Quantum Question often elicits *the primal feeling that underlies the persona.* This feeling will often be directed at the therapist. This point cannot be overemphasized: How a person reacts to the Quantum Question will yield a clearer diagnosis than a whole battery of psychological tests. For example, in the case of Bruce and Joan in chapter 2, Bruce's response to the Quantum Question was anger. He became angry at us, the therapists, for even suggesting that his current situation had something to do with him. He had previously projected the problem entirely onto Joan. This moment, when feelings underneath a persona get beamed at the therapist, is what the therapists get paid for handling. Therapists must welcome this moment, not ignore or avoid it. Frequently a Quantum Question triggers sadness or fear instead of anger. Sometimes it produces a knee-jerk "I don't know." These reactions are also diagnostic; the "I don't know" client is likely to be a habitual ignorer of feelings, while the "anger" client may be a habitual denier. Although anger is certainly a feeling, it typically masks a deeper feeling such as fear. Many of the most hostile clients are those the most scared of self-exploration. They are deeply afraid of the level of pain they will find if they allow themselves to turn their attention inward.

As people begin to see their personas with some clarity, it is useful for the therapist to ask:

Given this persona, what kind of people are required to play the other actors in the script?

One of the most gratifying moments as therapists is seeing the aha! of awareness break over their faces when people realize that they are creating the very things they are complaining about. A person with an Abandoned persona suddenly sees that he requires Abandoners, and we know as therapists that once a person sees this, he will never see the world in the same limited way again.

The verbal answer a client gives to a Quantum Question is important, but there is something else of much greater significance: The therapist must learn to notice *how* the client responds to the Quantum Question, not merely what the client says. Of particular importance is the client's body language, for the body reaction often replays exactly the stance that the client originally took when the persona was first assumed.

One young man reacted to this Quantum Question with a puzzled look on his face. At the same moment, he reached down and began to vigorously scratch his right leg. Upon asking him to go further with the leg-scratching, he realized that his projections were based on a persona he had adopted when, as a child, he was required to wear leg braces for a year. He had buried a great deal of anger under a Good Boy persona, and this feeling did not emerge until a casual-seeming leg-scratch put him back in touch with it. As the famous diagnostician Sir William Osler once said, "Listen to the patient—he is telling you his diagnosis." We would expand this important idea by saying that words alone may tell a therapist the diagnosis in time, but if a therapist watches the client's body language, the process of diagnosis and treatment is speeded up enormously. We will cover the reading of body cues in greater detail in our next chapter.

THE FEELING QUESTION

This Quantum Question is designed to allow the client to get in touch with the feelings on which his or her personas are based. The question is:

What were your feelings when you learned to experience the world that way?

An example: Matt and Laura talked to us about a problem that kept repeating in their relationship. She would open up to more of her creativity and power, and he would appear to withdraw and become distant. They both agreed that the pattern occurred; they could not figure out why or how to stop it. On the surface they agreed that they were completely committed to Laura's full development. They had already exhausted their projections before they came to us. Laura had said "He limits me!" and Matt had blamed her for being "pushy and bitchy." However, they quickly saw that there was little potential happiness in their running these projections.

We first had them tell their respective stories, eliciting the projections. We then asked them, "How is this familiar?"

Laura's projection was based on her Supercompetent persona. In growing up as the eldest child of alcoholic parents, she had developed a stance of "I have to do it all myself." This persona had had great survival value for her, but now it was causing trouble. She was bringing it to a situation that no longer wanted to limit her, that in fact wanted to support her power. Her hidden requirement, based on her "I've got to do it myself" persona, was that Matt had to pull away when she opened up to more power. Laura then realized that she did little things to push him away, out of her fear that she could not be powerful and close to someone at the same time.

Matt caught on to his part of it, too. He got in touch with a Loner persona, developed out of his attempts to dodge his powerful mother. The only way he could preserve some space and privacy for himself was to pull back from relationships.

This Quantum Question yielded a deep resolution for them. When we asked Laura, "What feelings were you experiencing when you learned to be that Supercompetent person?" she burst into tears. She talked about her sadness at feeling all alone, at realizing that her parents were woefully inept at the job. Sadness is what we call a Lead Feeling, because it first appears in response to the Quantum Question. Often though, the client's Lead Feeling is not the only one. There are frequently one or more Masked Feelings that need to be explored. A Masked Feeling is one that is hidden behind the

Lead Feeling. As a rule of thumb, the Lead Feeling of anger often is accompanied by a Masked Feeling of sadness. A Lead Feeling of sadness often hides anger.

We suggested to Laura that it might be appropriate for her to feel anger in such a situation. At first she denied it, saying that her parents were too pitiful to feel much anger at. We inquired about fear. Almost as soon as the words left our mouth, she realized that she had experienced a great deal of anger but had been afraid to express it lest it upset her younger siblings. A flood of other fears and angers came forth. But even this wasn't the end of it. As we pressed on, it emerged that Laura's sexual feelings were actually the source of the problem.

And so it was with Matt, in a very different way. Laura's parents' battles had had a strong sexual component, and they had resolved into noisy lovemaking about as often as they resulted in someone storming out the front door. She sought refuge from this type of conflict by assuming her Supercompetent persona. In the busy, neat, and tidy world of her Supercompetent persona, there was no room for the messy feelings of sexuality. Years later, in her relationship with Matt, she would experience more sexual energy as she opened up to more of her creativity and power. But since she did not yet know how to embrace this deeper sexual energy, she created a problem with Matt to bring herself back down to something more familiar.

Matt's script interlocked perfectly with hers. He had felt a sexual threat from his mother. His father had left early in his childhood, and Matt had become the Little Man of the House. As he tuned in to his persona, he identified a sexual component to his Loner act. He felt it was crucial to protect his sexuality from his mother, possibly out of fear that he might feel sexual feelings toward her. As we explored this aspect, he recalled her often coming to his bed late at night to cuddle him as she cried. He would feel his muscles tighten when this occurred, as if he were trying to stifle his feelings by stiffening himself. Finally, he told his third-grade teacher about it, and shortly thereafter the visits had stopped. He suspected that the teacher had mentioned it to his mother and that there had been words between them. But both his mother and his teacher had seemed to relate to him with distance from that point on, and he never quite knew if he'd done the right thing.

The Quantum Question for feelings may yield material that takes much time to integrate. Often there are walls of denial and avoidance that people must deal with just to gain access to their feelings. There is also the issue of whether people are willing to go all the way to completely experience and express their feelings. Once, for example, a highly intellectual corporate executive was in our office. She was exploring her Hard Case persona and discovered that underneath it was a fear of her own vulnerability. To give her a break from her nonstop flow of concepts, we invited her to take a moment simply to feel this fear in her body. She paused for about half a second, then resumed her monologue by saying "Okay, I guess this is what they call getting in touch with your feelings. But I still don't see what good it does."

It takes considerable practice to be able to experience feelings rather than to talk about them, but this skill is essential to opening to essence. Essence is developed by giving ourselves permission to be with our feelings and ourselves. Like any other skill, this one takes time to cultivate.

Therapists can speed up the process a great deal by inviting clients to locate their feelings specifically in time and space. The two questions that we have found most useful in helping clients pin down their feelings are:

Where are you experiencing this feeling in your body?
What are the specific sensations you are feeling?

The more clients can be specific about their feelings, the faster they can clear up. One reason these questions are so helpful is that many of us become awash in our feelings, resulting in a state of emotional overwhelm. Feelings can seem bigger than we are at times. Locating the feelings in the body, in a specific place or places, brings about an important shift in perception. Suddenly the feeling is something that is happening in a particular location. It is no longer bigger than we are. It has been restored to its proper place in the totality of ourselves. In addition, these questions anchor a person firmly in the present. Self-exploration often draws people into the past, to consider the source of the patterns that are playing out in their present lives. But it is important to anchor these explorations in the somatic reality of the present, and these questions readily accomplish this goal.

THE REALITY QUESTION

One of the most important Quantum Questions is:

Exactly what happened?

There was a moment in time and a location in space when a specific event happened that triggered the feelings that led to the persona that led to the projections. The therapist is after a statement of what happened, not of what meaning the client has made of it. The reality of what actually happened is usually obscured by the client's assessment of it and the meaning the client has made of it. Sometimes the client can remember what happened, sometimes not. In one sense it does not matter whether there is a memory of it, so long as the client accepts that something happened. In other words, the important thing is to open up the inquiry into what happened, not necessarily to come up with a perfect memory of it.

By the time most of us are adults, our personas, feelings, and projections have become so mixed up that it is not easy to separate them. We often have no idea of what actually happened to us, the events on which our personas were based. One client remembers being thrown off the back steps by his brother, but he forgot what had happened immediately before, until his mother reminded him of it. According to the mother, our client had stuck a crayon in his brother's eye first, triggering the fight. In other words, he remembered the part where he was the victim, but forgot the part where he was the perpetrator.

An experimental study has been designed to find out whether four- and five-year-old children can accurately remember whether their genitals have been touched during medical exams. The experimenters set up a situation in which doctors specifically touched some of the children and did not touch others. (All this was being done in the presence of their parents.) The results were not encouraging to therapists who encourage their clients to recall incidents of early abuse. Even one day later, the children's memories were unreliable, and a week later were extremely hazy. There is even now a growing backlash against the use of memories recovered in therapy. A new diagnosis—False Memory Syndrome—is being proposed, and a foundation has been organized to promote its premise.

Our position is that sometimes people can recover accurate memories of what happened, but often they cannot. For healing to occur, however, it is not necessary to recover accurate memories of past events. What is important is for the person to realize that *something happened*. There was a moment in time and space when the issue came into being. This realization disrupts a common illusion: that problems are pervasive and permanent. Once a client realizes that the problem started at a particular point in life, he or she can conceive of himself or herself as free of the problem.

THE ESSENCE QUESTION

Several Quantum Questions lead to essence. One of the most important is:

Can you conceive of yourself completely free of this issue?
Another is:

Who is the you that was there before this problem occurred?
A third is:

**Would you be willing to feel and tell the truth of this
event until it is complete?**
This third question may lead immediately to the emergence of something key to the healing process, but even if it does not yield an immediate payoff, it opens up the inquiry.

All these Quantum Questions can reveal essence on the spot, but they are more likely to open a space, sometimes only for a split second, that can give the person a flash of freedom. Ultimately, if people are willing to experience their feelings deeply enough, essence will appear spontaneously. Everything resolves in essence if the deepest truth of a situation is completely experienced and expressed.

This example is drawn from one of our relationship seminars. Stephen and Debbie volunteered to work on an issue in the front of the room so that the other participants (approximately a hundred people) could observe the process of a couple working down through the layers of projection, persona, and feelings to the experience of essence. The initial statement of the problem from Debbie was: "He's so inarticulate and inexact in the way he talks. It just drives me nuts." From Stephen: "She's always criticizing me. I can't stand it." They had been together only about six months, having experienced bliss in the first few months of their relationship until this issue had slammed on the brakes.

Our work with them started very slowly, largely because she defended her point of view very vigorously.

"The English language is so beautiful," she proclaimed righteously, "and I hate to see it abused."

"See!" he exploded, pounding his fist in exasperation. "Why do I have to put up with that tone of voice?"

We persisted with asking the Quantum Question for personas: What did this current situation remind them of from the past? Finally we broke through to the persona level. It emerged that Debbie's mother had been a librarian and an English teacher, forever correcting her English as a child.

And how had she felt when this occurred?

"Furious," she said, wrinkling her nose in disgust at the memory. We asked her to go further, to find out if there were other feelings beneath this persona. She burst into tears, saying that this critical aspect had prevented a close connection from developing between her and her mother. She felt robbed of the opportunity for intimacy. Then a wave of horror and amazement spread over her face as she realized that she was wholeheartedly running the identical persona with Stephen, preventing intimacy between them.

At this point a woman in the seminar raised her hand. "Did you plant these two in the audience?" she asked. There was a roar of laughter from the audience, and Debbie and Stephen walked hand in hand back to their seats, gazing at the essence in each other's eyes.

Such happy occurrences are the result of courage, not luck. It takes real courage for people to let go of their righteous projections and open up to the persona beneath. It takes a further leap of courage to explore the feelings underneath the persona. Essence is the big payoff, though, and is such a rewarding experience that people usually get hooked on it the farther along they go. The courage of jumping off into the unknown is replaced by a growing sense of inner certainty that there is a resting place inside ourselves.

ENTERING THE DOMAIN OF
BODY-CENTERED THERAPY

These Quantum Questions are the blueprint for powerful therapy. Used by themselves, without body-centered techniques, they will allow a great deal of healing to occur. Therapists skilled in working with the body will go far, far beyond these questions, however, into the domains of breath, movement, and body language. Projection, persona, and feelings are all revealed with exquisite precision through shifts in breathing and body language. Therapists who learn to speak this subtle language seldom have to rely on the verbal questions. Ultimately, the realm of essence itself opens up, because essence is always there, covered over by only the thinnest veil of illusion. All of the questions—and the whole inquiry into movement and breath—are designed to uncover essence and give the person an opportunity to celebrate it in self and others.

The body-centered therapist can move rapidly to essence by using the techniques and principles introduced in the next chapter. One couple, Sam and Lori, both in their midforties, came in to see us on the verge of divorce. They had been stuck in an intractable struggle for months. Both were exhausted and about to give up. For the first few minutes of the session, we listened carefully to their complaints. According to Sam, Lori was uptight and on his case about money. According to Lori, Sam was completely irresponsible about money and needed constant policing to stay motivated to keep his spending under control. As we worked with them during the hour, the source point for this polarization was gradually revealed in a most surprising way. Using the strategies in Part II, we assisted them in moving down through their polarized personas to the feelings underneath the battle. When Sam got underneath his persona and put his attention on the actual sensations he was feeling, he reported that he felt as if he were in the middle of "a mucoid sac." Lori said that she felt that she couldn't "see any way out of this situation." We were immediately alerted to the possibility that they were replaying a script from very early in life. The metaphors they were using suggested that the issues might be coming from prenatal or birth experiences.

As Sam talked about his sensations, his hand unconsciously began to cover the left side of his face and tug the skin at the side of his left eye. We asked him to tune in to this movement and make it a little bigger. He said that his vision had been blurry on this side for a week. As he mentioned this point, his left hand unconsciously moved again, this time touching his left lower back in the kidney area. We asked him to pick up on this movement and to feel what it was saying. He reported that he had been suffering from a kidney infection. We invited him to tune in to what feeling was being expressed through his hand movement, his left eye, and his kidney infection. "Fear," he said. "It's where I'm hiding all my fear." Staying with the inquiry, he let himself feel the fear in his body. Suddenly he blurted out that it felt like just before his birth, when his mother was overwhelmed with pain and given heavy anesthesia. He said that his mother had been enraged at not having any support and terrified at having to do it all alone. At the peak of her rage and fear the anesthesia had taken her into unconsciousness.

This finding tied in with one of the first things Sam had mentioned in the session—that he had felt numb all week. It also fit with the pattern that kept repeating in his life: He actually *was* being irresponsible about money. When the subject came up with Lori, he would get angry and take refuge in being spaced out. The pattern seemed to him directly connected to his prebirth experience. After the session the pattern cleared up, along with the relationship conflict and the real-life money troubles.

Now for Lori's interlocking issue: As we invited her to open up to her feelings, she, too, headed in a prenatal direction. Her mother had developed cancer during the pregnancy, and Lori felt as if she had little cellular support for living, being locked in a struggle to keep from being overwhelmed by her mother's cancerous cells. A pattern of rigid determination, fueled by a rage to live, had dominated her relationships. As she explored the prenatal origins, she saw how they were replaying in her current struggle with Sam. Neither of them, of course, had suspected that the battle actually had its origins in the womb. As a result of getting underneath the polarized struggle at the persona level, they uncovered a shared background. It made a huge difference in their relationship, because both of them lost interest in the battle and became allies again.

In summary, the absolutely crucial element for therapists to embrace is that essence lies below all conflict. If we as therapists feel this fact down in our cells, we can use practically any technique and it will work. On the other hand, if we are not acquainted with essence, even the fanciest technique may never take the person all the way to essence. The preceding example is testimony to how deeply we need to go to find essence. In Sam and Lori's case, essence was buried under a survival struggle of four decades ago.

Their case also speaks to the need for therapists to do a great deal of work on essence. Since we personally spend most of our time training therapists, we have developed a strong position in regard to this issue. We think that the main problem holding back the field is that therapists operate from their beliefs rather than from essence. When this occurs, therapists become their beliefs—their beliefs *have* them—instead of realizing that all beliefs are like lifeboats in a friendly ocean of essence. When therapists do not rest comfortably in essence, they cannot see it effectively in their clients. This shortsightedness may lead them to settle for their clients' simply changing one overcoat for another. Indeed, it may even lead them to mistake the overcoat for the real person. Once therapists experience a breakthrough to essence and learn to hold out for this same event in clients, they will never again settle for anything less.

The practical value of this knowledge is that therapists can proceed with confidence, knowing that conflicts are simply points of view that are preventing essence from being experienced and appreciated. Conflict causes human beings to lose touch with essence. In other words, we get busy defending our own lifeboat against the lifeboats of others and forget that we are all sailing on the same ocean.

SIGNPOSTS TO ESSENCE: READING THE SUBTLE LANGUAGE OF THE UNCONSCIOUS THROUGH THE FIVE FLAGS

Think with the whole body.
—Taisen Deshimaru

Thinking is what gets you caught from behind.
—O. J. Simpson

We experience stress when body and mind are not in harmony. If your body is scared, for example, but your mind is trying to deny it, the resulting disharmony will probably be obvious to you and to those around you. We have witnessed a fascinating phenomenon many times as we worked with clients on a biofeedback machine. If a client is scared, saying "I'm scared" will cause their stress level to drop. In other words, the very act of acknowledging fear puts mind and body in harmony again.

Reducing stress is certainly a valuable outcome of restoring harmony to body and mind, but even greater value has come to our therapy clients as they learned to live in alignment. Happiness and creativity are natural byproducts of harmony. As body and mind become unified, becoming a bodymind, people express themselves more creatively, make better decisions, and spend more of their time feeling happy.

THE FIVE FLAGS

All of us can benefit from learning to notice and understand the signals of disharmony from mind and body. There are five readily observable ways the bodymind sends out signals when unexpressed emotions need to be felt and communicated. Our term for these signals is *flags*. The Five Flags can be seen in breath, movement, posture, speech patterns, and attitude. These flags nearly always communicate faster than the conscious communications, and they are more reliable indicators of what is actually going on. There are many other flags through which the body and mind communicate, such as muscle tension and brain wave changes, but they are generally not visible to the naked eye. The flags we will discuss in this chapter do not require any procedures to detect them other than our own consciousness.

We consider the Five Flags first-line methods of diagnosis and treatment. In our experience recognizing them is a skill that is absolutely crucial to the therapist. Actually, any sensitive human being who wishes to communicate more effectively can benefit from an awareness of the flags. Business people and other professionals have told us that they were able to put awareness of the Five Flags to immediate use in their own work situations. One of our former clients, a general at the Pentagon, even mentioned that he employs what he learned about the flags at meetings that include the highest authorities in the land. Whatever your perspective, we believe that an understanding of the flags can add to your ability to communicate with people.

The Five Flags all indicate cracks in a persona. They point to places where the stress of living in a persona is so great that a tiny breakdown is occurring. One couple came in for their first session of counseling when the woman was convinced that her partner was having an affair. We turned to him and asked, "Well, are you?" His left eye twitched wildly, his breath shifted up into his chest, he crossed both arms and legs, and he said, with a righteous indignation, "What kind of question is that?" We pointed out his breath shift, his eye-twitching, the way he had crossed his arms and legs, and the fact that he had not answered with a clear yes or no. With this he slumped forward, burst into tears, and confessed that he had been conducting a relationship with another woman for *over ten years*. Interestingly, both of them became extraordinarily grateful for this moment, which, after the uproar died down, took them into a rebirth of their relationship. All we had really done was to point out three of the Five Flags that had occurred in the same moment. The stress of wearing his persona was so great that three cracks were observable in one response.

In two decades of training therapists, we have had the opportunity to study many of our students' taped sessions. We have also watched ourselves on videotape hundreds of times to improve our own skills. One learning stands out: People are a lot more telepathic than they think they are. Human beings are extraordinarily sensitive to each other, and just because many of them have learned to override this sensitivity does not mean it has disappeared from them altogether. Therapists' conscious minds are always far behind their unconscious minds. Dozens of times we have observed a client change positions, perhaps leaning to one side; a split second later, the therapist makes an adjustment to match the client's new posture. Inevitably, when we point this out later, the therapy student was not conscious of changing position. This is good news. It means that some deeper part of the therapist's mind was watching for how it could resonate with the client. Matching the posture change was what this part of the mind came up with. It is fascinating to speculate about what else in the therapist might be changing in response to the client. Perhaps subtle brain wave changes could be detected in response to changes in the client. But in our work we are most interested in the changes that anyone can be trained to perceive. In this section we will be working toward conscious use of these changes on the part of the client, in order to make the work proceed more rapidly.

The Five Flags can be thought of as signposts to essence. Because they are stress reactions, it is sometimes easy to think of them in negative terms. But we encourage our therapy students and our clients to think of them as friends, as winks from the soul. They are signals that the stress of separation from essence is too wearing, and that there is an opportunity to surrender the persona and reclaim the connection to essence. Many if not most of our clients have been so accustomed to censoring the signals from their inner selves that they think they have done something wrong when we point out one of the Five Flags.

Listen in on this moment from a therapy session with a new client.

GAY: I notice that as you talked about changing jobs, you were gently stroking your left arm.

REBECCA (*quickly removes hand from arm, as if caught doing something wrong*): Oh, I'm sorry. I didn't realize I was doing that.

We went on to explore why Rebecca had so interpreted an observation by a therapist who had no interest in judging her or in catching her doing something wrong. It turned out that Rebecca, like many people, had built a whole lifestyle around concealing her inner self. Finally, when the pain of concealment became great enough that she sought help, she interpreted an opportunity to inquire into the inner self as censure.

THE FIVE FLAGS IN BRIEF

Let's begin our exploration of the Five Flags with a brief example of each. On the videotape of a therapy session, we noticed that the client's breathing was deep, full, and observably moving her relaxed lower abdomen. This pattern indicates that she was using correct diaphragmatic breathing. In the next session we brought up an issue from a previous session: "How is your daughter?" Immediately the breathing in her abdomen stopped, shifted up into the chest, and became labored. This is a **breathing flag**. It indicates a shift to the Fight-or-Flight Breathing mechanisms of the body (see chapter 9). Practically speaking, a breathing flag tells the therapist that the client is withholding some unexpressed emotion. As it turned out, this woman still had a lot of anger about a situation with her daughter that had not been effectively expressed. Interestingly, as we watched the videotape later, we noticed that our own breathing shifted slightly up toward the chest right after her breathing changed. Then, a second later, ours shifted back to our bellies, although her breathing remained up in her chest until after she had communicated the unexpressed feeling. Then it shifted back down into her belly.

A **movement flag** can be any motion the body makes. Movement flags range from the comically obvious to the extraordinarily subtle. An obvious one: One of our therapy students was doing a session with a teenage boy.

The boy hesitantly brought up a sexual issue with which he was struggling. Our student, who had been sitting quite relaxed, suddenly crossed her legs and arms. She turned out to be personally quite defensive about sex. In fact, she grew quite defensive when we showed her the videotape. The client had unwittingly found the therapist's blind spot, and the therapist had reacted to it equally unconsciously.

A more subtle movement flag may reveal a particularly deep emotional issue. One of our clients was talking about something that seemed relatively trivial. At one point we noticed a tiny split-second squint of his eyes. We said, "Something just passed through your eyes. What's that saying?" He sneezed. We waited. Suddenly his head slumped down, and he began to cry. This emergence of emotion signaled a breakthrough for him out of his usual controlled way of being. The unconscious flag had said, "It's time to cry." Had we not noticed it, his breakthrough might have been delayed.

A **postural flag** is more static than a movement or breathing flag. It usually signals a chronic issue that has settled into the physical configuration of the body itself. A common postural flag is one shoulder that is lower than the other. Another is when one side of the jaw bulges more than the other. A third is a sunken chest. A good way to think of postural flags is that they can be observed in still photographs. In fact, we frequently have clients bring in childhood photographs to identify when in their life they adopted the personas that sculpted their body tensions.

Some people argue that their postural flags are genetic. Some of them may be, but more often we have found that they are learned. We know of a family, for example, where the father and three sons all have a distinctive postural flag in common: Their chests tend to cave in and their heads jut forward. The youngest son has the most pronounced version of this flag, and we assumed that it was genetic. But later we discovered that he had been adopted into the family when he was four. In his first two years of photographs, the flag is not visible. It slowly appears in his elementary school years and is well in place by high school. Despite the fact that he was adopted, he had the same postural flag as his family.

Verbal flags may appear in both the tone of a person's voice and the content of the person's communication. Are the words said in a flat tone or in a whine? Are they clipped, or are they mumbled? The most common verbal flag is a word that is repeated or underscored. If a person uses the word *awful* several times to describe things, it may turn out that *awful* has a special meaning to that person, stemming from a specific moment in life. A prominent example occurred in the first session of therapy with a thirty-five-year-old woman, Georgia. In the first ten minutes of her session she used the phrase "I can't get past it" seven times. Each time it came out slightly different. Once it was "I just can't seem to get past it," while another time she asked "Why can't I seem to get past this?" As we worked with Georgia, it turned out that not being able to get past things had been a theme of her life. She was deeply competitive with her twin sister, whom she had always struggled to "get past" academically and athletically. It may have even started at birth: According to the birth records the twins had jammed up in the process of getting out, and our client had literally not been able to get past her sister.

The chronic lifelong pattern had given her a cringing and apologetic manner. This **attitude flag** was made up of posture, voice, tone, and speech patterns. Exactly what makes up an attitude is harder to pin down specifically: What is it that makes James Dean's attitude different from John Wayne's but somewhat similar to Elvis Presley's? It is probably possible to take it apart into its components, but the overall picture is what is important with an attitude.

WORKING WITH THE FIVE FLAGS

It is not possible for the therapist to be aware of every flag that goes by. Nor would it even be helpful to the client to mention all of them. We train our students to focus on repetitive flags—those that a client tends to use over and over—as well as on flags that have a particular charge to them. With practice, the therapist begins to recognize those that are important and to let the others pass by. The beginning student can be comforted by realizing that any flag will do for the basic purpose, since all flags lead to the same place: They are all signals from the unconscious. They all indicate a need for the person to go within, to inquire into the deeper self, and to communicate the truth of the inquiry to the outside world. The therapist who recognizes a flag is simply picking up on a communication that the person desperately needs to make but is unable to articulate on a conscious level.

The Five Flags are also signals from the unconscious that it is ready to change. This news is important for therapists, because timing is one of the central issues in helping people change. Gifted therapists are able to see subtle flags before they become major symptoms. In some ways the workings of the unconscious are like the underpinnings of a car. Sitting in the driver's seat, we may not pick up on a subtle communication from the underpinnings that something is wrong. Once, for example, Gay thought he felt or heard something a little "off" in the sound of his car, a *whrrr* that had not been there before. It was so faint that he disregarded it, even though it flickered through his awareness several times over the course of a week. Then on the inconvenience of a country road, a belt gave way, stranding him twenty miles from town. Later a mechanic confirmed that the initial sounds of the belt fraying would have been detectable by a change in the sound of the engine. The unconscious is like that. We often overlook or override the initial faint signals that something needs to be handled. We may notice a thought that hurries across the crowded back corner of our mind, or a fleeting feeling that can be easily ignored. But if we continue to avert our attention, the unconscious must take a stronger means of expression. Hence the flags. When the unconscious cannot make its wishes and feelings known to its owner, it may start flashing signals to the neighbors.

The Five Flags are signals that the bodymind is under stress. Consider a movement flag that is often seen in couples therapy: the twisting of a wedding ring. This mannerism nearly always signals that there is an unexpressed communication that needs to be delivered. The stress of withholding the communication produces a logjam of energy in the bodymind that leaks out through the twisting of the wedding ring. In fact, flags may be considered as "feeling leaks." If we cannot say something directly, it usually finds expression in some roundabout way.

Freud called dreams the royal road to the unconscious. Perhaps they are, but not everyone can pay the toll. Dreams are not easy to recall, and they are even more difficult to interpret. Plus, the therapist cannot see the raw data, only the secondhand report filtered through the client's conscious mind. The Five Flags are the freeway to the unconscious, because they get both parties there the fastest. We are certainly not saying that dreams are a waste of time; in fact, they can often be deeply revealing. They only appeal to a small segment of the population, however, whereas flags like movement and breath are paths to the unconscious that everyone can travel.

Let us now explore each of the Five Flags in more detail.

BREATHING FLAGS

The first thing we usually notice about a person's breathing style is *where* the breath is. For example, the breath may be high in the chest, with little or no movement in the lower abdomen. The second thing we focus on is *how* it is: It may be labored, effortful, and hesitant. Taken together—where and how—these elements form a person's breathing signature.

Although there are some broad categories, each person's breathing signature is slightly different. The combination of shallow chest breathing and effortfulness is a signature common to asthma patients. As one client cleared up his asthma through practicing the Daily Breathing Program described in chapter 10, his breathing signature changed to its exact opposite: He learned to breathe diaphragmatically, as nature intended, rather than staying trapped in permanent Fight-or-Flight Breathing.

THREE MAIN BREATHING PATTERNS

Although there are subtle differences in breathing patterns that make everyone's breathing unique, there are three general patterns that can be recognized. A distinguishing characteristic is whether the breath is found largely in the belly or largely in the chest.

- CENTERED BREATHING. In a relaxed state, breath ideally should move the lower abdomen dominantly, with some movement in the chest. We call this pattern Centered Breathing. Centered

Breathing is the ideal pattern for most of human existence. It is deep and relaxed; it occurs at a rate of eight to twelve times a minute. It is the pattern you will learn in the Daily Breathing Program described in chapter 10.

- AEROBIC BREATHING. This pattern is in effect when we are in a physically aroused but not frightened state—such as during exercise or sex. In Aerobic Breathing the breath moves the chest and the belly together, rapidly and deeply. Upon closer observation, there is usually more movement in the chest. We will not discuss this pattern in detail, because it has little relevance for therapy or personal growth.

- FIGHT-OR-FLIGHT BREATHING. This breathing pattern is a major source of difficulty for human beings. When a person is scared, angry, or hurt, the stomach muscles tighten, curtailing movement in the belly and forcing the breath up into the chest. Breathing speeds up to a rate of fifteen or more times a minute.

The problem is usually that people are using Fight-or-Flight Breathing when they ought to be using Centered Breathing. At this stage of evolution human beings have the ability to create symbolic fears in their minds. This is not the case with other animals. A cat will go into Fight-or-Flight Breathing when a feared dog comes into view. When the dog is gone, the cat's breathing goes back to Centered Breathing. By contrast, humans have the ability to keep a steady stream of unpleasant images coursing through their minds all day long, whether or not those images have any relationship to reality. Our physiology responds to mind-stuff just as it does to real-stuff.

Therapists are generally concerned only with Centered and Fight-or-Flight Breathing. Clients often come in with Fight-or-Flight Breathing; with skilled intervention, they leave with Centered Breathing. In our work we train people to notice when their breathing shifts from Centered to Fight-or-Flight Breathing. When they become skilled at noticing this shift, they are able to discern better what emotions they are experiencing. We also train people directly in the skills of Centered Breathing. (Both of these approaches are explained in chapter 9.)

For a therapist, the easiest way to notice a client's breathing pattern is to keep the eyes mainly on his or her chest and belly. Breath does move other places like the back and the pelvis, but these areas are often harder to observe. We have found that with an hour or so of training, nearly everyone can reliably distinguish between Centered and Fight-or-Flight Breathing.

THE HOW OF BREATHING

To observe *how* a client breathes, considerably more art and intuition are required. There are hundreds of adjectives that can be applied to breathing styles. Whether a client's breathing is ragged or hesitant can be a meaningful distinction, but it takes quite a bit of practice to see and hear the difference. For the present we would like to focus on just one dimension of breathing: the force of the breath. Does the breath have a weak or strong quality? Is it shallow or deep? Does it seem to support the person's full expression, or is something held back? Another aspect of breathing force is whether too much effort is being used: Is there an effortful quality to the breath? Is it easy or labored? Macho or wimpy? By noticing this dimension, the therapist can get great insight into the client's persona before a word is even spoken.

Here is a bit of dialogue in which a breathing flag reveals a major pattern. It occurred approximately ten minutes into Alan's session.

GAY: I notice that your breathing is mostly up in your chest.

ALAN (*pauses*): Yeah, I guess that's where it is most of the time. I can't ever seem to get a deep breath, even if I really inflate my chest.

GAY: Right. There's not much room up there. The only way to get a full breath is to use your diaphragm. And to do that you have to fill your belly, not your chest.

ALAN: How do you mean?

GAY: I'll show you, but first, magnify the way you're breathing right now. Breathe way up in your chest. Make it real effortful like that.

ALAN (*exaggerates the effortful quality*): God, that hurts!

GAY: Yes. Notice what that kind of breathing reminds you of? What time in your life?

ALAN: I'm not sure.

GAY: Stay with it. Check it out.

ALAN: Okay. (*Pause.*) Well, it reminds me of when I would cry as a kid, and try to keep from it so I wouldn't get in trouble with my father. He hated me crying. "I'll give you something to cry about" is what he would always say.

GAY: Yes. Take a moment to feel all the feelings you have about that. (*Alan spontaneously takes his first centered breath.*)

GAY: Did you feel how you breathed down into your belly? Let that happen again. Yes—let the breath fill your belly, so that it feels like you are filling up a balloon down there.

Sometimes a breathing flag reveals a specific incident in which the breathing pattern itself was directly traumatized. Kathlyn was working with a new client one day when the following interaction took place.

KATHLYN: So sometimes you feel out of control?

RHONDA: Yes, the body does these things, and it doesn't have anything to do with me. At those moments the body doesn't seem real.

KATHLYN: What else do you notice?

RHONDA: Sometimes I can't breathe into my chest. (*As she says this, she unconsciously touches her throat.*)

KATHLYN: Be with that thing your hand is doing—touching your throat. Do that a little more, and tell me what it reminds you of.

RHONDA (*her chest flutters, her face gets flushed, and she starts to choke up*): I—I can't get my breath.

KATHLYN: Feel what that's connected to. When in your life?

RHONDA (*suddenly begins breathing deeply*): Omigod, I remember my uncle sitting on my chest. I couldn't breathe. I was just a kid, maybe ten, and he was a teenager. (*Pauses and gulps big, deep breaths.*) Yeah, it seemed as if it had a sexual component, too. He was turned on. But I think I went unconscious and left my body.

It was a combination of breathing and movement flags that yielded Rhonda's breakthrough. In fact, these two flags often accompany each other, since when the bodymind is under stress, breathing and movement are both compromised.

MOVEMENT FLAGS

Three key areas in which movement flags appear are the extremities, the eyes, and the position of the head. The extremities—arms, legs, and fingers—are perhaps the best place to observe movement flags. Clients often cross their arms and/or their legs when sensitive issues are discussed. They may pick at a fingernail or twist a wedding ring. These movements of the extremities are nearly always revealing to the therapist and client, if handled skillfully.

Similarly, the eyes (the proverbial "windows to the soul") are movement flags par excellence. As the only place where the brain fronts directly on the world, the eyes give a sensitive portrayal of the inner world of the client. There are several easy-to-observe movement flags that the eyes give off. One is averting the eyes. When a certain subject is raised, do the eyes go up, down, or off to the side? Is this a characteristic pattern, and if so, what is the meaning of it to the client? Another frequently encountered eye movement flag is defocusing: The person "goes off," as if in retreat. A third such flag, somewhat harder to see, is when the size of the pupil shrinks or gets larger.

In this dialogue from a therapy session, one of these eye flags is being discussed.

KATHLYN: Marty, I noticed that when you start to talk about your anger, you look off to the left. Look off to the left a few times and see what that reminds you of.

MARTY (*darts eyes to the left several times*): I don't know. It makes me feel a little nauseous, though.

KATHLYN: Do it a little more. Let yourself breathe right through the nausea.

MARTY: Ugh—it's like the worst part of me, the part I don't want to look at.

KATHLYN: Which is . . .

MARTY: Feeling unwanted, unloved. Like I don't belong here.

KATHLYN: Let yourself really contact that feeling. Notice where you feel it in your body.

MARTY: Yeah, I feel it all over, like it's in my blood.

The position of the head also reveals an enormous amount of information to the observant therapist. Some people chronically tilt the head to the left or right, while others chronically jut forward or pull back the head. In some people these head positions are not chronic, but emerge as responses to specific emotions. If the head positions are chronic, they are considered postural flags instead of movement flags. In Joyce's case her nonchronic head position was the starting point for an important learning on her part. Here she is discussing a problem she kept having with her boss.

GAY: Joyce, as you were talking about your issues with your boss just a moment ago, I heard a kind of "little girl" tone in your voice. Does that sound familiar to you?

JOYCE (*cocks head to the right*): Gee, I don't really know. (*in the "little girl" tone*) It's like, just out of my reach.

GAY: Tilt your head even farther to your right side. Make your voice a little more "little-girly." Talk to your boss as if you were a real little girl.

JOYCE (*mincing, whiny*): You never appreciate me. All you want is nine to five. You don't want to know the real me.

GAY: Who are you really talking to?

JOYCE (*starts crying*): Dad. I'm talking to my dad. He's just like my boss. He doesn't see me. I'm just somebody to get the job done. He doesn't want to know who I am.

Joyce explained this issue further, discovering how her Little Girl persona interlocked with the "Critical Father" persona of her boss. One of the flags that came in handiest was that her head was out of the vertical when she talked to her boss. Noticing this movement flag was much easier than noticing the whole persona and its accompanying projections.

POSTURAL FLAGS

Chronic patterns of tension in the body gradually express themselves in postural anomalies. This is a subject that could easily fill an entire book. For the present discussion, however, we will focus on three kinds of postural flags: left/right splits, top/bottom splits, and front/back splits. Here are several examples of each:

- LEFT/RIGHT SPLITS. One shoulder higher than the other; one eye more open or more closed than the other; one leg shorter or longer than the other; the left hip higher or lower than the right; one side of the jaw more muscled or bulgy than the other (see figure 2).

- TOP/BOTTOM SPLITS. Weight help in hips and legs while torso is thin or underdeveloped; barrel chest with underdeveloped legs.

- FRONT/BACK SPLITS. Pelvis pulled back while belly juts forward;

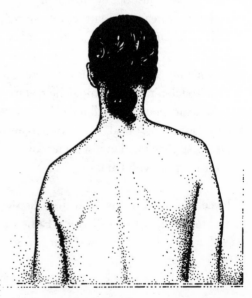

FIGURE 2. A Left/Right Split

head pulled back while chest juts forward; head straining forward, in front of torso and lower body (see figure 3).

It must be emphasized that, as much as some therapists would like there
to be a universal language of the body, there is none. In our twenty-some
years of body-centered therapy, we have found no pattern that always
means the same thing in everyone. We learned what we know by noticing
what people spoke of when they explored certain splits and imbalances in
their bodies. We did not start out with a theory that we then fit to our
findings. Working the other way around, we developed our theory from
what people uncovered as they explored themselves.

Bearing this point firmly in mind, here are a few generalizations that we
have found to be true.

Left/right splits often reveal a male/female distinction in the person's
psychology. For example, if the person's trauma has largely been with the
mother rather than with the father, it tends to be expressed in more tension
on the left side of the body. We have found over the years that psychoso-
matic problems tend to be found on the left side rather than on the right
side of the person's body. Freud himself mentioned this odd finding a
hundred years ago. This may be due in part to the right hemisphere's
intimate relationship with the left side of the body. The right hemisphere,

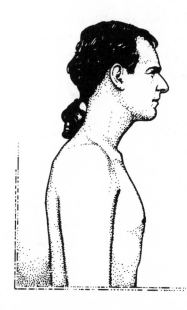

FIGURE 3. A Front/Back Split

the repository of image and emotional memory, runs many of the functions of the left side of the body. This finding could also mean that many of us have deeper wounds with our mothers than with our fathers. For whatever reason, the sensitive observer will soon discover that left/right asymmetry is the norm rather than the exception.

Left/right splits may also reflect our relationship with our internalized male and female. As the Buddha said thousands of years ago, enlightenment involves cultivating all the feminine and all the masculine elements of ourselves, regardless of whether we are biologically male or female. For a man, it is urgent to befriend the feminine elements of himself: the intuitive, the feelingful, the receptive. For a woman, it is equally important to come to terms with the forceful, the outgoing, the active. When left/right splits are discerned in a person, imbalances in their internalized male and female are often found.

Top/bottom splits often reveal the differences between support and expression in the person's psychology. The upper part of the body is very expressive—the arms, the heart, and the head. The lower part of the body is where most of us experience support or lack thereof. Moshe Feldenkrais expressed this principle well with his slogan, "You *are* where your pelvis is." If your pelvis is tucked back out of the way, you will experience the world very differently from the way you experience the world if it is underneath you, supporting you solidly.

Front/back splits often reveal a person's relationship with time. If the head is forward, out in front of the body, the person may well have a "hurry-up" script. This pattern can be contrasted with a posture in which the head is pulled back. Frequently this type of person is in retreat from life. Similar front/back issues can be seen in the pelvis, which can either be held back in retraction or held forward, as if it were leading the body.

Another set of issues that emerges from the exploration of front/back splits are those involving experience and expression. The front of the body seems to be more associated with experience—most of us feel our emotions along the front of our bodies. The back of the body often holds more of the issues relating to expression. This is perhaps because it has the muscles involving pushing, a primitive form of expression. Long before people developed the ability to say "Push off!" they had the biological capability to push someone away. Our own clinical experience has shown us that problems involving inability to *experience* feelings tend to show up on the front of the body, while those involving inability to *express* feelings are often found along the back side, usually from the low back to the back of the head.

Here is an example of working with a left/right split in a first session with a new client, Charles. We were about halfway through the hour when this set of interchanges occurred.

CHARLES: I keep being stuck in this one place, where I go completely wishy-washy when my wife's mad.

GAY: Something I keep noticing, that I saw when you first walked in, is how the left side of you, especially your upper body, is so different from the right side.

CHARLES: What do you mean?

GAY (*walking over and placing his hand on Charles's right shoulder*): This shoulder, for example, is much longer and lower than your left shoulder.

CHARLES: Really?

KATHLYN: Here, come look in the mirror. (*Charles goes over to the full-length mirror in the adjoining room.*) See how your left shoulder is shorter and sits up higher than your right shoulder.

CHARLES: Oh, yeah! I never noticed that before. What do you think that means?

GAY: I've got a few ideas. But what do you think it means?

CHARLES: I don't know.

KATHLYN: Play with it a little bit. Lift your left one higher and make your right one lower just a little. (*We ask him to exaggerate the split, taking each shoulder a bit further in the direction it is already going.*)

CHARLES: That feels really strange. I feel some nausea in my stomach.

GAY: Yes, feel that nausea. Stay with it as long as you can.

CHARLES: Ugh, I feel sick.

GAY: Feel what that reminds you of.

CHARLES (*becoming quite uncomfortable*): It's just like watching my parents fight. It used to make me sick to see them tear each other up. They were such great people on their own, but together they just never could get along.

KATHLYN: What other feelings are down in there, underneath the sick feeling?

CHARLES: Uh, I just had a flash of my mother, the day she had the breakdown and had to be taken away to the hospital.

GAY: And you saw her having the breakdown?

CHARLES: Yes—the worst day of my life, pretty much.

GAY: You were how old?

CHARLES: Eight.

KATHLYN: You must have felt terrified.

CHARLES: Yes. Who was going to take care of me? What was going to happen to my mother? I didn't know if she was coming back. Two men hauling her off in an ambulance, with her yelling and all, and my father was out of it, too—he just sat in the corner.

GAY: And feel what the connection is to your left shoulder.

CHARLES: It feels tucked up, as if I'm pulling it in toward me.

KATHLYN: As if you're protecting yourself?

CHARLES: More to make sure I'll never be like her.

KATHLYN: Oh, yes—as if you'll never let yourself get in that kind of state.

GAY: And so when your wife gets mad, you go into that same kind of posture.

CHARLES: Oh, I get it. Maybe my wife getting angry throws me into those feelings I had when my parents split up.

KATHLYN: Feel if it fits in your body.

CHARLES: Yes, and also I want to make sure I don't get angry.

GAY: Because if I did . . .

CHARLES: Well, I'd explode.

GAY: Like your mother did.

This example shows how an event of long ago can settle into the structure of the body. It also illustrates how an inquiry rooted in body awareness can speed up the process of healing. Had we not assisted Charles in delving into his left/right split, we might not have been able to cover the same amount of territory so quickly.

VERBAL FLAGS

The body-centered therapist must learn to focus intently on how clients speak, as well as on what they are saying. *How* reveals personality quite accurately—in fact, much more accurately than *what*. Think of the utter difference in personality that is revealed when the emphasis is placed differently in a sentence. Here are two versions of the same sentence:

How could *he* do this to me?

How could he do this to *me*?

There are several key areas in which the therapist can listen for verbal flags: tone, repetition, emphasis, and paraverbal communications. *Tone* is the attitude the person is projecting onto the words themselves. Are the words issued in a challenging, hostile tone? Or are they delivered as a supplication? Is the sound grating, wheedling, or contemptuous? The ancient Latin roots of the word *personality* are *per* and *sona*, "through sound." The actors on the Roman stage wore masks, so that their personalities had to be revealed through the sounds they made.

In twenty years of supervising therapists, we audiotaped many sessions. Nowadays, with the widespread availability of video technology, we tend to videotape sessions. But in the first decade and a half of work, we were able only to use audiotape. Still, it is remarkable how much diagnostic information we can pick up by listening to the tone of the client's and therapist's voice. Often, in fact, a therapist can come up with a more accurate diagnosis and treatment plan from listening to the person after the session on tape than in the session itself.

Noticing the *repetition* of words and phrases is a reliable way to tune in to what a client's unconscious is saying. For example, on one tape we heard a client use the word *awash* several times. Another person on the same tape (it was a group session) used the word *stuck* more than once. It is crucial for the therapist to notice whether the person describes himself as *awash* in feelings or *stuck* with them. These two states—awash and stuck—are completely different sensory experiences inside the person. In addition, the words themselves can reliably direct the therapist to the correct healing metaphor for the given client. The client who is "awash" may need to get his feet on the ground, while the client who is "stuck" may need to find a way to push herself through.

Emphasis is another key area in which verbal flags may be noticed. Which words or phrases does the client emphasize? In working with one young professional, Carl, we noticed that he consistently underscored the word *can't*. Whenever he used it, he would land heavily on it, often with an accompanying head bob.

GAY: What about your job situation these days?
CARL: It would be nice to do something different, but you just *can't* go around switching jobs every year or two.
GAY: Whose voice is that? The one who's saying you *can't* switch jobs?
CARL *(long pause)*: Well . . . that's my grandmother's voice. She was full of *can'ts*.

This successful person, not yet thirty, was getting his career counseling from the internalized voice of a seventy-year-old woman who never had a job outside the home. As Carl began to learn more about his long-dead grandmother, he saw how her negativity dominated his life. But the initial insight came from noticing that a simple word had a greater emphasis than it warranted.

Another example comes from the first moments of work with Clara, a woman studying to become a movement therapist herself:

KATHLYN: Let's get started, Clara. Tune in to what you are feeling right now.
CLARA: Okay.

Kathlyn thought she perceived in this single word *okay* a tone of resignation. There was a heaviness to Clara's emphasis, as if she were having to go along with someone who was resisting.

KATHLYN *(mimics the tone)*: Okay. Tune in to the tone of voice you're using, Clara. Where does that heaviness come from?

CLARA (*thoughtfully*): Okay. Okay. Okay. . . . You know, that's the way I feel about a lot of things—that I've got to do it just because I've got to.

KATHLYN: Because if you didn't . . .

CLARA: I wouldn't get anything—any approval.

For Clara, a single word, uttered in a distinctive tone, brought on a productive inquiry into the source of a major life pattern.

Paraverbal communications are all the sighs, sniffs, coughs, and stutters that accompany words. The prefix *para* means "alongside" or "by the side of." Once people begin to tune in to paraverbal communications, they cannot help but be astounded by how much they determine the meaning of human speech. Perhaps the most important thing we ourselves have learned about the paraverbal realm is that these communications *are* the meaning of human speech. A sigh or well-timed sniff will reveal the real meaning of the words that are being used. The unconscious speaks its meaning "between the cracks," and it speaks directly to the other person's unconscious. Therapy is one of the few institutions where the real meanings of human communications can be noticed and revealed. Listen in on this section of Sally and Len's session.

KATHLYN: What are you experiencing right now?

LEN: I guess there's not much to say (*coughs politely*).

SALLY (*becoming instantly furious*): That's exactly the problem! You never say anything about anything that's real!

KATHLYN: Something about his cough brings up a lot of anger for you.

It emerged that Len's polite cough was the trigger for Sally's rage. It had rich meaning for both of them. As they unwound the set of issues that the cough concealed, it came forth that for Len the cough held the relationship between his wimpy father and his domineering mother. For Sally, the cough symbolized the chain of men she had known who had concealed their feelings underneath a bland exterior. Sally carried the anger for both of them, as Len was completely out of touch with his own rage.

ATTITUDE FLAGS

An attitude flag often involves a combination of the other flags, adding up to an overall approach to life. For example, the attitude of the early Elvis Presley could be discerned through a combination of flags: the sneer, the slouch, the mumble. Taken together, they added up to the misunderstood punk with a sensitive soul that he portrayed in movie after movie. As he matured in his development, he became a caricature of himself; as his fame grew, his attitude gradually became first a joke, then a subject of derision to him. He was able to make jokes about his lip and his sneer. But later the derision came out. We recall seeing Elvis on television late in his life and being somewhat sickened by the contempt he obviously had for himself.

We mention this point because people are often lost in their attitudes of their teens and twenties. In fact, we become so thoroughly identified with our attitudes that they do not seem like attitudes. They have us, rather than the other way around. As psychological development progresses, however, people are usually able to joke about their attitudes. There is enough separation for this to occur. If their attitude does not shift, it may become an object of derision for themselves and people around them.

Some attitudes play particular havoc with the therapy process if they are not confronted and dealt with squarely. These are: seductiveness, hostility, worshipful reverence for the therapist, and needy dependence.

Attitudes can be difficult to confront, because of common blind spots on the part of the therapist. Many therapists have unresolved sexual issues, for example, that make them blind to seductiveness on the part of clients. If therapists' own sexual issues have not been worked through to satisfactory completion, they run the risk of violating clients. Approximately 10 percent of therapists, according to surveys, have had sexual contact with their clients. Similarly, hostile clients may be difficult to confront because many therapists have not dealt with their own anger satisfactorily. If therapists have self-esteem issues, depending on clients to make them feel good about themselves, they may form a bond with supplicating or worshipful clients that is unhealthy and damaging to both parties. It is our view that these attitudes should and must be brought to light and dealt with squarely in the early stages of therapy. If therapists are sufficiently observant, they are usually able to bring them out in the first session.

This bit of dialogue is from the first ten minutes of a client's first session with one of our student therapists:

JOHANNA (*in a very soft, somewhat pleading voice*): I'm not sure why I'm here. I guess a lot of people have said I might be able to benefit from counseling. And I have heard so much about you, how you've helped other students here at the counseling center.

THERAPIST: I, uh . . .

JOHANNA: So I thought I could come in, get acquainted with you, get a feel for whether I could really trust you, open up to you. (*She gives her hair a careless toss and bathes him in a radiant smile.*)

THERAPIST: Maybe you could give me an idea of what kinds of things you're wanting to accomplish.

JOHANNA: Well, you can show me what I ought to be doing with myself. I feel as if I'm at loose ends. I don't really like my classes and stuff. You seem to have your life all together, and I really want to learn how you do that.

Here we see several attitudes that, unless they are confronted and cleared up at the outset, will come back to haunt the therapist and halt the process of healing. Specifically, three attitudes are conveyed in Johanna's tone: (1) an overly worshipful attitude toward the therapist, accompanied by a possible delusion that the therapist can provide something that she cannot give herself; (2) an overly trusting attitude, suggesting possible dependence; (3) the use of the phrase "open up" so close to the trust issue—a further confirmation that there has been a violation, possibly sexual in nature, that has caused Johanna to close up.

The student therapist, upon watching the videotape, reported that he had felt uncomfortable with Johanna from the moment she opened her mouth. This is evident in his tongue-tied ("I, uh") inability to respond to her. Her attitude was worshipful and reverent, where her neediness and disownment of responsibility were masked beneath her seductive demeanor. Many therapists find such clients hard to confront, partly because they seem so needy, and partly because it feels good to be so well regarded. In fact, this complex of attitudes masked a pattern that had caused Johanna a great deal of grief. She had been violated sexually by her uncle, whom she trusted as a child, and later by a therapist who was much older than she.

The therapist learned this only after Johanna attempted a seduction with him. On the third session, she made an overt sexual offer, following an elaborate series of compliments. Fortunately, he was able to extricate his hand from the trap. He declined the offer and invited her to look at whether this pattern was familiar to her. When he went over the videotapes of the first two sessions, he saw that he had missed dozens of attitude flags that had made him unconsciously uncomfortable, but he had not been able to take action due to his own blind spot.

Quite often therapists are not able to identify accurately the attitudes that they are seeing in the client. We wish we could say that we always spot and label the attitude in the first session and break through it effectively to a clear communication with the client. We don't. Sometimes we see it and cannot label it, and sometimes we see it and label it but still cannot communicate it so that the client hears it. Sometimes we miss the boat entirely, only to wake up to what is really going on a few sessions later.

Here is an example of a session where we noticed some sort of attitude going on from the first moment in the client, Peggy, but were not able to identify it specifically.

PEGGY (in a controlled tone of voice): . . . so I'm not sure if this is what I
    need. Just wanted to check it out and see if body therapy is what I
    need.

A verbal flag ("what I need") appeared in the first minute or two of the session. But what did it mean? We missed it the first time around, only seeing its impact upon watching the videotape later.

GAY: So you're not quite sure if this is exactly what would work for you.
    What can I tell you about the work to give you a sense of whether it's
    right for you?
PEGGY (backing up slightly, looking slightly frightened): Uh, well, maybe just
    give me some information about it.
GAY: What would you like?

PEGGY (*averts her eyes*): Well, you know . . . (*lets the sentence trail off, looks confused*)

Up until now, Gay was caught up in the content of what Peggy was saying and asking about. He missed the underlying process of *how* she was asking for the information and mistakenly thought she actually wanted information. But she was not asking for information at all. Rather she was making a statement. Although Gay did not pick up on it at first, he saw the error of his ways and changed direction.

GAY: You know, I'm feeling confused. It feels like there's something going on between us, and I can't exactly put my finger on what it is. It seems as if you're uncomfortable—I notice you backing up and looking down—and I'd like to know if something's going on that I don't know about. Maybe it's something in me.

PEGGY (*looking quite scared now*): I—I don't know.

GAY: Do I remind you of somebody? Or is this whole situation somehow feeling familiar to you?

PEGGY (*pause of about twenty seconds, during which she wrings her hands and her eyes dart around*): Well, I feel kind of like when my dad would call me on the carpet.

GAY: You see some of your dad in me, in this situation?

PEGGY (*laughs nervously*): He's a doctor, too. Always in a hurry. The way you came into the room was just like him, as if you were putting on brakes. He's a brain surgeon, actually, and he was always yelling at my mother that his time was worth $1,500 an hour so don't waste it. It seemed as if he had about ten minutes a day for us kids, and then it was always for something wrong.

GAY: So when you're here talking to me, with me asking you what you want and all, it brings up how scared you were of your dad.

PEGGY (*smiles*): Yeah, I guess you're kind of like him physically, too. He was a big man, especially when I was a kid. (*The unwittingly humorous nature of this comment causes both to laugh.*)

Therapists need to be reminded frequently that it is all right not to know it all. Many of our biggest breakthroughs come from acknowledging that we do not know what is going on. This "beginner's mind" place often gives miracles the space to appear.

A LIFELONG PROCESS

At one of our week-long trainings for mental health professionals, we were teaching the Five Flags and the material in this book to a group of about twenty in California. On the third day of the training, after working intensively on these skills for many hours, we took a break. During the break, one of the participants began playing a set of three conga drums that belonged to the center where the training was being held. He was a professional musician and proceeded to thrill all of us with a spontaneous performance of brilliant, intricate drumming. At the end, one of us asked him, "How long would I have to practice to be able to do that?" He replied, "About as long as I am going to have to practice to get good at spotting flags." He was in the state of overwhelm that many of our students feel when they first begin to work with the powerful messages people broadcast with their bodies.

For a therapist, noticing and working with flags can best be thought of as a lifelong process. Do your best not to be too self-critical along the way. We have been working with this approach for over two decades, and next week at this time we hope to be better at noticing flags than we are now. Getting the attention focused on process as well as on content is a great leap. Once your attention shifts to include *how* people are communicating in addition to *what* they are saying, it is almost like having a third ear or eye. Your ability to notice what is really important expands sharply. Gay remembers asking his mother why the minister in church had a tic that would fire off when he talked about the collection. "Shhh," she said. "It's not polite to notice things like that." That was too bad, because the congregation would probably have felt great relief at knowing why the collection plate induced anxiety in the minister. Too bad, also, for the child who was desperately trying to see reality, to find out what was really going on. It probably does not take too many incidents like this for children to focus in on content and become oblivious to what the whole of the bodymind is saying.

A societal blind spot keeps us all from noticing and discussing the flags we see. We see the darting eyes and the sweaty lip of a Richard Nixon, but we look the other way, only to pay the price for this avoidance later. We refuse to confront the sexuality of our children, and we end up with a million pregnant teenagers a year. There is obviously a major commitment to not seeing reality in many realms of human life. As therapists, we work with people every day who avert their eyes, metaphorically speaking, to avoid seeing something that they absolutely should be paying attention to. The same people who take their car to a garage as soon as they notice a wobble in the front wheel may spend years avoiding an emotional issue in themselves or a troublesome pattern in their relationship.

Clearly, a great deal of healing needs to take place in our ability to notice how things really are. While our conscious minds are busy preserving illusions, the deeper parts of ourselves are busy communicating through the only signals they have. These are the Five Flags, and therapists who become fluent in reading their messages are much more likely to be able to experience harmony in themselves and to lead others toward unity.

THE NINE
STRATEGIES OF
BODY-CENTERED
THERAPY

THE PRESENCING PRINCIPLE: THE STARTING POINT OF MIND/BODY HEALING

You do not need to leave your room. Remain sitting at your table and listen.
Do not even listen, simply wait. Do not even wait, be quite still and ordinary.
The world will freely offer itself to you to be unmasked, it has no choice,
it will roll in ecstasy at your feet.
—*Franz Kafka*

No mind is much employed upon the present; recollection and
anticipation fill up almost all our moments.
—*Samuel Johnson*

Problems persist to the extent that we fail to be present with them and with the feelings associated with them. When we can simply be with an issue (rather than judging it or trying to change it), the issue has room to transform in the desired direction.

The most important healing strategy is being present. For all of us, but especially for therapists, giving a person space to feel whatever he or she is feeling is the fundamental healing technique. Everything we do either enhances or interferes with our ability to be with what is going on in ourselves. The act that initiates healing is a moment of nonjudgmental attention. Our term for this moment is a verb that is not yet in the dictionary: *to presence.*

When we presence something, we let our attention rest fully on it. Presencing has no judgment, no agenda. It simply is. The reason this moment has such a powerful healing effect is that it is a replica in miniature of the end-state. Being—pure consciousness—is the longed-for result at the end of the quest for liberation. A tiny taste of it begins the whole process.

AN EXPERIMENT IN PRESENCING YOU CAN PERFORM RIGHT NOW

If you would like to experience presencing, take a moment right now to tune in to something you are feeling in your body. You can use presencing with many different things, but it is easiest to begin with a body sensation or feeling. It could be hunger or tiredness or a pleasant feeling of happiness. It could even be something highly localized such as a tooth-ache or the pinched feeling of a too-tight belt. Just let your attention rest on the sensation. Put your attention on it without doing anything else to the sensation. Don't try to fix it or make it change. Simply be with it. Rest your attention on it without doing anything else.

Notice what happens when you get your attention fully connected with the sensation. Can you keep your attention on it, or does it jump away onto something else? There are no right answers; just notice what you notice.

Presencing is the nonjudgmental placement of attention. As you work with the ideas in this chapter, you are invited to use the Presencing Principle as often as you like. Find out what happens to your overall sense of aliveness as you presence various things about yourself. Many people find that presencing enhances their whole-body sense of well-being.

THE POWER OF PRESENCING

Ken Hecht, a television producer and writer in Los Angeles, is one of the rare people who lost a great deal of weight (over 120 pounds) and kept it off for many years. A remarkable moment changed his life direction. He wrote of the experience in *Newsweek* magazine and has given us permission to share it with you.

How does a person summon the strength to lose the weight?
The brutal part is the anxiety-ridden moments leading up to the

eating binge. Those moments when it's all internalized and it all seems to be about food. You know you want the food, lots of it, but you know you shouldn't eat it; you know the disgust you'll feel for yourself. But you really want the food, and you know that if only for a few moments—those moments you spend eating it—the food will make the anxiety go away. So then you cave in and gobble, gobble, gobble. Then you hate yourself. The cycle never ends.

For me the key to breaking that cycle was to finally decide one night to give in to the anxiety. Not numb it with the food, but instead go, rather than eat, cold turkey. I wanted to just sit there and see if the nightmarish anxiety I so feared would in fact total me. So I sat and felt god-awful and eventually felt feelings of self-loathing and disgust and worthlessness. And finally the panicky desire to eat passed. It lasted less than 30 minutes. It was an awful experience, and one that I highly recommend. Sit with yourself. Don't eat, don't go to a movie, don't turn on the television. Do nothing but sit quietly, be miserable and feel what you're terrified of. It is the part of yourself you've been using food to run from. It is a part of yourself you need to know.

Doing this just once changed my life. No, I didn't immediately and easily diet the weight off from that point forward. There were many binges. But there were also many times when the anxiety came and I drew upon that one experience and knew I could tough it out. And the next morning there's a wonderful feeling: an absence of self-loathing.

What Ken is describing so passionately is a moment of being present with a feeling. Eating was a way to avoid being present with his fear. The fear was right now, the present. The food fantasies were his unconscious's way of saying, "Let's do something—anything!—else to get out of the present." So he dropped the addiction for a half an hour and sat with his fear. His advice to others: "Have this one experience that lets you know you can survive what you dread." In our work as body-centered therapists we have been with thousands of people as they have done exactly what Ken is suggesting. The other principles and techniques in this book all rest on this fundamental idea.

THE BARRIERS TO BEING PRESENT

There is a general human tendency to avoid presencing. Ken Hecht avoided his fear by eating, finally waking up 128 pounds into this bad dream. Other people avoid dealing with issues in their lives by watching too much TV. There are hundreds of different ways to avoid, but only one way to become present.

Mary, a former client of ours, told us about an experience of presencing that changed her life long after she learned the skill in therapy. She was sitting at home alone on a Friday night, watching TV and reading a book. Images of a co-worker to whom she was attracted kept popping into her mind. Mary knew from other colleagues that he had been separated from his wife for a while, and she thought she picked up some indications that he was attracted to her. It occurred to her to presence her feelings, and when she did so, she found that she was both excited and scared. Then, she told us, it was almost as if she went into a trance. She raided the refrigerator looking for something to eat. Finding nothing that appealed to her, she went into her bedroom and cleaned out a closet. Along the way she tried on a lot of clothes and set out some shoes for polishing. Then she "woke up." She realized that she was avoiding presencing her fear and excitement. So she went back and sat down in the chair where it had all started. She let herself tune in to her sensations of fear and excitement. She sat with them until they passed. Suddenly it occurred to her to call the co-worker at home. This idea brought up another wave of fear and excitement, which she presenced. Then she decided to risk it and reached for the telephone. The co-worker seemed surprised but happy that she had called. Instead of making small talk, Mary basically summarized the experiences she had been through over the past hour or so. Her candor inspired him to tell her about his feelings of attraction to her. They ended up meeting for a late-night snack at a nearby coffeehouse.

Being present is exquisitely simple, but most of our clients do practically anything they can to avoid it. Listen in on a bit of dialogue from a therapy session. We are talking with Lisa, who wanted to be rid of her fear of speaking in public. She had recently been promoted to a job with more public exposure, and her stomach had been aching every morning since the promotion. Earlier in the session she learned that the stomachache was a signal to her that she's scared. As a result, the stomachache has just disappeared. Now she is "underneath" the pain, moving toward a resolution of the fear itself. Our first move is to tune in her awareness to the sensations she is experiencing in her body. Then we want to pinpoint exactly where they are located.

US: Now that your stomach isn't hurting, what actually do you feel down there where the pain used to be?

LISA: Uh, nothing really.

US: And what does the nothing actually feel like?

LISA: Maybe a little sick feeling, like nausea.

US: Kind of nauseous. And feel if there's more.

LISA: Well, kind of antsy, too.

US: And the antsy feeling feels like what exactly?

LISA: Like a speedy, itchy feeling.

US: Where do you feel that?

LISA: Under my skin, in my chest. And along my forearms.

US: Good. Now let yourself be with those sensations.

LISA: What do you mean?

US: Let your attention rest on them.

LISA: Why?

US: It's a new idea for you. It's not a familiar thing to do.

Notice that we did not get into a lengthy intellectual answer to her "Why?" To do so would have played into the trap that her unconscious was setting. It wanted to avoid presencing the fear. The moment the unconscious lets go, it gets subsumed into being. It loses its power. One part of Lisa wanted to get clear, but her programmed unconscious had a vested interest in her staying stuck. Her unconscious thought: We've been stuck with this fear for a long time and we've survived. Let's keep things the way they are.

LISA: I don't know how to do that.

US: Yes. It's something brand new. Just being present with the sensations without trying to do anything about them.

LISA: But if I do that, they'll be there forever. I want to get rid of them.

US: Yes, but they've been there forever anyway. Maybe it's time to do something new. Maybe trying to get rid of them is what's keeping them there.

On watching this videotape later, we were not exactly proud of this response. It seemed a little snappy and glib, as if we were trying to talk her into a more enlightened point of view. Fortunately, it turned out not to slow the process down too much.

LISA: Well, okay. (*She closes her eyes for a moment and focuses inward; a big frown appears on her forehead.*)

US: There's a frown on your forehead. What's that about?

LISA: I guess I'm still confused. It's hard. Not *doing* something about the feelings.

US: You're used to judging things like that pretty severely, it seems.

LISA (*bursts into tears*): I've always been that way.

These last three exchanges held the key to the ultimate resolution of the issue. A split second of presencing her fear brought forth her fundamental personality issue. Her persona was built around judging herself harshly for all her feelings. Her attempt to be with her fear was clouded by her persona. When she gave herself a moment of being present and when her persona was pointed out nonjudgmentally, everything shifted for her. She could now see her fundamental approach to life. Her fear was not the problem at all: It was her way of being with her fear and everything else in her life. As Lisa focused on this issue, it became clear to her that she judged her husband, her son, and particularly her daughter. Finally she was able to grant herself a deep experience of presencing.

US: So let yourself just be with what you're feeling. Fear, sadness, the nausea—whatever.

LISA *(pause of about ten seconds)*: It's strange, but when I do that, the stuff disappears. The fear, the nausea—everything. It just isn't there.

The payoff for being present to feelings is the one Lisa just enjoyed. Our feelings are locked into place by our resistance to them, and the moment the resistance is dropped they have freedom to change. Often the change is dramatic and immediate.

If you remember how your feelings were likely dealt with as a child, you will see why as adults people have little familiarity with being present. In one of our seminars we asked the roomful of people what they had been told as children when they told an adult they were scared. We filled up a chalkboard with their answers: "Don't be scared." "There's nothing to be scared of." "It'll be better tomorrow." "Go out and play." "Big boys/girls aren't afraid." Several people remembered practicing the Boy Scout remedy for fear: smile and whistle. None of these pieces of advice are all that bad; it's just that they are all ways of avoiding being with the fear. Feelings like anger often engender even more repressive reactions than fear on the part of our caretakers.

By contrast, one of Milton Erickson's students remembered watching how the great psychiatrist dealt with his son's pain when the little boy hurt his leg. Dr. Erickson, knowing the value of being present as a healing and pain-reducing strategy, said something like, "It hurts, Robert. It hurts awfully. And you know what? It's going to keep on hurting for a while." One moment of this brilliant and caring communication could set in motion a lifetime of successful handling of feeling.

Ask yourself a question: In your life, particularly your young life, has anyone ever asked you just to be with a feeling? We do not know how Ken Hecht got the idea to be with his anxiety after a lifetime of eating to quell it. One thing is for sure: He probably did not learn it in school. In Western culture there is not much information available on the value of being present with feelings. When we turn on the TV, we usually don't see commercials for being present. Imagine a kindly white-haired doctor/actor saying "Got a headache? Suffer from nagging backache? Don't take a pill. Instead, be with that pain. Open up to it, and acknowledge the feelings under it."

One barrier to our being present, then, is our lack of training in it. A second barrier is that the power of being present generates resistance to itself. As we saw in Ken Hecht's example, a few minutes of being present sparked the loss of 128 pounds and a major lifestyle change. Most of us are fairly well addicted to the way things are, however, and we resist experiences that could shake up the status quo. Being present has a great deal of power in it: the power to alter irrevocably the structures and assumptions by which we live. Of course, most of us desperately want to change the status quo, but before we can, we need to acknowledge the part of us that is deeply invested in staying stuck in it. When we are split, one part of our mind is working against another part. The part that wants to grow and change is fighting with the part that knows that we've done things the same way for years and we've survived. Why change? Why risk a sure thing? Then, too, many of us are equipped with a troublesome mechanism, an internal Luddite who trashes the machinery when we begin to make progress.

We recently worked with Michael, a Vietnam veteran, who had come in to resolve some recurring relationship issues. His wife Teri was complaining about his lack of communicativeness. She felt she had to draw him out or else try to read his mind to find out what was going on with him. Michael was a great stonewaller. In the first few sessions with us his expression was blank, and he imparted little information about himself. In one particular session while he was opening up, he had begun to see the cost of not being with himself and his feelings for years. He talked about feeling lonely and isolated at work and out of touch with any possible intimacy. He had recently begun to share with Teri. As is often the case when the doors open to a feeling, incomplete past experiences become available. At that point in the session Michael was experiencing the simultaneous pressure of trying to feel (the good feelings of sharing) and trying not to feel (the bad feelings of loneliness and isolation).

We asked him simply to let himself be with that pressure. He stared straight ahead for a few minutes, breathing more and more deeply. Suddenly his eyes darted to the right and back to center, and he paled slightly. We asked him, "What happened? What did you see?" "Dead bodies," he replied, and started to sob. Being present for a brief moment had given

Michael direct access to feelings he had been holding since the end of the war. Over the next three sessions he let himself consciously feel many different emotions—fear, anger, sadness—that he had sealed off when he was in the military. As he softened to allow these feelings to come into his awareness, Teri noticed a striking difference in their relationship. As she put it, "Michael became more easygoing and easy to touch. He would seek me out to talk to me about feelings, something I had been wanting him to do for years."

THE INTERNAL CRITIC

Another common barrier to being present is the dictatorship of the internal critic, a nagging or harsh voice whose function is to make wrong. Thousands of our clients have described to us the internal critic and its paralyzing effect. The internal critic is by nature a judge, and we have rarely heard it make a favorable judgment. Here are some of the commands and criticisms the critic makes:

- "Can't you just sit still and pay attention for a minute!"
- "How many times do I have to tell you?!"
- "Has your brain gone out to lunch?"
- "Listen! It's very simple if you'll just pay attention!"
- "You don't seem to have the brains God gave a cow."
- "That was the stupidest thing I've ever seen. What were you thinking of?"

The internal critic can speak only when we are separate from our experience, and it works hard to keep us from becoming present. In therapy, when we invite clients to tune in to a feeling or a body movement, they often think they have done something wrong. "Uh-oh, I've done something wrong" and "I'm in trouble, gotta hide" are common responses. The effect of this constant internal criticism is mistrust of their internal impulses and separation from being. We spend much time in initial therapy sessions assisting clients in identifying the style and timing of their internal critic.

For Lewis, the emergence of the critic was always signaled by a fleeting look of disdain. At first Lewis wouldn't speak when the critic was present; he shut down and felt blank. Gradually, he began to bring the critic out into the light of consciousness. He would say, "I just had a critical thought, 'You sure are stupid, Lewis.'" Lewis is dyslexic and had a lot of discouraging experiences in school. He is in his forties, and he attended grade school well before the time when learning disabilities were acknowledged. His frustration and failure evolved into his internal critic. We had him spend time being present with the internal critic, reclaiming that hidden voice and embracing its need to control, to protect Lewis from looking stupid. Gradually, Lewis learned to turn his attention to his body with no attempt to do anything about his feelings, including judge them. Lewis describes the result of being present: "It's a sweet freedom I've never experienced, as if I had a permanent smile in my belly."

Hundreds of other clients have expressed tremendous relief when they acknowledged the internal critic's tone, loudness, and characteristic judgments. For them, being present with the critic created the space for them to recognize that their experience was greater than the broken record that the critic played.

Sometimes a client fights with the critic or tries to ignore it. When we asked Sharon, an exuberant professional in her thirties, to describe her battle with her internal critic, she said, "I realized I was holding my breath and getting really tense in my shoulders. I almost felt like putting my hands over my ears and screaming, 'I won't listen to you!' But I really see that the more I do that, the more power the critic has." In contrast, when Sharon could let herself simply be present with the critic, the internal voice quieted, and she could expand her awareness to include more of her experience.

Karlfried Graf von Durkheim, in a hard-to-find book called *Hara*, wrote fifty years ago that "the separation from [a person's] Being is what produces the basic tension in life: the release of it is imperative for the integration of [the] I-self with [the] essence." In anticipation of the body-centered revolution, he went on to localize the "I-Self" (what we call the persona) in the chest, in what we call Fight-or-Flight Breathing. His theory was that when the breathing drops from the chest to the belly, the consciousness changes from I-centered to Essence-centered.

The family background of one of our clients illustrates why being present to the truth is not more popular than it is. Denying feelings was a societal strategy that Wolfgang's family turned into their profession: diplomacy. The son of an Austrian ambassador, Wolfgang had grown up knowing he had to be "perfect" and literally to get back on the horse if he fell. Much of his daily life involved appearances at public functions, where behavior was exactly prescribed and any emergence of feelings was considered an unforgivable weakness and breach of protocol. In therapy, Wolfgang's presenting problem was an incapacitating fear that his voice would shake when he was speaking in public. He wanted to go into public service, but he was terrified that people would notice his anxiety. When we suggested that he let himself experience the trembling, to just be with and notice it, he heard his father's voice in his head demanding his professional demeanor: "We never tremble or show *any* feeling!"

The cost of not being present became clear as we continued to explore Wolfgang's life. His father had dropped dead of a heart attack in his early fifties. His mother had followed a few months later, from a viral infection. And his sister had committed suicide a year earlier, leaving a note that said she just couldn't face all the feelings welling up inside her. Wolfgang had lost his entire family because they couldn't be with their feelings. Even when he was confronted with this terrible cost, however, Wolfgang responded with what he came to call his "Austrian" persona. This involved pulling his body and chin up, narrowing his eyes, pressing his lips tightly together, breathing high in his chest, and tightening almost all his muscles.

For Wolfgang, learning to be with his feelings, particularly the paralyzing fear of making a mistake, has started a long untangling of parental and cultural admonitions against the natural state of being. He recently said, "I can see that after generations of soldiers and civil servants, my family became marble sculptures instead of human beings, beautiful and perfect, but cold and hard."

In therapy, clients commonly repeat their life strategies for avoiding being present in their relationship with the therapist, especially when threatening memories or feelings start to emerge. A common maneuver is to divert awareness away from the issue at hand and put it somewhere else. Some clients do this by "thinking about something else." One client, Marcia, had learned to remove her awareness to a little box in her mind where she felt safe and quiet. Several sessions of work allowed us to trace the source of this strategy to her first experience of sexual abuse as a little girl. During that experience she had looked over her uncle's shoulder to the jewelry box on her dresser and had willed herself there to separate from what was happening to her. The breath and movement flags that signaled this separation were subtle but distinct. Marcia would glance up to the left and hold her in-breath, then continue the conversation in disguise; her body was still in the room but her presence had fled. When we gently encouraged her to stay present, vivid memories and upwelling sadness and fear immediately surfaced and could be experienced and claimed.

THE FLOWERING OF PRESENCE

Now we will look at what creates the space for the Presencing Principle to flourish. We will also explore the value of distinguishing between being and other states of awareness. To begin, let's take a close look at what happens when someone risks really being with herself.

Deborah's persona was scattered confusion. She couldn't finish a sentence without digressing on a multitude of tangents. Her gestures dissolved without impact; they faded into the air. Her eyes constantly swept the horizon, never settling on anything. Her breaths overlapped the previous ones like waves against a sea wall. Even her hypersensitive hearing was a problem for her: She felt she couldn't keep anything out or sort out what was important. When we asked Deborah to be present with and express this confusion, she uncovered several layers of feeling. First came her Scattered persona strategy.

"I don't know how to get out of this." Most people feel they need to *do* something immediately when a feeling occurs. They need to get rid of it, control it, or change it into something different. A long time ago, when basic human feelings evolved, they were usually designed to mobilize us for action. Now, after several thousand years of civilization, we are learning not to take many of the actions our ancestors were programmed to take. It is not socially acceptable for us to flee the office or swing a fist when the boss is criticizing us, although that is what our physical machinery might like us to do. So Deborah encountered the first obstacle to being; the leap into doing. As she returned to presencing the scattered confusion just as it was, another layer of feeling emerged.

"I feel like I'm not good enough." Tears came with this awareness. Deborah realized that she had created the Scattered persona to cover her intense sadness about feeling that her being was not good enough. If she wasn't always dashing around doing something useful, she felt she was worthless. We asked her to be with those feelings and to see what emerged. Very quickly a memory came.

> I just saw an image of my mother holding me straddled over her hip while trying to manage six older siblings. I am very aware of my ears burning as I say that. I think I developed sensitive ears because I was always trying. I had my ears out there all the time so I wouldn't miss anything. Really, so I wouldn't get left out.

Deborah took several minutes to breathe and be present with this memory. We encouraged her to love the truth of her experience just as it was. She cried deeply and shivered with fear as the waves of feeling flowed unimpeded. As they subsided, she said she realized that she had duplicated exactly her mother's fragmented pattern of attention. With this awareness she could begin to distinguish her own being from what she had learned in order to survive in an active and tumultuous family.

Ultimately, our ability to be present with the truth in ourselves opens the space for love. The same attention that we bring to ourselves will flower into love for ourselves if we are patient. But the act of loving ourselves is often the very last thing we think of. Even when someone reminds us, we still are likely to resist it, as Henry's story illustrates.

Henry was a fifty-year-old business executive who had some issues that had been bothering him for years. In therapy, as he peeled away layer after layer, he finally came to his "bottom-line" feeling, as he termed it. It was a feeling of bitterness that seemed deep down in his cells.

HENRY: What am I supposed to *do* with all that bitterness?
US: Love it.
HENRY *(long pause)*: You mean I have to love it?
US: That's the best thing we know of.
HENRY *(another long pause)*: How about if I love something right next to it and let it spill over?

We broke up into laughter, and soon he joined in. There was something about the poignancy of the moment that we will never forget. It's as if there is something deep in us all that knows that we need to come into love and harmony with ourselves. Then there's that other part, the one that fights it every step of the way. Love resolves all, though, and it's inevitable that if you keep the quest going long enough, you will eventually come to that resolution.

Let us open a window on a session where the client, Don, is arguing with being present. Don is a professional counselor with a city agency. We later laughed with him over the irony that a professional therapist was having this much trouble learning how to be present. But he was.

Don's son Tony was living with Don's ex-wife. Their relationship had been conflicted for years. Don recently decided to resolve it and clear up all the obstacles to his having a close relationship with Tony. As you read this example, it may look at first as if we were "badgering the witness," trying to find a problem where there may be none. But in his case our persistence paid off. After the session Don's relationship with his son shifted dramatically toward the positive.

DON *(stretching)*: Well, I finally wrote a letter to Tony *(grimaces)*.
KATHLYN *(mirrors Don's expression)*: What were you thinking just now?
DON: I just kind of *(long pause, another grimace)* feel cranky.
GAY: Let yourself go more into that feeling.

DON *(shakes his body, puts his hands in his pockets)*: Uewh!

KATHLYN: Don't make it go away. Stay with it, open up to it.

DON: I don't know how to do that.

KATHLYN: You're already doing it—just let yourself feel what you're feeling.

DON: If I don't want to be something, I should be able to change it.

KATHLYN: All right, change it.

(Don laughs.)

KATHLYN: Really, if you can change it, change it.

(There is a long pause as Don struggles with his impulse to feel and his impulse to control.)

GAY: You say you're feeling cranky. That's what you're experiencing. So for you to say I want to change it, I'm not having the right experience—I want a different experience—

DON: Yeah? *(shrugs)*

GAY: The moment you do that, where does your awareness go? Where do you go? *(Pause.)* If you're cranky, and you don't want to be experiencing that, where are you going to go?

DON *(smiling)*: Well, I was going to think about something else.

GAY: Yeah? That's a popular strategy—"I'll just think about something else." Notice how thinking about something else often brings more separation.

(Don leans back into the couch and looks down for several minutes.)

KATHLYN: What are you doing? *(Long pause.)*

DON: Well, I *know* that intellectually, but—it's not working right now. I started thinking of something else.

KATHLYN: You look annoyed.

DON: Well, *apparently (much louder)* you're attacking me, and I don't know why.

(Don is trying to change the subject here by adopting his Hostile persona, engaging us in an argument.)

KATHLYN: Wait a minute, please answer my question.

DON *(grins)*: Which question?

KATHLYN: Are you angry or irritated? You said *apparently* with emphasis.

(There is a long pause as Don's feet tap and tears well up.)

GAY: Listen to your feet, listen behind your eyes. Here's another opportunity to experience yourself, to be with yourself.

(Don's body wiggles and shifts, as if he cannot get comfortable. More tears come.)

GAY: Let that happen more.

(Don brings both legs up, hugging them to his chest, and rocks his body side to side. He sighs deeply several times.)

DON: I'm mad 'cause I don't know what I'm mad about, but I don't want to know what I'm mad about—but I'm mad 'cause I'm mad.

GAY: You're mad at yourself for being mad. You're mad and cranky, and you won't let yourself be cranky.

DON: Well, who the hell wants to be cranky!

GAY: But you don't have any choice about that. The only choice you have is to feel or not to feel. You don't get to choose what you feel. You have feelings just like you have tears or brown eyes. (Long pause.) What is happening right now is that you're cranky—or whatever that is—but you don't like that. (Don rubs his nose and puts his hand on his hip.) So you won't let yourself be with it. So you abandon yourself; you take your awareness elsewhere. You think of something else. When we do that, there's nobody home. You're not at home for yourself. . . . Your eyes just started to drift (long pause as Don holds his breath, fidgeting).

DON: It might not be so bad to be cranky if I knew what I was cranky about.

KATHLYN: We call that putting the cart before the horse. You don't get to know what you're cranky about until you let yourself be cranky.

DON: Well, aren't I being cranky?

GAY: Are you being with yourself being cranky? Are you keeping yourself company while you're being cranky? Where is your awareness?

DON: I don't know.

US: It's valuable to let yourself find out where your awareness is.

DON: It keeps moving around—a little bit in my head—every now and then my feet or something.

KATHLYN: Would you be willing to let yourself be present with what is

going on right now? To be present with your feelings and open up to
them?

DON (*rubs his face as more tears come*): Has to be yes or no, right?

KATHLYN: Well, it really is yes or no, not "has to be." Either you're willing
or you're not.

DON: Maybe that's what feels like it bounces around.

GAY: Would you be willing to be present with the bouncing around?

DON: It's like I don't know what it really *means* (*sighs*).

GAY (*softly*): A kind of openness, a sense of acceptance, a potential.

DON: Gosh, it just seems so *stupid*.

US: What's stupid?

DON: Not being able to just *do* it. (*His fingers touch his mouth, and he begins
to cry more deeply.*)

GAY: Let yourself do that more. Let more of you participate.

DON (*shifting, rocking, as he whispers*): I just feel stupid.

KATHYLN: Is the movement matching the intensity you feel inside?

(*Don shakes his head vigorously as his mouth grimaces.*)

KATHLYN: What would happen if you let that occur?

DON: The image that comes to mind is blowing up. What I think of is
stabbing someone (*gestures with hand*).

KATHLYN: So what is going on now?

DON (*through strong crying*): I was having flashes of wanting to kill my
father when I was real young.

KATHLYN (*softly*): You were really angry at him.

Talking ceased for several minutes at this point as Don cried and shook
more openly. In reviewing the videotape, we noticed that our own breathing synchronized with Don's here, which let us know that we were being
present with his experience. As we began to wind up the session, Don had
an insight: that his unresolved feelings about his father played a large part
in his own conflicted feelings toward his son.

This long example illustrates the common obstacles to being present for
experience. Life is full of distractions; there are lots of ways to avoid being
present. But it is well worth doing the work, because presencing is in itself
healing. Many of life's problems begin to be resolved the moment we focus

the pure power of attention on them. When Don was finally able to be with the truth of his experience, he discovered a core feeling that had shaped his life with his son. The power of presence created the opening for immediate healing.

THE PRIMACY OF ATTENTION

For many of us, the initial wound to our wholeness *was* the withdrawal of attention. Human beings need attention in order to grow and flourish. Ideally this attention is a loving and responsive presence that allows us to develop our unique being. When that attention is distorted or withheld, the infant or child experiences intense pain and often interprets this absence personally. We frequently hear from clients, "I'm too much"; "I ask for too much"; "There's something wrong with me"; or "I don't deserve anyone to love me." These same people, as infants, may have been left in the hospital for days or weeks because they or their mother was sick after delivery. One woman, an RH negative twin, had been whisked away immediately after her birth to have nine-tenths of her blood transfused. She could not bond with her twin or any of her family for ten days. As an adult, her strongest feeling was, "I don't deserve anyone's attention. I'll just settle for what I can get." Another man had been abandoned by his mother at six months of age. As an adult, he believed that women would love and attend to him only if he bribed them with money and gifts. He managed to recreate abandonment with two wives before he woke up to the initial pattern.

The withdrawal or distortion of an attentive presence can be very subtle and yet still script the person's relationship to attention. Parents or primary caretakers whose fundamental presence is disapproving or fearful can instill approval-seeking or supergood behavior patterns that mask the person's need for genuine, direct contact. The repetitive sigh, the tight-lipped glance, and the narrowed-eye stare are powerful distortions of presencing that impact the receptive child. We learn who we are first by the responses we receive. The way we are looked at, held, and spoken to gives us our first sense of aliveness and contact. Wounds given through distorted or withdrawn attention can be healed through clear, loving attention.

There is a distinction between presencing and other kinds of attention. Concentrated attention, for example, is useful in situations that demand focus, but in therapy we find that clients often confuse concentration with effort and judgment. New clients often *try* to pay attention, wrinkling their forehead as if therapy were school and a grade were going to be given. We often hear "I'm doing it wrong" or "I need to do it right" when we invite presencing initially. Concentration involves a narrowing of attention. In contrast, being present is similar to keeping company with a good friend—or "hanging out," as our son calls it.

Much of the time our attention is loaded down with other baggage, such as expectations and feelings. We have all heard the sharp reprimand "Pay attention!" This command teaches us to concentrate and be scared at the same time. Similarly, attention may be "loaded" with an intention to fix something. This "loaded attention" should be distinguished from "bare attention," or what in Oriental philosophy is sometimes called emptiness. In emptiness, we are not looking for anything specific; it is pure attention with nothing added. An extraordinary immediacy evolves from this kind of attention. In healing ourselves it is helpful to learn pure attention, to be present with our feelings and issues with no agenda attached.

Let's look at Carole, a woman in her thirties who has come in for her second session. As therapists, we could focus on her stated concerns: her despair over unfulfilled relationships, her career dissatisfaction, and her indecision. But a perspective of bare attention was needed, since her cocoon of weightiness was immediately and vividly clear. With slumped shoulders, receding chin, collapsed chest, and droopy eyes, she entered the room looking beaten down.

What was obvious to us, however, wasn't obvious to Carole. She began to describe her week. We interrupted and asked if she was aware of her severely slumped shoulders. Tears came immediately. "Oh, that!" she said. "I thought I had gotten rid of that." The impassioned story of the development of her Hard Worker persona followed. As the only college graduate in her working class family, she had spent her whole life trying to escape a feeling of being "the underdog." We invited her to be present with the underdog, using the Moving Microscopic Truth (described in chapter 12). Within a few minutes of this feeling and expressing, Carole was reliving her first fearful reaction to her father's frustrated and random violence—abuse that had left her huddling "like a dog in the corner." At the age of five she could not make sense of his anger and despair. She had tried desperately to figure out what she had done wrong. Out of this confusion, she had made a decision to rise above her background. But up until this session, Carole was unaware that she still carried her initial pain as an excruciating burden that pulled her whole body down.

Bare attention includes what we call bare listening. When a therapist is resting in presence, the undertones, meaning, and mystery of communication open. A student of ours described a session where she had been listening fully, without agenda. "My client opened layer after layer of memories that he was so surprised to find. He had vivid images and could even smell the kitchen he grew up in. He broke into tears when he remembered his grandfather holding him in front of the fire." Our student was pleasantly surprised to notice how energized she was at the end of the session. Presence takes no effort and actually increases aliveness.

THE LOOP OF AWARENESS

Presencing is created in a therapy session by letting attention flow between therapist and client. The flow of attention, or what we call the Loop of Awareness, includes both participants in its circle of wholeness. Since awareness is intrinsically healing, the process of letting it circulate between therapist and client provides a living model for the client that there is an abundance of love and attention. The Loop of Awareness is the central skill we teach our therapy students. It is the underlying river along which all other techniques flow. The therapist simply notices his or her experience, then notices the client, in a continuing Loop of Awareness. Here is an example of the Loop of Awareness in action.

When Nicole came in for her third session, we focused on practicing Loop of Awareness. Both of us would tune in to what we were feeling, then shift our attention to Nicole. We quickly noticed a sense of not being able to make contact with Nicole. When we looked at her, she would break eye contact or giggle. We brought this process to her attention after it had happened a couple of times. She was very surprised that we mentioned it, because she had felt we were hovering on the surface of her issues. In other words, she did not realize she was breaking off contact, projecting onto us that we were not interested in exploring deeply with her. She laughed when she caught herself in this projection. Then she asked us to give her feedback whenever her attention drifted. We stood facing her, mentioning each time she seemed to take her awareness away. Whenever it would happen, we would ask: "What are you experiencing now, right here?"

After several Loops of Awareness, Nicole said, "If I drop this Giggly persona, I'm afraid there'll be nothing inside." It became clear that she had constructed a pleasantly spacy persona over her fear of the emptiness inside. With these seemingly simple Loops of Awareness, she healed her basic split, no longer dividing her attention between the fear of emptiness and the defensive maneuvers. With this extra free attention she presenced her fear. She sat with it, placing all her awareness on the sensations of it. An extraordinary stillness came over her. She now seemed an utterly different person from the nervous, giggly woman of a moment before.

This is the power of the Presencing Principle, and it does not take much of it to bring about major healing. In the next chapter we will show the practical steps and instructions for putting its power to work for you.

THE FUNDAMENTAL PRESENCING TECHNIQUE

The present moment is a powerful goddess.
—Goethe

TOM SEAVER: *Hey, Yogi, what time is it?*
YOGI BERRA: *You mean now?*

There are two psychological moves that allow people to come into the present and put the Presencing Principle into action. The first is to take their attention from everything that is keeping it somewhere else. The second is to place their attention on what actually is present: right now. By removing the attention from fantasies and distractions, by placing it on something that is unarguably right here and right now, we immediately start moving at the speed of life.

Part of the art of living is to be present with our inner selves as we go about the outer requirements of life. Many of us find this is a challenge. There are many temptations to lose ourselves in the busy-ness of life, and few supports for staying in touch with our inner selves as we live in the world. The art of therapy is to be able to handle the various resistances in which people engage to stay away from the present. This art can be learned only by experience, because clients will always find the therapist's blind spots—those places where the therapist has not developed self-awareness. In other words, as therapists we tend to get stuck on those feelings in ourselves that we have difficulty presencing.

Of particular concern are those feelings that clients may have about therapists and vice versa. If clients have feelings of anger or sexual attraction toward the therapist, for example, they may have two reasons to resist presencing those feelings. First, they are naturally afraid of the feelings themselves. Second, they are afraid to talk about the feelings in the presence of the person they have them about. In the past they were likely discouraged from talking about their feelings toward authority figures. As children, many of our clients were punished physically for sharing their anger or their sexual feelings with adults.

Although the two feelings that people have most difficulty presencing are anger and sexuality, others, such as grief and fear, are also hard to confront directly in ourselves. From many years of watching videotapes of our therapy students, we notice that they will go to the greatest lengths to hide their sexual feelings and their anger toward their clients. We tell our students to dedicate the first ten years or so of practice to discovering these blind spots. In addition, our students have a great deal of difficulty giving their clients the space to discuss openly their feelings toward them.

BARRIERS TO PRESENCING

The barriers to presencing are formidable. Imagine that you are home by yourself, feeling lonely. Presencing would mean placing your attention on your feeling of loneliness, noticing how you are experiencing it in your body. Presencing, though, is often the last thing we do; we might raid the refrigerator first, to try to escape the loneliness through oral gratification. Two brownies later, feeling stuffed but still unsatisfied, we might vow to start a diet and call a friend to find out about the latest "Lose Ten Pounds in 24 Hours!" article in the *National Explorer*. Reaching an answering machine, we give up on aural gratification and turn to the solace of the TV, spending the rest of the evening with our thumb poised over the remote control. Finally, boredom overtakes us and we fall asleep. We have attempted to satisfy ourselves through mouth, ears, and eyes to escape a problem that still lives in the body, a problem that can be effectively confronted only through feeling it.

The therapist confronts this problem every day. In the following conversation we are attempting to bring a client into the present.

US: What are you experiencing right now?

MILT: You should have seen those morons on the freeway this morning! That's why I was late.

US: And so what are you feeling in your body right now?

MILT: I'm not sure what you're getting at. Are you saying, what did they do that bugs me?

US: Not exactly. More like we're inviting you to feel what you're feeling at the moment.

MILT: You mean now?

US: Right.

MILT: I don't know.

US: For example, you sound angry.

MILT: Well, no, of course I'm not angry. That'd be pretty stupid. I wouldn't get angry about something stupid like a bunch of jerks on the freeway. Why do you think I'm angry?

US: Well your face is kind of flushed, and you have your jaws clenched together.

MILT: Oh, that. No, that's the way I always am. Runs in the family, I guess.

US: Your father was like that, too?

MILT: Yeah, kind of.

US: So what are you experiencing right now?

MILT: Well, I'm sort of tired.

US: Tired.

We will depart Milt's story here, because it took us another twenty minutes of inquiry to bring him into the present. You can see, however, the different strategies of resistance that a simple question like "What are you experiencing right now?" can trigger. Within the space of a minute or so we saw denial, confusion, changing the subject, and faulty attribution. And this was with a willing client, someone who was paying to be there.

THE VALUE OF PRESENCING

One of the most important learnings we see people make in therapy is their discovery that they have the power to make an unpleasant feeling disappear simply by being present with it. We have had the pleasure of seeing a thousand precious moments like the following. Larry had a pain in the neck—a literal one. Not only that, he also had a metaphorical one: a nagging mother-in-law who just showed up unannounced for a visit. As he began to inquire into the pain and the psychological pattern that had put it there, he narrowed the whole problem down to a place in the back of his neck that is "tight as a drum." Along the way he unearthed a powerful insight—that he did not express his anger to anyone and therefore left it up to his body to act it out. As he realized this pattern, his pain began to subside, and now underneath the pain remains only drumlike tension. We asked him to place his attention on what was actually happening now, the sensation of the tension. There was a moment when he let go of judging his tension and simply placed his attention on it. His eyes flashed open wide: "It goes away!" he said.

This is the power of presencing. This moment—now!—has so much power for transformation in it that it generates powerful resistance.

Contrast Larry's story with this segment of dialogue from someone who is about to graduate from therapy after successfully clearing up a depression of long standing. Notice how quickly and thoroughly he is able to come into the present.

STEVE: Hi, I'm kind of out of breath. Traffic. (*He sits down on the couch and takes a deep breath.*)

GAY: So what exactly are you experiencing right now?

STEVE: I'm feeling kind of shaky inside. I guess I'm scared, come to think of it.

GAY: "I'm scared that . . ."

STEVE: I'm scared you're going to be mad at me for being late.

GAY: And what's that remind you of?

STEVE: Um, maybe like waiting for my father to get home to punish me.

Mother never hit us, but she would tell Dad when he came home, and he'd carry out the punishment.

GAY: Notice what you're really afraid of.

STEVE: I'm feeling more of the quivery feeling in my stomach. Some also up in my chest. I'm afraid you won't like me.

GAY: Afraid, too, that you'll lose your father's love?

STEVE: Yeah, I guess so. I did lose it. Gradually he withdrew from all us kids.

GAY: So being late is an extension of worrying about losing your father's love.

THE FUNDAMENTAL PRESENCING TECHNIQUE

The Fundamental Presencing Technique is *to invite the person to put his/her attention on a feeling or a sensation as it is experienced in the body.* We use feelings and sensations in the body because they cannot be argued about. By placing the attention on something that cannot be argued about, the client presences the truth. The resulting communication—the report—must be a simple description of the feeling or sensation. We are interested in a specific experience and description of the feeling or sensation, not an analysis of it. In body-centered therapy, insight and analysis must always follow experience.

Although the technique is quite simple, it may take a lifetime to master. The reason is that the client may do an infinite variety of things to delay or avoid presencing, and the therapist must somehow dance with all these defensive maneuvers to keep the process moving.

Here is an example of what the Presencing Technique looks like, followed by an example of what it does not look like.

KATHLYN: Jeff, take a moment to be with what you are experiencing in your body.

JEFF: Right now I'm feeling nervous.

KATHLYN: Notice the actual sensations that nervousness is for you.

JEFF: Yeah, I'm feeling a tight gut and a speedy feeling in my chest and throat.

This is presencing. Jeff is placing his attention directly on something that actually exists for him in his awareness. He is not explaining it, analyzing it, or judging it. Contrast Jeff's responses with those of another client, who has not yet learned how to presence.

KATHLYN: What are you experiencing right now, Leon?
LEON: It's the damnedest thing. You know, I trusted her and then she really let me down. Sometimes you put your hopes on something, and then it doesn't work out—you feel really let down.
KATHLYN: Tune in to that "let down" feeling. What does that feel like?
LEON: She didn't really even give me a chance. She just—

Leon went on for a while in this vein until Kathlyn was finally able to help him focus in on his feelings.

A SIMPLE TEST OF THE POWER OF THE PRESENCING TECHNIQUE

Any clinician can put the power of the Presencing Technique to a simple test. Select a symptom that a client is actively complaining about, and use the Presencing Technique with the symptom for a few minutes. Here is a case example of this test, followed by a broader experiment. We used the symptom of anxiety, partly because it often responds quickly to the Presencing Technique and partly because many of our clients experience it.

Sonya, age thirty-five, arrived for her third session feeling quite anxious. Work was not going well, her relationship with her husband was fraying at the edges, and she had to do the daily juggling act of dealing with a preschool child, sitters, and the inevitable complexities of life as a working woman. Since she seemed so rattled—very much in need of presencing—we asked her if she would partake in a brief experiment. She agreed. We asked her to give us a number from zero to ten that represented how anxious she felt.

We entered her number—an eight—on the following scale:

0	1	2	3	4	5	6	7	8	9	10
NONE		LITTLE		MODERATE		SIGNIFICANT				MAXIMUM

The scale is generic and can be used with any number of different symptoms. By indicating an eight, Sonya was saying that she experienced significant anxiety. To our eyes, she had selected correctly.

Next, we did the Fundamental Presencing Technique with her for ten minutes. Every two minutes we asked her to select a new number that represented her current level of anxiety. The conversation between us was repetitive. It went like this:

US: Feel the anxiety. Tune in to where you feel it in your body. Keep
    bringing your attention to it.
(*Two minutes of repeating these and similar instructions pass.*) Now, Sonya,
    pick a number that represents how much anxiety you feel.
SONYA: Now it's a five.
US: Fine, now go back to feeling the anxiety. Tune in to where you feel
    it. . . .

After ten minutes of the Presencing Technique Sonya reported zero anxiety. This finding confirmed what we had experienced many times in the clinical setting, but it was heartening to see the actual numbers on paper.

Symptoms like Sonya's are often a mask for a deeper issue. When her anxiety decreased, she was able to contact the issue that was driving the anxiety. In her case it was rooted in self-esteem issues: She was afraid that she was worthless. When the anxiety was presenced and dissolved, she could see the problem much more clearly.

We went further and designed a simple experiment that we administered to a group of graduate students just before a major examination. We invited twenty of them to fill out an anxiety scale, just as Sonya had done. Then we put ten of them into a Presencing Technique group and the remaining ten into a reading group. The reading group sat quietly and read about the Presencing Technique for ten minutes. Meanwhile, in another room, the Presencing Technique group actually practiced the Presencing Technique for ten minutes. The results were striking and are illustrated on the following chart.

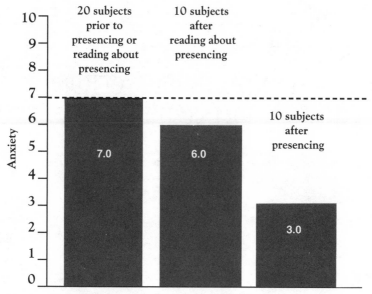

FIGURE 4. **Effect of Presencing on Test Anxiety**

In our experience the Fundamental Presencing Technique is a sine qua non for therapists. If you are a therapist, we urge you to put it to the test with the problems with which you and your clients are concerned. Encouraged by the intriguing results of simple experiments like the ones we describe above, we look forward to more elaborate experiments on the effectiveness of the technique by the scientific community.

C H A P T E R 7

THE MAGNIFICATION PRINCIPLE

Things're gonna have to get a whole lot worse before they get better.
—Satchel Paige

Many troublesome symptoms and feelings disappear rapidly when the person consciously magnifies their frequency or intensity. Magnification is also a reliable method of revealing the authentic feelings beneath symptoms.

A couple enters our office, locked in the troubled posture of conflict. Stuart slumps in his chair; Bonnie drums her fingers, flickers of irritation playing around her mouth. His body language says "I give up," while hers communicates bristling impatience.

KATHLYN: Stuart, I notice the way you're slumping down in your chair. You look sad and depressed, discouraged.

JOHN: Yeah, I guess I am.

KATHLYN: And Bonnie, you seem agitated, impatient. (*Bonnie bobs her head rapidly in acknowledgment.*)

GAY: Both of you, if you'd be willing, just let yourself do those things a little more. Stuart, slump a little more and magnify that discouraged feeling. Bonnie, drum your fingers a little faster. See if you can feel that impatience more and more.

This is the Magnification Principle in action. The therapist notices something—often one of the Five Flags—and invites the client to make it bigger, to fight fire with gasoline. What is the purpose behind such a seemingly paradoxical action? Why invite someone to do more of something that is already an expression of misery?

We will take a careful look at this question in this section, because when artfully used, magnification is one of the most powerful body-centered techniques in the therapist's toolbag. Just why it works so well is a complicated question, but before we turn our attention to the philosophy behind the Magnification Principle, let's look more closely at the actual technique.

A MAGNIFICATION EXPERIMENT
YOU CAN PERFORM

Here is an experiment you can do right now to test the power of the Magnification Principle. Tune in to some thought, feeling, or sensation you are having that you would like to get rid of. It could be a worry thought about something or perhaps a hurt or fear you are carrying. It could even be a simple sensation like hunger or tiredness. Notice it and be with it for a moment. Once you have tuned in to it, see if you can make it bigger. Exaggerate it, amplify it. If it is a rapid anxious thought, speed it up. If it is a sluggish depressed feeling, make it even more torpid and heavy.

Notice carefully what happens to the item you focused on. Many people find that magnifying it has the paradoxical effect of making it go away. Others find that it shifts, or that something deeper is revealed.

HOW WE FIRST LEARNED ABOUT THE
MAGNIFICATION PRINCIPLE

The first time we saw the Magnification Principle in action was in the gifted hands of Fritz Perls, the originator of gestalt therapy. Perls was something of a miracle worker, triggering rapid breakthroughs in clients who had proven intractable to other therapists. As we watched him work, the one tool he used in every session was magnification. He would pick up on some nuance—a tone of voice or the twitch of a lip—and ask the person to do it more. Sometimes this technique would lead to outrageous maneuvers on his part. But whether or not you liked him—and many people loathed him—it was hard to argue with his results.

Magnification was Perls's therapeutic panacea. When he saw a tapping toe, he would ask the person to tap faster. When he saw a look of supercilious disdain etched into a face, he would ask its wearer to become even more disdainful. He was like a mirror that reflected his clients back to themselves in hugely magnified close-up. Not everybody liked seeing themselves that way, and we saw people go into explosions of rage at Perls when he caught their act perfectly. Even now, more than twenty years later, occasionally we run into people who are still extremely grateful to or extremely mad at him.

In our own work, we have found ways to use magnification without prodding people into such escalated reactions. We definitely do not recommend that anyone try to imitate Perls. In addition to being a genius, he was also a lonely, misogynistic chain-smoker who delighted in getting people mad at him. He loved being the center of attention—an attribute that can be very limiting in therapy. Our view is that therapists should be so skilled that they seem to be not there. Therapy is about the client, not the therapist, and the therapist definitely should not be the star of the session, as Perls often was. But he left us the legacy of a very powerful tool, and we will always be grateful to him for it.

MAGNIFICATION ELIMINATES JUDGMENT

Now that credit has been given where it is due, here is an example of the Magnification Principle in action.

GREG: . . . and so I'm feeling a kind of heaviness all over.
US: And it's been there for how long?

GREG: Basically all week. No, since Tuesday, when I got the evaluation at work.

US: Oh, so that seemed to bring it on.

GREG: Yes.

US: Tune in to the actual sensations of the heaviness. Notice where exactly you feel it in your body.

GREG (*pause*): Over my shoulders, up my neck, and over my head. And oh, yeah, there's like a pressure on my chest.

US: Pressing down on your chest.

GREG: Yes.

US: Okay, let yourself exaggerate that feeling of heaviness. Make it heavier.

GREG: How?

US: Don't know. Feel how you could make it bigger and heavier.

GREG (*pause*): Wow, holding my breath makes it bigger very quickly.

US: Yes, go ahead and experiment with that.

GREG (*holds breath*): Yes, and then I start feeling irritated.

US: Yes, go ahead and magnify that irritated feeling.

GREG (*pause*): Oh, you know what? I see now, I didn't do anything with the anger I felt about the evaluation. So it's as if this blanket of heaviness settled in around me because I didn't handle the anger.

US: And you didn't handle it because . . . ?

GREG: I don't want to make things worse with my boss. And also there was a grain of truth in what he said in the evaluation.

US: Go a little further with that, if you would. Keep magnifying that irritated feeling.

GREG (*grunts*): You know, this is my father's whole life we're talking about here, not mine. He walked around in this irritated state all the time.

US: So when you got that evaluation, you started reacting in your father's style.

GREG: Yeah (*excitedly*), I do that, and it doesn't even feel like me, but I do it anyway.

US: Don't fight it, make it bigger. Be your father for a moment. Go ahead and swell up like that, put his expression on your face.

GREG (*tears coming*): He was such a lonely man underneath all his bluster.

US: And you're replaying that yourself.

GREG: Yeah, I am. Boy am I glad to be catching on to all that while there's still time.

US: Your father never caught on?

GREG: Not really, and he's seventy-nine now. Maybe he never will.

Using the Magnification Principle assures that the therapist will not shame the person for having the symptom. Here lies a supremely important issue in healing. The client has almost invariably been caught up in a cycle of blaming and shaming the symptom. Each time we make a symptom wrong, it seems to get worse, which leads to making it even more wrong. The more the client attempts to get rid of the symptom by controlling it or pushing it away, the more the symptom seems to escalate. The Magnification Principle breaks up this cycle by turning it on its ear. When the therapist welcomes the symptom or the problem feeling and invites the person to make it bigger, the judgment of "wrongness" is eliminated. Someone in the relationship—the therapist—has broken through to a new reality, and the client soon follows.

If someone is scared, for example, the act of trying to control the fear or get distance from it inevitably makes it worse. If the person uncovers this fear in therapy, the single most important act that promotes healing is for the therapist to refrain from trying to control it or get distance from it. To do so would perpetuate the very problem that brought the person in. In fact, this moment—when the client brings forth an issue that the therapist himself or herself has not resolved—is what makes the practice of therapy endlessly fascinating and growthful. Client and therapist are engaged in a dance in which each other's edges are being revealed. Therapists are always getting the opportunity to expand their own awarenesses, to go beyond their edges into new territory. The edge is always where acceptance ends and the possibility of making some aspect of ourselves wrong begins. If the client is expressing fear and if we as therapists judge that fear as wrong, there is no room for healing in the relationship. But skilled in the Magnification Principle, the therapist can never really make this mistake.

This client dialogue is an example of just what we are talking about:

US: What exactly are you feeling right now?

GEORGE: A kind of butterfly feeling in my stomach. I guess I'm scared.

US: Scared. Butterfly feeling. Is there more?

GEORGE: Yes, I'm feeling shaky in my knees. A weak feeling.

US: Be with that, all that for a moment. Be with the butterfly and the weak feeling.

GEORGE (*pause*): Yeah.

US: Now see if you can magnify those feelings. Be more scared, get weaker in the knees.

GEORGE (*breathing deepens, lets the feelings overtake him*): I see how much energy I waste trying to control those feelings.

US: Yes! Instead of controlling them for a moment, put all your energy into magnifying them.

The Magnification Principle can transform the whole practice of therapy. Every moment of a session is charged with the potential for receiving feelings—therapist's and client's—with an embrace or a cold shoulder. What is censured within becomes the outward symptoms that capture the therapist's attention. When the inner wrinkle is ironed out, the outer symptom often spontaneously disappears.

WHY THE MAGNIFICATION PRINCIPLE WORKS

There are several reasons why the Magnification Principle works. First, it is a powerful way of making the unconscious conscious. The unconscious produces an action of which the person is not aware—for example, the twisting of a wedding ring—then magnification brings consciousness to bear upon it. When the unconscious is greeted with a welcoming embrace, a healing moment opens. Freud said that the whole purpose of therapy is to make the unconscious conscious. Magnification is an exquisitely simple and to-the-point method of bringing consciousness to an unconscious element of ourselves.

Second, magnification breaks the "vapor lock" of a recycling symptom. The unconscious tends to repeat itself over and over because it is stuck in a pattern. One person, when scared, may idly stroke his mustache, while another may tug an earlobe. These elements may repeat themselves hundreds of times until something happens to break up the pattern. Magnification does just that.

Third, the magnification of a surface symptom gives us direct access to the deeper element just below the symptom. When the mustache-stroking is made consciously bigger, the person becomes more aware of the feeling that is hidden under the symptom. A superficial mannerism must always be regarded as a flag of a hidden feeling. Often these feelings are buried so deeply that they are far from the person's awareness. By magnification of the surface symptom, the person is able to clear space through which the deeper issue may emerge.

Fourth, magnification gives full expression to something that the symptom may be expressing incompletely. For example, a person who was talking about anger was making a small repetitive movement with his clenched right fist. When he was asked to magnify it, he made it bigger and found that it was a withheld punch directed at his long-dead abusive father. The unconscious remembered the withheld punch from childhood and was still reproducing it faithfully forty years later.

A fifth reason magnification works is that the person who magnifies a symptom or a feeling goes benignly out of control in order to do it. Control is often what is keeping the symptom or feeling locked into place. The willingness to magnify something risks going from the unknown into chaos. The happy surprise for those who make this jump is that there is a deeper order just beneath the chaos waiting to support the person.

At a more philosophical level, magnification works by inducing transcendence by paradox. There is a principle often encountered in Eastern religions, symbolized by the Chinese idea of yin and yang. The underlying unity of the universe seems on the surface to be two. There is existence and nonexistence, you and me, black and white, up and down. By going deeply into yin, however, one arrives at yang. By deeply getting to know another person, one inevitably finds an underlying unity with the person. The opposite is true, too: By pushing hard against a wall—a yang activity—one eventually surrenders to an acceptance of one's weakness, the yin concept. By occupying both sides of the paradox, one can let go of both and surrender to the oneness that is always greater than the duality.

WHEN NOT TO USE THE MAGNIFICATION PRINCIPLE

There are places in therapy where the Magnification Principle is clearly inappropriate. Three such areas are sex, physical violence, and self-destruction. If the client has developed feelings of sexual attraction toward the therapist—or vice versa—it would be unwise, illegal, and unethical to magnify any behaviors related to the attraction. But the feelings underneath the behavior could and should be magnified without expressing them in inappropriate actions. Doing so will give the person deeper insight into why these feelings are being called forth in therapy. Likewise, in regard to physical violence and self-destructive activities, the therapist must take care to build in a clear distinction between the feeling and the action. Magnification of the feelings underneath the expression is often a rapid path to healing. But the client must not be encouraged to act out any of these feelings, unless therapist and client can agree that the expression will not hurt anyone. If the therapist invites the angry client to express the anger by pounding a bed with a tennis racket, for example, both of them need to agree that it will be done safely. To be absolutely safe, the therapist may wish to stick to magnifying feelings and behaviors that do not have destructive potential for self or others.

THE POWER OF MAGNIFICATION

One of the most dramatic healing experiences we have had the privilege to facilitate made use of the Magnification Principle. A woman, Marie, came in for her regular therapy session—the seventh hour of what would be a twelve-session series—with a hideously twisted expression on her face. The session took off so quickly that Gay did not even invite her to sit down.

GAY (*alarmed*): What's wrong?

MARIE: I feel like I'm dying. I've got this migraine—I get one or two a year. But this is horrible, and nothing I do has helped. Even the medicine isn't working. I got a stronger prescription from my doctor, and it just isn't doing anything.

GAY: And does it feel like you might be able to work on it here? Or should you be home?

MARIE: I've been home all day. I want to see if I can do something with it here.

GAY: Okay. How long have you had the headache?

MARIE: Two days. But it's getting worse.

GAY: Okay. Tell me about the exact sensations.

MARIE: My vision is off, as if I'm seeing double. Most of the pain is on the left side of my head. It's horrible.

Note that she has used the word *horrible* twice. This is a verbal flag.

GAY: What other sensations are you feeling?

MARIE (*cocks head to left, a movement flag*): I've got irritation, an irritated feeling, all over my arms, under my skin. On my chest, too.

GAY: Anything else?

(*Marie shakes her head*)

GAY: What about the "horrible" feeling? Where do you feel that in your body?

MARIE (*pauses, cocks head to left again*): It's a kind of nausea in my stomach.

GAY: Okay, see if you can be with all those feelings for a moment. Feel them in your body—the horrible feeling, the irritation, the pain on the left side of your head. Maybe tilt your head a little farther to the left.

MARIE: Be with them?

GAY: Yes. Give your full attention to them without trying to do anything with them.

MARIE: Oh. (*After a five-second pause, she takes a deep breath.*)

GAY: Yes, do that some more, make that breath bigger.

(*Marie takes three or four big breaths, then sighs.*)

GAY: What's happening?

MARIE: The pain's getting less, but the nausea is getting more.

GAY: Okay, do your best to make the nausea bigger. Breathe, or do whatever you need to do to get more nauseous.

There is a possibility that magnifying the symptom of nausea will result in actual vomiting, but in practice it seldom does. We have invited several hundred people to magnify this sensation, and fewer than a dozen of them have needed to use the rest room to vomit.

MARIE: Why?

GAY: Sometimes things get better when you consciously make them worse. But don't worry about figuring it out right now. Just experiment with it.

MARIE (*breathes deeply, a very sick look on her face*): Oh, God, I feel horrible.

GAY: And that horrible feeling—go back to when you first felt that in your life.

MARIE (*starts to cry*): I felt it all the way through the first grade. My parents were splitting up, and I couldn't keep any food down. I was skinny as a rail, and they had to put me on these special milky drinks to put calories on me. God, I kept throwing them up, even a couple of times in class.

GAY: That sounds awful.

MARIE (*sobbing*): Why is all this coming up right now?

GAY: Not sure. What happened the day you got the migraine that reminds you of when you were in the first grade?

MARIE (*long pause*): Omigod, that's when I found out they were going to split up the class I've been teaching all year and give half of the kids to another special ed teacher. Part of me is glad, but I guess another part of me is heartbroken. I won't get to see how they turn out.

GAY: Ah. And what does that remind you of?

MARIE: Well, when my parents split up, I had to choose between going to the school near my father's or go to a new school if I wanted to stay with my mother. I had to leave the class and my best friend Margie and go across town. It was horrible.

(*Marie stands quietly in the center of the office, head bowed in thoughtful silence, for about two minutes.*)

GAY (*curious*): What kinds of sensations are you feeling right now?

MARIE: I was just feeling myself all over. It's all gone, the headache, the itchiness, the nausea.

She went on to decide what actions she could take to support these powerful insights. She decided to tell the truth to her special ed class, about how sorry she was to see them go. She planned a party and made arrangements to go into the new teacher's class from time to time to check in with her former pupils. The amazing feature of this session, from a therapist's point of view, is how quickly the symptoms disappeared. Here was an intractable headache of two days' duration—one that medicine had bounced off—and all it took was a few minutes of applied consciousness to transform it. Things do not always go quite this smoothly, but when they do, body-centered therapy seems the most graced of professions.

THE FUNDAMENTAL MAGNIFICATION TECHNIQUES

N ow, let's look at two Magnification Techniques that therapists can
use to put the Magnification Principle to work.

THE FLAG-TO-MAGNIFICATION PROCESS

The Magnification Technique that we use most is the Flag-to-
Magnification Process, abbreviated by many of our students as Flag-to-Mag.
This process involves picking up on one of the Five Flags and inviting the
client to magnify it. Here are several examples of the Flag-to-Mag Process at
work. The first example uses both movement and attitude flags as objects of
magnification.

KATHLYN: Hi, Mark, come on in.

MARK (*enters and sits nervously on the edge of the chair; in a clipped, staccato
voice*): I'm late. I'm sorry. Traffic.

KATHLYN: Yes. Take a moment to be with that. Sense what is going on in
your body right now.

MARK (*shakes his head impatiently*): Oh, it's nothing. I'm just hassled by traffic and too much to do. I've got four deals closing this week, and my daughter's sitter is sick, and so I had to make a whole bunch of other arrangements on the car phone while I was trying to get here—

KATHLYN: Take a moment to be with all those feelings—the hassled sensation, having too much to do—

(*Mark shakes his head again.*)

KATHLYN: And experiment with that head-shaking some more. Make it more exaggerated.

MARK (*shakes head consciously, tunes in to body feelings for about five seconds*): I don't like the way things are going lately. I'm feeling out of control.

KATHLYN: Take that out-of-control feeling, and notice how you experience it in your body.

MARK: It's like being off-balance, almost a dizziness. Things moving too fast.

KATHLYN: Let yourself feel it even more, risk being off-balance.

MARK: I hate it.

KATHLYN: This harried pattern is something that has come up for you a lot in the few times we've been together. What does it remind you of?

MARK: Everything! I've always been that way. My mom says that I would be finished and away from the dinner table in five minutes if she would let me.

KATHLYN: So you've been in a hurry for a long time.

MARK: Yeah.

KATHLYN: I'd like you to really exaggerate that hurriedness. Go around the room, acting it out as far out to the edge as you can go.

MARK (*goes slamming around the room, furiously rearranging things, looking at his watch, saying "I'm late," then breaks out in laughter*): Oh, man, this is the story of my life.

KATHLYN: What does that really feel like you're reacting to, with all that hurrying?

MARK: I gotta get it done, gotta be somebody, gotta survive.

KATHLYN: Whose voice is saying that?

MARK: I think it's Dad. See, he was desperate for a son. They had three girls in a row, only they had wanted to have just one girl and one boy. The boy didn't come and didn't come, and then my mom miscarried with a boy just before me. So I think they were loaded with fear that I wasn't going to survive.

Here, then, is how a lifetime pattern can be generated. An attitude of hurriedness begins very early, in response to a specific set of attitudes in the home. Then it generalizes and expands into all corners of life, culminating in the way the client enters the room. This is why we often tell our students that their first five minutes of contact with a client will tell them everything they really need to know.

Let's look at another example, one that magnifies a breathing flag. This excerpt is taken from the middle of Betty's session.

BETTY: There's always been this sense of not being enough. I notice it most around my husband and kids—as if nothing I do will ever be enough.

GAY: Tune in to how long you've felt that not being enough.

(*Betty holds her breath at the top of the in-breath.*)

GAY: I noticed you stopped breathing. Hold that breath a little while longer. Notice what that's connected to.

(*Betty holds her breath about ten seconds, then lets go with a big sigh.*)

GAY: Yes—make that sigh even bigger. Do it a couple of times.

BETTY: I'm so ashamed of myself. It seems as if I've always felt that I did something wrong.

This moment led into a productive inquiry about where Betty's sense of shame had developed. It is always remarkable to see how powerful a simple thing like holding the breath can be in revealing the depths of what is going on with a person. Gay invited Betty to tune in to a certain feeling—and her unconscious responded with a command of its own: Hold the breath. Then, when consciousness was brought to bear to the breath flag, a new world of information was discovered. This is the magic of the body-centered approach.

Our next example shows how a postural flag can be magnified. It is drawn from the first session with a new client, Val. We join the session about halfway through.

VAL: The other thing that's happening in my life right now is that I'm getting some acupuncture treatment for shoulder pain, some sort of bursitis.

KATHLYN: When did that start?

VAL: I guess I first noticed it after aerobics class one day. We'd been doing a bunch of stretches up above our heads, and maybe it pinched something. But I've had things up in that shoulder before, on and off.

KATHLYN: The most recent version of it is pretty new, but you've noticed pain up there for years? Months?

VAL: I can remember it back in college, even, and I'm thirty-two now. So I guess about ten years.

KATHLYN: You know, I noticed something when you first walked in. I don't know if it's connected or not, but it might be. Look how your left shoulder sits up higher than your right shoulder.

VAL: What do you mean?

KATHLYN: Here, come over to the full-length mirror. See how your left shoulder is higher and shorter than your right one.

VAL: Oh, uh-huh. That's the side I carry my purse on, though. Maybe it's just that.

KATHLYN: Possibly. Experiment with it for a minute, though, if you'd be willing. Make the left shoulder a little more tense. Just tighten it some more, and as you do that, lift it a little higher. Be with that a moment.

VAL (closes her eyes, concentrates as she magnifies the shoulder flag): Hm, if I do that, it hurts the place where I've got the bursitis.

KATHLYN: So it's connected. Be with that as long as you can. Be easy on yourself, but stay with it. Feel if there are any other connections you can make.

VAL: I just had a picture pop into my mind of my mother criticizing me about something.

KATHLYN: About?

VAL (nervous laugh): My shoes not being polished just right. She had a thing about that. But it could have been just about anything. She was critical of just about everything me and my dad did.

KATHLYN: I wonder what the connection is between your shoulder and your mother's criticism.

VAL (*spontaneously begins raising and lowering her shoulder, experimenting with it*): You know, I think I somehow tensed up around her a lot. She never hit me or anything, but we were never close, either. She really was never close to anybody. She didn't have any good friends, and her relationship with her own mother was awful.

KATHLYN: So your main support was your dad.

VAL: Yeah, he and I were buddies, kind of like allies against her. He respected her, but I don't think he really liked her.

KATHLYN: Back to your shoulder. Does it feel like you're still tensing your shoulder because you really haven't resolved things with your mother?

VAL: I never really thought about it like that. Maybe you're right. How do I resolve it, though? She's been dead five years.

KATHLYN: You can start by acknowledging the feelings you may be carrying around in your shoulder. Like anger toward her. Go ahead and let that shoulder be angry for a moment. Make some angry sounds and do something angry with your shoulder.

VAL (*growls and shakes her shoulder up and down and around*): That feels good.

KATHLYN: Do it more. Really go all the way.

(*Val roars and growls and hits out with her left arm. Suddenly she bursts into tears.*)

KATHLYN: You must have so much wanted a connection with her. It must have felt sad not to be close.

VAL (*crying*): Yeah, I saw my best friend, Joanie, always laughing and joking with her mother. Her mother was this jolly lady who just worshiped Joanie, and my mother was stiff as a board. I was jealous of a lot of girls because of that.

The Magnification Principle allows the body-centered therapist to begin with the obvious and then reveal the deeply hidden. It is accomplished by using both the consciousness of the therapist and the consciousness of the client. A shared dance of exploration, the process goes as rapidly as the client allows. If the person is open and willing, a tremendous amount of information can flow forth in a short period of time. In Val's case, her willingness created an opening into which a powerful awareness could be invited.

THE FEELING-TO-MAGNIFICATION PROCESS

Feelings can also be effectively explored and resolved through magnification. Many therapists come to grief by trying to talk clients out of their feelings. We have found that feelings must be honored and embraced, and there are few more effective ways of doing so than magnification, in the Feeling-to-Magnification Process, the second Magnification Technique. There are three main feelings that people have difficulty in expressing: fear, anger, and sadness. In the following example, all three of these feelings are magnified, with an overall healing result.

We are doing a couple's session with Daniel and Dianne. It is our second session together, and they are deeply polarized at the moment.

DIANNE: You see! He simply doesn't care anything about my feelings.

DANIEL (*his arms crossed defensively, a stubborn, derisive expression covering his face*): There you have it, ladies and gentlemen, round number four hundred and twenty eight of the Daniel and Dianne soap opera! Dammit, Dianne, you don't ever seem to get it, do you? You think everything's my fault and that you are completely blameless! It just is not that way!

KATHLYN: Step out of each other's range for a moment. Okay, go all the way with expressing that anger. Yell as much as you like. Get your arms and legs into it. That's it.

(*Daniel and Dianne go full out into their angry, aggrieved personas, stomping and yelling and calling each other names. The outburst lasts about thirty seconds, then subsides.*)

It usually works this way. Early in our careers, when we first began inviting people to magnify their negative feelings, we feared that people would lock into an escalated version of their conflict and stay there. In fact, it almost never happened that way. Having permission to escalate the conflict speeded up the process and gave clients access to the deeper feelings under the veneer of anger. This is what happened with Dianne and Daniel.

GAY: Notice what else you're feeling under all that anger. Be with what's underneath that.

DIANNE: I'm just exhausted.

DANIEL: I feel scared that it's always going to be like this. That we'll never get it together.

GAY: Okay, Dianne, exaggerate that exhaustion—let it really overtake you. Daniel, feel the fear down in your cells. Be with it and make it bigger.

(*Both of them stand transfixed, focusing on their inner sensations.*)

DIANNE: You know, I'm really hurt, too. I've been living in this state of being hurt and not getting what I want for so long that I feel exhausted.

KATHLYN: Yes, notice where you feel that sadness.

DIANNE (*she touches her chest*): Deep in here.

KATHLYN: Feel it and let it spread as far as you can. Feel it all over you, as many places as you can.

DIANNE: I can feel it out into my arms.

GAY: Let your arms move with that sadness.

(*Dianne reaches out with her arms, as if to embrace the air. As she does this, she bursts into tears.*)

KATHLYN: Who is it that you're really reaching out for?

DIANNE: My father. When he died, I was lost. My mother had been in and out of treatment centers, and he was my only stability. Then he died and I had to grow up overnight. I feel like my childhood stopped when I was in the second grade. I want it back! (*She sobs. Daniel comes to comfort her.*)

One of the most beautiful moments that we get to witness nearly every day is two people finding a feeling that they share under the raging battle on the surface of their lives. In this case, Daniel and Dianne discovered that the positions they were taking about each other were simply masks for deep feelings that they needed to face. When they dropped the battle (which happened only after they magnified it), they were able to find out what was under it. In Dianne's case, part of the battle had begun twenty years before she met Daniel, in the grief of her loss. This ancient sadness fueled her anger in her present relationship. As long as the focus was on being right and proving Daniel wrong, she was not able to get to the real issue, nor was Daniel. This is the seduction of conflict; it has an addictive quality, and like many addictions, it prevents the person from confronting the real problems of living.

THE BREATHING PRINCIPLE: USING BREATHWORK IN THE HEALING PROCESS

And now I see with eye serene
The very pulse of the machine;
A being breathing thoughtful breath,
A traveller between life and death.
—William Wordsworth

Breathing patterns precisely reflect the emotional difficulties people are experiencing or have experienced in the past. Several specific breathing techniques can serve as the first-line methods of diagnosing and treating psychological issues.

If we could do but one thing with people who are in emotional pain, we would most likely focus on breathing—both ours and theirs. As our therapeutic vision has expanded over the last twenty years, we have found a universe of rich possibility in each moment of breathing. The Breathing Principle holds a major key to know how human beings get stuck and how they can achieve liberation.

A MOMENT OF DISCOVERY

Gay recalls the moment of first discovering the power of the Breathing Principle:

"I learned the power of breathwork by a happy turn of fate. One day in the early seventies while I was walking in the woods, I had a powerful enlightenment experience that changed the direction of my life and work. This experience, which lasted less than an hour, has organized my existence ever since. The experience had such coherence and integrity that even twenty years later I can resolve problems in my material, psychological, and spiritual life by referring back to the moment. Here is what happened.

"While walking that day, I found myself thinking that I had been on an unconscious quest for a psychospiritual grail for much of my life. I wanted to know what the one thing was that brings about transformation. I thought: Life is so complicated. There must be one thing we are doing wrong, one thing that needs to be changed, in order for clarity, spontaneity, and harmony to replace the programmed, muddy, disjointed state of being that many of us experience.

"I realized that I had been seeking the answer to this question outside myself for years, and I hadn't found it. This unconscious quest had motivated me all the way to a Ph.D. in counseling psychology and to familiarity with every major psychological and spiritual tradition, but I still could not say that I knew in my heart what it takes to generate transformation. A very subversive question arose in me: Could it be that the act of trying to find the answer outside myself was the very thing that kept me from finding it?

"In a moment of supreme clarity, I simply asked the question of the universe and myself and awaited the answer. I looked up at the skies and trees and asked out loud what I and humans in general needed to know or do to be free.

"When the answer came, seconds later, it rocked the foundations of everything I knew. It reorganized my knowledge of myself, it revealed what I had been doing wrong, and it showed me how to do therapy, all in one fell swoop. For a few seconds after I asked the question, there was a charged silence. Then a roaring cascade of energy and light poured through me. It was so strong and ecstatic that I could only revel in it, moving and stretching to accommodate its power. The energy and light lasted probably about half an hour. When it subsided, it left several truths behind in its wake. I still don't know where these truths came from, although I'm quite sure they didn't come from any conscious process of logical thinking on my part.

"The truths: I had been living my life in a state of conflict between mind and body. I would have a feeling, for example, such as fear or anger. I would use my mind to ignore, deny, or minimize it. I realized that I merely needed to link up my mind and body, to acknowledge my feelings and communicate them clearly. The only thing required was to experience— instead of conceptualize—life. To live in a state of harmony, I simply needed to be with what I was feeling. To live in a state of ecstasy—the frosting on the cake—I needed but to love myself for whatever I was experiencing. Certainly there is a place for concepts, but I had been using them to create distance from myself. A moment later, I put this truth to the test.

"I said to myself: Okay, I'm willing to experience whatever is necessary for me to learn to live in a state of harmony. What do I need to experience? Seconds later, a lifetime of unfelt feelings poured through me. I sobbed for losses in my childhood, I shivered in fear and went popeyed with rage. I felt joy and excitement and misery and love. I let go of my resistance to myself and let whatever was there come through. For an hour or so wave after wave of feelings rolled through me; I simply felt them. The feelings literally came in waves, with pauses of clear space between them. And I learned that I could open up to even more feelings simply by breathing a little deeper. Actually, the learning was more subtle than that. I learned that breathing more completely allowed the feelings to pass through unimpeded and effortlessly. If I tensed up or held my breath, the feelings got rough and painful.

"All my feelings—even rage and grief—felt good as long as I *breathed with them*. This news was astounding to me (and still is). I realized that I had held my breath to hold my feelings in check as long as I could remember. Specific memories came up of holding my breath to deaden the pain of my grandmother's death and to choke back the anger and humiliation of receiving physical punishment from my mother. I realized that I had always held my breath to handle pain and my feelings.

"As I stood in the forest that day, I took breath after joyful breath, celebrating the passion of feeling that was coursing through me. After a while all the emotions disappeared, and I felt a uniform sensation of energy and bliss throughout my body. Another truth formed in my mind as I breathed: At the bottom of all feeling is peace and bliss. Peace and bliss are our natural birthright, but we keep them covered with painful feelings that we are afraid to *breathe into*. If we can risk going into our unpleasant feelings consciously, using our breath as the searchlight, we can come out on the other side into an organic state of clarity and happiness.

"During the five years following the original revelation, it seemed that every session I had with a client revealed something useful that complemented the original learning. Just a day after I had the experience in the woods, I sat down with a woman for her therapy session. She described some fears and angers that were dominating her mind and body. Armed with my new knowledge, I invited her to feel the emotions in her body and to amplify the sensations by breathing into them. She held her breath and said something quite revealing as the intensity of the feelings began to mount: 'I don't understand why I ought to be having all these feelings.' I pointed out that she had stopped experiencing her feelings in order to understand them and that the act of understanding them (or not understanding them, in her case) had stopped her experience and her breath. Her jaw dropped in amazement as she got the message. She went back to participating with the feelings by breathing with them, and within seconds she released a torrent of tears. She immediately felt better. Beyond that, she spontaneously thought of some creative solutions to her real-life issues. I was in awe at how the completion of the feelings through participation with them had unlocked her creativity. I recalled many effortful sessions in which clients and I had batted our brains out trying to figure out how to resolve some issue. Could we all actually have a hidden reservoir of creativity just on the other side of our resistance? Could the keys to the treasure be a breath away?"

BREATHING PATTERNS

Human beings are equipped with two different breathing patterns that everyone can benefit from identifying. Learning how to spot these two patterns in ourselves can be of great benefit in many life situations. Therapists in particular will find much value in knowing about the two basic patterns. It will allow them to notice at a glance when their clients are in the grip of emotions with which they are not comfortable. The first breathing pattern, called Centered Breathing, is found when we are relaxed and do not perceive a threat. The second breathing pattern, called Fight-or-Flight Breathing, is found when we are in a variety of circumstances involving perceived threats. A third breathing pattern, which can be called Aerobic Breathing, occurs during exercise and does not directly concern us here.

A BREATHING ACTIVITY YOU CAN TRY OUT
AS YOU READ

Right now take a conscious breath. Breathe all the way in and all the way out. Notice how it feels to take a conscious breath. Do it again. Take a full breath in, and let it go completely. Notice the feeling in your body as you breathe consciously. As you read the material in this chapter, pause now and then to take a full, conscious breath.

We emphasize the concept of perceived (rather than actual) threats in Fight-or-Flight Breathing. Fight-or-Flight Breathing evolved a long time ago, when physical threats were the order of the day. Running and punching were two popular options for dealing with a world of exotic and hungry beasts. Later, sticks and stones were added to the defensive repertoire, followed much, much later by language. Nowadays, we encounter far fewer physical threats, but we have generalized our Fight-or-Flight Breathing to cover situations where we think our ego or identity is under threat. Unless one's identity is exceptionally strong, most of life can be seen as a threat to identity. Typically, by midmorning, many of us may have already perceived threats from fellow commuters, the bus driver, the boss, and the daily newspaper.

Centered Breathing moves the abdomen observably—hence its nickname "belly breathing"—and it occurs at a rate of fewer than fourteen times a minute. Fight-or-Flight Breathing occurs mainly in the chest, at fourteen or more times a minute. Fight-or-Flight Breathing is nearly always accompanied by tense abdominal muscles. One can see how this breathing pattern could have evolved. The primitive human under threat would have wanted to protect the organs of the belly by tightening the muscle wall and would have also needed to halt digestion, which takes enormous energy, in order to mobilize for action. When a person is under a physical threat, the breathing moves rapidly in the chest, accompanied by massive secretions from the adrenal glands. The heart rate goes up, and the muscles tighten. The organism is at the ready. In the primitive environment, this buildup of energy was discharged immediately by either running or fighting. In modern life, neither is usually appropriate, so we get all revved up with no place to go.

When we first began to distinguish between Fight-or-Flight and Centered Breathing, we were profoundly amazed at how much of the former we saw. We were particularly humbled to discover how much of the time we ourselves were locked into Fight-or-Flight Breathing. Was everyone walking around in a state of fear? At first we thought our profession might be giving us a skewed vision of the world, because most of our clients were in emotional turmoil. But then we began paying attention to breathing as we waited in line at the grocery store or sat in a subway train. What we saw was basically the same: Most people were locked in Fight-or-Flight Breathing, or if not, they are breathing just barely enough to stay alive. We even spent a couple of hours observing breathing during a visit to Disney World— where people are supposed to be having fun—and we saw about as much Fight-or-Flight Breathing there as we had seen on the New York subways.

We have also seen Fight-or-Flight Breathing in an elementary classroom, where we observed twenty-five students as they were each called on to deliver a two-minute oral report. All but three of the students went into Fight-or-Flight Breathing just before their turn came. The majority stayed in Fight-or-Flight mode for a while even after their report was over. Apparently the common fear of public speaking begins early. On another occasion we were sitting in the board room of a major high-tech firm during a corporate consulting engagement. All but one of the seven participants were men; two of the men and the lone woman stayed in Fight-or-Flight Breathing throughout the whole meeting. Later, interestingly enough, we found that those three people were of particular concern to the company because they had cost it a great deal of money in lost days and medical bills over the previous few years. On still another occasion we were observing breathing patterns during a long wait in the post office line. We could see most of the postal clerks from where we stood, and none of them were doing any exertion heavier than handing out stamps and making change. Yet four out of six of them were in Fight-or-Flight Breathing. What fear could be gripping our postal clerks?

One of our first observations of the shift from Centered to Fight-or-Flight Breathing had amusing overtones. One afternoon in the early Seventies, we were sitting on the back porch watching our English sheepdog breathe. Gay had set himself the task of learning about breathing from the inside out by watching a hundred different organisms breathe. This research included studying the breathing of babies, women in labor, animals, and amoebae, as well as dozens of people in emotional crisis. He had been closely watching the rise and fall of Millie's breathing as she sunned herself at his feet. Suddenly the neighbor's cat, a fat old tabby named George, wandered into the yard. Millie emitted a low growl, and her breathing immediately shifted into Fight-or-Flight. With Millie, the archetypal coward, one could not be sure whether she was contemplating fighting or fleeing, because she had at least on one other occasion been frightened into hasty departure by a hissing cat.

BREATHWORK

In this chapter we want to show how breathwork can be integrated, with great benefit, into every moment of daily living. Once you master the basic Breathing Principles, you will have a skill that you can take with you everywhere. Breathwork is of particular importance to therapists: We think it can enhance therapeutic contact immensely. Therapists can focus on their own breathing to eliminate the stress of conducting therapy, and they can use their awareness of their clients' breathing to make the whole therapy enterprise easier and more effective. In daily life as well as in therapy, we ourselves use what we know about breathwork to pay attention to our own breathing. Frequently we will be discussing some issue in our marriage, for example, when we will notice that we are both holding our breath. This awareness usually signals us that some deeper feeling—perhaps something we are scared about—is being left out of the discussion. Even if we cannot locate a hidden feeling, taking a few deep breaths never fails to enliven the conversation, particularly if we are feeling stuck.

We would like to show you some ways we use the Breathing Principle in a typical therapy session. It can be used to enhance being and feeling, to enhance unity, and to enhance mastery.

USING THE BREATHING PRINCIPLE
TO ENHANCE BEING AND FEELING

Our therapy office is a big, sunny room with a teal-colored leather sofa and a massive wooden rocking chair. There are two videocameras at the ready so that we can tape sessions for the client to take home and for us to review. Music is playing in the background softly, and rainbows shimmer on the walls from the crystals resting on the windowsill. We open the door to the waiting room and greet Bob, a middle-aged man whom we have not seen before.

He trudges in wearily. His every movement broadcasts heaviness, not just because of his middle-age paunch but because all the vectors of his body seem tugged by gravity. His chin sags, his chest slumps, his footfalls thud. When he takes the couch, his head slouches forward. Even the chunky gold Rolex on his wrist suggests a burden rather than an emblem of prosperity. Our eyes are immediately drawn to his breathing, which is very shallow and seems to be moving only a tiny bit in his chest. (Healthy breathing moves the belly substantially and the chest somewhat less.) His abdomen looks gripped with tension; it seems to move not at all. It is our practice not to engage in pleasantries but to move right toward the heart of the matter. We invite him to sit down.

GAY: I notice a lot of heaviness in your posture. Your breathing seems very shallow. You seem quite depressed.

BOB (his eyes coming up for the first time): I've been very depressed this week. All week long.

We take a moment to resonate with his depressed feeling. We try on his tired heaviness in our own bodies, feeling the leaden deadness of it.

GAY: Take a moment to feel the depressed sensations in your body. Just be with them.

BOB: What do you mean?

GAY: Feel where you feel the depression in your body. Notice the exact sensations that let you know you're depressed.

(*There is a long pause.*)

Clearly, this is the first time anybody has asked him to do such an unusual thing. In fact, there are no places in society other than a certain type of therapist's office where this kind of thing is suggested or encouraged. In fact, one could say that the whole trend of society—including advertising, schooling, and religion—is toward keeping us from tuning in to what we are actually experiencing. When we have a headache, the TV tells us to take a fabulous new pain reliever, recommended by nine out of ten doctors in the known universe. When we go to our minister and say, "I have lust in my heart," chances are we won't hear him say, "Feel it, be with it, celebrate it."

There is no verb in the dictionary for what we are asking him to do. That is why we had to coin our own term—*presencing*—to describe this action. We ask him to place his attention on sensations in his body, with no attempt to *do* anything with them. All his life he has probably ignored, denied, censured, or drowned out his sensations. Chances are he will even hear our basic instructions as a suggestion that he judge or attempt to get rid of his sensations. Fortunately he has found his way to one of the few places that can help him. He has tried just about everything else, from motivational tapes to antidepressants. Both irritate him, and the latter made him either manic or sleepy. Now he is doing something absolutely radical: He is taking time out from everything he knows how to do to leap into the unknown. In short, he is feeling what he is feeling.

How a person responds to a request to do this is itself remarkably diagnostic. Some people get hostile when we ask them to tune in to their body sensations. They glare and ask, "What good is *that* going to do?" Others cannot do it at all, and they retreat into asking questions about it or seeking information about it. On one memorable occasion, a burly man went sound asleep after pausing for a few seconds to tune in to what he was feeling. We thought he was having an exceptionally deep communion with his feelings until the rumbling snore began. The therapist who invites clients to be with their feelings can expect the clients' favorite defensive maneuver—whether it is sleep or anger—to emerge in response to the invitation.

Bob, being highly motivated by his desperation, did not spend much time resisting the basic instruction.

BOB: I feel a heavy sensation on my chest, like something pressing down on my chest.

GAY: Um-hm. What else?

BOB: There's a burning sensation around in my stomach. And it's real tight.

GAY: Could you point to where it is burning and tight? (*We wanted to be absolutely clear about where he felt it, since most of us only have the vaguest idea where our stomachs actually are. Bob points to his navel.*)

GAY: What else are you feeling in your body?

BOB: Well, I guess there's a kind of speedy feeling in my chest. And I feel a little sick to my stomach.

GAY: Stay with it. Notice anything else you can.

BOB: I have a slight headache.

GAY: Where do you actually feel the pain?

BOB (*pauses for ten seconds or so*): Well, I guess it's here in my temples.

GAY: Do you notice anything else in your head?

BOB: The back of my neck is really tight.

Just as he says the last sentence, he takes his first belly-breath and appears to relax somewhat.

This short conversation has communicated an enormous amount to us about how to help Bob. It has also accomplished something very important that has resulted in a shift in his internal state toward releasing his tension. When people talk about their problems in vague terms like *depression*, the problems seem immense, certainly bigger than they are. But the moment they can point to something specific—a heaviness in the chest or a burning in the belly—they locate the problem in time and space. Suddenly they become bigger than it is.

An incident from Gay's childhood illustrates the point: He recalls a time when he thought he saw a ghost in his bedroom. His mother wisely gave him a flashlight to shine on it, and it turned out to be a curtain hanging in an unfamiliar way. Until he located it in time and space, though, it was bigger than he was. Bob had metaphorically done exactly the same thing, and his deep breath told us that it was beginning to have an effect. Here are a few other things we learned in our conversation.

First, several of the sensations he was calling "depression" were actually the physical sensations that come from not breathing diaphragmatically. Correct breathing must move the diaphragm, which does not move properly if we hold our belly tightly. Unless the abdomen swells and expands with the in-breath, the diaphragm cannot make its full excursion. If this large and crucial muscle does not move with each breath, some predictable, unpleasant sensations begin to happen. There is a pressure in the chest and a feeling of heaviness. An antsy sensation seems to flutter in the blood itself. Speediness and nausea float around the chest and belly.

Some of these sensations also signal the presence of fear. There is, in fact, an intimate relationship between fear and breathing. As the gestalt therapist Fritz Perls once said, "Fear is excitement without the breath." When we are breathing deeply and fully, we experience fear as excitement and energy. What Perls was really pointing to was the diaphragm. If the diaphragm moves through its full excursion with each breath, it is physiologically not possible to feel those sensations of heaviness, pressure, and speediness. Not possible. Those symptoms are all caused by poor diaphragmatic breathing.

We learned something else from our brief dialogue with Bob. Two of the sensations he described sent us a message loud and clear: hidden anger. We have found that the majority of all headaches, especially those that are accompanied by tight neck muscles, are caused by the tension of muscles being used to hide and control anger. We decided to move in the direction of his anger.

KATHLYN: How do you deal with anger?

BOB (*his eyes flicker and his in-breath is interrupted*): Well, uh—I'm not an angry person.

Note that Bob answered a different question from the one we asked. We had asked him how he deals with anger—a process—and he answered with a description of his being. Whenever anyone changes the subject like this—technically called "redefinition"—it is a good bet that a fundamental split in the person has been spotlighted. The flicker of his eyes and the shift in his breathing are telegraphing this split.

GAY: And so what happens when you—who aren't an angry person—feel anger?

BOB (*his eyes glaze over for a split second*): I guess I don't ever really let myself tell anybody when I'm angry.

KATHLYN: "Because if I did . . ."

BOB (*pause and deep sigh*): They wouldn't like me.

GAY: So, Bob, someone way back there withdrew love from you for being angry.

BOB (*laughs harshly, eyes tearing*): It's the story of my life. Nobody in my family could be angry. We all had to tiptoe around.

KATHLYN: Tell us what exactly happened one specific time.

BOB (*holds his breath again*): I—I—

GAY: Breathe deeply. Let yourself breathe into your feelings. Breathe right into where you feel anger and sadness or whatever else you're feeling.

BOB (*gasps, simultaneously trying to breathe and not breathe, to feel and not feel*): This is hard.

GAY: I know. Take full deep breaths. Notice when you're fighting your feelings by holding your breath.

(*Bob contacts his sadness and his anger. He is breathing more deeply, and there is a flush of color in his cheeks. In spite of the fact that he is fighting his feelings, he looks remarkably more alive than he has since the start of the session.*)

KATHLYN: Tell us about the first time you can remember feeling these kinds of feelings.

BOB (*pause of about half a minute*): I guess it was when my grandmother died. I was eight.

GAY: And you felt sad and angry.

BOB: And lost.

GAY: Yes, lost.

BOB: She was all I had to hold on to. My parents were so volatile. Always angry and off the wall. My grandmother was steady. And one day she just had a stroke and died.

KATHLYN: And how does her death connect with your being depressed right now in your life?

BOB: Well, I promised my grandmother I'd be responsible, hold a steady job. And now I hate my job and want to quit it and can't.

GAY: Like you're afraid you'll let her down?

BOB (*hangs head and cries*): Yes, like that.

Bob might not have revealed himself quite so rapidly if he had not learned to *be with and breathe with* his feelings in the session. As soon as he stopped fighting what he felt, his inner self was quick to step forward with a learning that changed everything. His conflict—to feel or not to feel—was obvious from the first moment in his breathing. The decision not to feel had won, for the time being. When he walked in the door, he was breathing enough to stay alive but not enough to feel good and prosper. With courage on his part he resurrected himself, by being willing to use his breath and consciousness to heal the split in himself. He left after three sessions, feeling well and with a new life-plan under development.

So the first fundamental way we have learned to employ the Breathing Principle in therapy is to notice when clients are using their breathing to restrict their ability to feel or be with themselves in some way. When we see this pattern, it leads us to one or both of two therapeutic moves. We can zero in on the feeling that they are denying, inquiring into the fear, anger, or sadness that is being held back. We can also intervene directly on the breathing, inviting them to break free of the restrictive pattern by deepening the breathing, using the Fundamental Breathing Techniques described in chapter 10. (You can put this skill to use every day in your own life. Notice when you are holding your breath or when your breath feels restricted. Notice what you may be feeling in your body at that moment. Open your awareness and your breath to it.)

USING THE BREATHING PRINCIPLE
TO ENHANCE UNITY

Another visit to the therapy office can give us a close look at the consequences of Fight-or-Flight Breathing. As we said, this type of breathing is intended to mobilize the organism. In evolution, it was based on two alternative concepts of crucial importance to the primitive human: "I'm here, and I want to be somewhere else" (flight), and "You're here, and I want you to be somewhere else" (fight). Each of these concepts expresses a fundamental division. When we are in the grip of them, we are not unified, and we are separated from others. The very nature of Fight-or-Flight Breathing is opposite to being, and when it is in charge, it overshadows being completely. Sometimes breathwork is the quickest way to promote unity in a person who has been living in a split for a long time. One of Gay's clients Gladys, a fifty-seven-year-old woman, called for an appointment because she had experienced a lingering depression for six months accompanied by a growing sense of anxiety and dread. When Gay greeted her in the waiting room, he met a stout, pleasant person of meticulous appearance. Gladys was a nurse-receptionist for a team of family-practice physicians. She described an all-too-familiar pattern of depression. Her husband of thirty years had divorced her, and a number of people, herself and others, had subsequently tried to talk her out of her feelings. Her minister told her divorce was a sin and implied that it was her fault, while her physician/boss urged antidepressants on her. She wished that one of them had simply listened to how she was feeling rather than trying to judge her or fix her. No one invited her to be present with what she was feeling, and as a result, she pulled back from church and work, feeling that no one really cared.

At a deeper psychological level she was experiencing a disturbing conflict that is quite prevalent in our society. She had fulfilled her roles in life—wife, mother, hard-working employee, churchgoer—but the plug had been pulled on two of them. Her children lived across the country from her, and her husband was living with a younger woman. Nearly everywhere she turned, she felt rejected or used up. She tended to portray herself as a victim, and although some people would agree with her assessment, the therapist must never make this foolhardy error. The therapist's job is to empower the client in any way he or she can, and the worse possible thing to do is to support a victim position. Every moment so spent is a lost moment that could have been spent taking action to change.

Gladys's problem was vividly reflected in her breathing. Gay could detect no movement of the breath in her abdomen: It looked frozen, as if she were encased in an iron girdle. The tension in her abdomen caused her breath to be forced up into her chest, in Fight-or-Flight Breathing. (Sometimes we call this upside-down breathing, because it is exactly opposite of what is healthy.) Gay acknowledged her problem, taking care not to place blame on her, her husband, or the world in general.

GAY: It seems like you haven't had anyone to just listen to your feelings. You're burdened with sadness and anger and maybe other feelings, too. And you haven't found a way to just be with those feelings yet. I also notice your breathing looks frozen.

GLADYS (nodding): I don't think I've been able to take a real breath in months. (Immediately after she said this, a slight movement took place in her abdomen.)

They spent most of the hour discussing her feelings. Gay did his best simply to listen with empathy to how she felt about what she had been through. In the last twenty minutes of the session, he undertook to retrain her breathing.

As you will see in chapter 10, the fundamental problem in retraining the breath is to get the diaphragm to move through its full excursion. Although breathing can usually be temporarily corrected in one session, it often takes many years of practice to have it stay that way permanently. One has to begin somewhere, though, and we feel strongly that even ten minutes of correct breathing, with its rapid improvement in mood, is enough to get a person moving in the right direction. So it was with Gladys.

Gay asked her to put her hands at the bottom of her ribcage, a few inches higher than her hips. This position enabled her to feel the rising and falling (or lack thereof) of her breathing. Indeed, she could not detect any movement of her belly. Gay did not ask her to relax her stomach muscles.

If she could have done that, she probably would have done it already. Instead, he asked her to tense the muscles of her abdomen. They were so tight, she could hardly feel any difference between tensing and letting go of the tension, but after several rounds of this, she was able to feel a shift. Now she had a map for relaxing and letting go. It was a small start, but it made the next step possible.

Now Gay asked Gladys to tighten as much as she could and to hold the tension as long as she could. When she could hold the tension no longer, he would say "Relax" or "Let it go," and she would let the muscles relax. A few minutes of this procedure brought some brightness to her face and an improvement in her mood. She was gaining mastery over something that had previously "had" her, and it felt good to be back in charge.

Next, Gay invited her to relax her belly muscles without tensing them first. In other words, she was to relax from a neutral starting position, allowing more relaxation than she had accomplished before. As she did this simple thing, she burst into tears and cried for a few minutes without stopping. She said that the tears had no reference but were simply tears of relief. He could well believe her. It must have been hellish to live in such a straitjacket of tension.

Now they could move further. When one inhales fully, the diaphragm flattens and moves downward. The contents of the abdominal cavity must get out of the way, which results in the swelling or rounding of the abdomen. Gay invited Gladys to let her abdomen round when she breathed in, and to feel it swelling with her hands. She did this once, then asked what we call the Woman's Question, since inevitably women ask: "Won't breathing this way make my belly stick out?" This culture has a particular taboo against rounded bellies on women, causing a good percentage of the population to go around holding their abdominal muscles tight. In addition to being a questionable idea culturally, it doesn't work. In fact, holding muscles in a state of unnecessary tension causes them eventually to let go and go slack. Then it is very difficult to retrain them to stay at the correct level of tension. Moreover, holding a set of muscles in one part of the body too tight will often cause a corresponding set to go slack. In the case of stomach muscles, the ones that go slack are in the small of the back, leading to many back problems as people age.

Gay explained all this to Gladys, making it clear that he wasn't asking her to protrude her belly—simply to relax it a little. Done properly, this subtle relaxation is not visible from the outside. It is very obvious from the inside, though. It feels wonderful.

As Gladys let go and began to fill her belly full with each in-breath, she let out a burst of giddy giggles. It had been so long since she had breathed properly that a little bit of it made her slightly intoxicated. The giggle of a person who was sunk in glum depression an hour before has to be one of the sweetest sounds in life. Gladys rested for a few minutes before continuing. Soon she was breathing full, steady breaths that moved her diaphragm as nature intended. The result was astonishing: Her skin color pinked up beautifully, replacing the sallow pallor with which she had walked in. When Gay asked her how she felt, she said, "Great."

He sent her out with instructions to practice her new-found breathing skill during one formal ten-minute session in the morning, and to take a few conscious breaths every now and then during the day. She also agreed to get ten minutes of extra exercise each day by taking a brisk walk during her lunch hour. She left in full sail, and her mood lasted all of two days.

Gay got a call from a very depressed Gladys later in the week. "It quit working," she said. She went on to explain that she had felt great for two days and then had started getting depressed again. Gay invited her to stop in for a minisession at the end of his work day so they could figure out what went wrong.

When she came in, Gay asked her to show him how she had been doing her breathing practice. What she demonstrated proved once again the power of our personas to sabotage us. She had completely forgotten how to breathe. In fact, she did a textbook demonstration of how *not* to breathe. Instead of relaxing and filling her belly with the in-breath, she tightened her belly muscles and forced the breath effortfully up into the chest. She sucked and pulled rapidly, inflating her chest like a bullfrog. No wonder she had stopped feeling good. Breathing that way would make anyone depressed and anxious.

Gay took her through the drill again, just as they had the first time. This time she got it much more quickly. Within minutes her depression lifted, and she felt fine again. Gay explained to her that it was absolutely normal to forget it all and relapse to her old breathing style. After all, she had spent a long time breathing incorrectly. It was unrealistic of her to expect a complete and permanent change after less than an hour of practice. They talked also of her "be perfect" programming, which had been part of her life for as long as she could remember. Gay asked her to give herself plenty of permission to learn how to breathe correctly, to forget it and relearn it. He told her that even after nearly twenty years of focusing on his own breathing, he still had lapses into his former unhealthy style.

Between this session and the next, Gladys became a breathing convert. One of the doctors she worked for called us up to ask "What did you do to her? She looks great!" Correct diaphragmatic breathing took hold, showing her that she was the mistress of her mood. As Gladys said, "The breathing does not take away all the problems in my life, but it gives me the energy to solve them one step at a time." Gay saw her one more time individually, then he invited her to join one of our breathing groups for a month or two. We lost contact with her for about a year, and then Gay received a card from her saying that she had moved to the East Coast to be closer to her children. She said she was still breathing (thank goodness!) and had taken a new job in an electronics firm.

Gladys's story illustrates how to approach emotional change through direct work on the breathing. It was very clear that at least part of her problem was due to Fight-or-Flight Breathing. As soon as the breathing was turned right-side-up, her mood changed dramatically. Of course, sensitive attention to feelings and psychological issues is always a factor. Combining breathwork with sensitivity simply speeds up the process of healing.

USING THE BREATHING PRINCIPLE
TO ENHANCE MASTERY

We use the Breathing Principle in therapy not only to enhance being and feeling, and not only to enhance unity, but to promote mastery of feelings and issues that seem bigger than the person. One of the remarkable properties of conscious breathing is that it often magnifies a feeling, then reduces or eliminates it. Early in his career, Gay was quite afraid of speaking in public to large groups. After his first book came out in the midseventies he had frequent opportunities to challenge this fear. One day he was speaking to a group of several hundred people in Kansas City, doing a morning workshop. After the workshop a man came up to him with a lopsided compliment. He could really relate to Gay, he said, because his voice shook like his own did when he spoke to groups. After this sobering feedback Gay vowed to get help quickly.

For some reason it had never occurred to Gay to use breathing for this problem, but before the afternoon workshop he put it to the test. As he stood before the group listening to the host give him a very long-winded introduction, he located the fear in his body. It was a butterflyish, slightly nauseous feeling in his belly and chest. Gay began breathing directly into the feeling. It got worse, more prominent. He continued, though, and in a few more breaths the feeling subsided. This moment was the beginning of one of our therapy mainstays, the Magnification Techniques (see chapter 8). From then on he would use his breath to magnify whatever feeling he was having. Inevitably by making it worse, it would go away.

There are two main reasons why this odd strategy is so effective. First, whatever we resist, persists. This is particularly true in the realm of feelings. Resisting feeling scared won't make the fear go away. In fact, fear stays in place until we embrace it. The energy that we use to keep the fear out of our awareness is wasted, and our effort to do so causes a split in us. Going toward the feeling with the breath is a key first step in healing the split. The second reason is that there is a subtle but enormous distinction between control and mastery. Control is the attempt to hold back, to restrain, to curb. Controlling feelings is a coping strategy from within a persona. Mastery of a feeling is the ability to produce it and make it disappear at will. By consciously breathing into a feeling, we get a happy surprise: If we can make it bigger, then we can make it smaller, even disappear.

When people learn to magnify their feelings consciously, it reminds them of who is in charge. Before they learn to make a feeling get bigger at will, they may think it runs them. Afterward, this illusion dissolves, replaced by their growing sense of mastery. (Chapter 10 shows how to apply this technique in detail.)

MAJOR BENEFITS OF BREATHWORK

Perhaps the most amazing effect of breathwork we have ever seen or heard of occurred a few years ago, when we were consulted on a case by a colleague, Dr. Loic Jassy. Dr. Jassy's patient was a woman who suffered from a lung disease so rare that only twelve cases of it had ever been seen in the western United States. The Stanford University School of Medicine had received a grant to study it and develop a treatment for it. The woman was part of the research project, but she had decided to take her treatment into her own hands. Rather than wait for a new drug to be tried on her (the focus of the Stanford approach), she reasoned that a lung problem might be well-treated by breathing. She found Dr. Jassy, who had conducted trainings for our institute on the West Coast. He told us that she had asked the research team at the medical school to teach her how to breathe correctly, but no one there could tell her or show her what healthy breathing was! As he described her breathing pattern to us, it became clear that she did not know how to breathe diaphragmatically, any more than Gladys had. Dr. Jassy took her through three sessions of breathwork, using the same processes you will find in chapter 10. Within a month her disease disappeared completely, and it has not returned. The woman is the only person in the research group who has to date been cured. In spite of this unusual finding, no one on the research team showed any interest in how she had healed herself. It appears in the records as a "spontaneous remission."

STRESS REDUCTION

For most of us, the greatest benefit of breathwork is probably its use as a technique of stress reduction. Under stress all animals tend to go into Fight-or-Flight Breathing—that is nature's way of ensuring their survival. It is unlikely that any of us could set up a stress-free environment for ourselves; nor can we expect to become relaxed enough to meet every situation with a relaxed body and a clear mind. What we need, then, are stress-reduction techniques that we can use to recenter ourselves after being knocked off center by some thought, feeling, or life-event. In our own experience, breathwork, particularly the first Fundamental Breathing Technique described in chapter 10, is the preeminent tool of stress reduction. It requires nothing (no mantras, no special shoes) and can be carried out anywhere. Once you learn how to breathe correctly, it is like riding a bike. No matter how long it's been since you have done it, you will always remember it in one breath.

TREATMENT OF ANXIETY AND DEPRESSION

From a therapist's point of view, the highest potential of breathwork is in clearing troublesome emotions from the bodymind. The two major problems that people bring to therapists are depression and anxiety. Breathwork can be powerfully effective in both these maladies. In fact, we predict that breathwork will come to be considered first-line treatment for both these problems within the next twenty years.

We have personally seen psychiatric medications work wonders with severe depression and anxiety, so we have great respect for this branch of science. There are definitely people who are not able to function without medicines. We send 10 to 15 percent of our clients to medical colleagues for prescriptions. But the majority of people who experience anxiety and depression do not need medication. Too many people today are put on medicines when they should be making adjustments in their lifestyle and in their way of handling tension. Growing numbers of people who have been prematurely put on medications are expressing disenchantment with them. Approximately a third of our clients are people who have been on antidepressant or anxiety medications and who are seeking natural healing alternatives with fewer side effects. We completely agree with them and advocate exercise, meditation, communication skills, and breathwork as healthful alternatives. We have personally worked with several hundred people who were able to get off psychiatric medications by learning breathwork and other natural methods.

Centered Breathing, exactly as you will learn it in chapter 10, is the technique that most people need, particularly those who experience anxiety and depression. The diaphragm is the fault line where the fundamental split shows up when we leave essence behind and lock into our personas. By tensing the abdominal muscles and freezing the movement of the diaphragm, we can cut off some of the unpleasant sensations of feelings that we do not want to feel. The benefit of this coping strategy is that we temporarily avoid the pain of emotions we judge as wrong. The cost, however, is profound in terms of aliveness. We may think we can make something go away by cutting off all feeling and sensation of it. But this strategy is about as effective as that of a four-year-old child who puts her hand up in front of her eyes and says, "You can't see me." In fact, the opposite is true. Splitting off from feeling guarantees that either it will come back stronger or it will fester just below the level of conscious awareness. By learning to breathe with proper use of the diaphragm, a great deal of anxiety and depression can be completely eliminated.

Most of us were born knowing Centered Breathing, but we seldom see a high school student who can still do it. By adulthood, most of us have been rattled so often by the vicissitudes of life that Fight-or-Flight Breathing comes more naturally to us than Centered Breathing. Using the Fundamental Breathing Techniques we will explore in chapter 10, we can usually get a person's breathing straightened out in less than an hour. To get it to stay that way, however, particularly under stress, is a far different matter. But if the person will practice the ten-minute daily program, correct breathing can usually be put into place within a matter of weeks.

CONTROL OF PHYSICAL PAIN

Physical pain can be reduced and sometimes eliminated through Centered Breathing. Nowhere is this process more observable than in birthing. Sometimes we are invited to coach women as they are giving birth. We often marvel at how fast the pain of contractions disappears the moment the woman begins to breathe with the pain rather than holding her breath against it. Once we arrived late to a birthing to find a friend of ours, an hour away from delivery, in a wide-eyed state of exaltation. We asked her what she was experiencing.

"It works!" she said, referring to breathwork. "I've been learning how to turn pain into ecstasy. When I match the pain with breath, it turns into pure sensation. Then if I remember to breathe into the sensation, it turns into ecstasy."

This testimony, offered during one of life's prime stressful moments, could serve as a motto for the potential of breathwork.

IMPROVEMENT OF PHYSICAL PROBLEMS

Many physical problems can be helped significantly through breathwork. When 153 heart-attack patients were examined in a Minneapolis hospital, the finding was startling: None of them were breathing diaphragmatically. All were using Fight-or-Flight Breathing, tensing their abdominal muscles and breathing shallow, rapid, choppy breaths in their chest. A related study conducted in Holland compared two groups of heart-attack patients. Each person had suffered one heart attack. One group of twelve people was taught how to breathe correctly, using techniques like the ones described in chapter 10. The other group was not taught the breathing techniques. Within a year, seven of the twelve in the nonbreath-trained group had suffered a second heart attack, while none of the breath-trained group had done so.

Asthma is another physical problem that often responds rapidly to breathwork. Working in conjunction with physicians, we have seen hundreds of cases of asthma, and Centered Breathing was remarkably successful with the majority of them. In the minority of cases in which breathwork did not help, the problem was usually that the patient had been on strong medicine (usually a steroid such as Prednisone) for so long that their body could not function without it.

Asthmatics are strikingly unable to breathe diaphragmatically, so directly retraining the breath is often immediately helpful to them. Quite frequently, breathwork helps them clear up psychological and emotional issues, such as a particular feeling that they are stifling. Asthmatic readers who practice the Breathing Techniques in chapter 10 will find that emotions frequently come to the surface. That is because the breathing pattern of asthma was often used to hide emotions that the asthmatic felt, often long ago in childhood. The professional who wants to work with asthmatics must be willing to handle the emotions that arise as their breathing improves. Frequently asthma patients must access and breathe through the feelings that were in their bodies when their asthma first began.

Treating long-standing cases of asthma with breathwork is a specialized activity beyond the scope of this book. The professional who wants to work with asthmatics through our body-centered methods is strongly urged to seek special training. Our institute conducts professional training for this purpose; a list of practitioners and seminars is available on request.

PERMISSION TO FEEL GOOD

Although we have great respect for the healing power of breathwork, we think the real potential of Breathing Techniques is to make already healthy people feel even better. You don't have to be sick to get better, and this truism applies particularly to breathwork. Highly functioning people have used the techniques to go even further in their chosen field. Not long ago, a forty-five-year-old marathon runner came in to us for some fine-tuning of his breathing pattern. We noticed that he was stopping short of full breath, not letting it go through the full excursion. It took about a half hour of breathwork to correct the problem. Shortly thereafter, he went east for the New York Marathon and shaved just over ten minutes off his personal best. Not only that, he went through the race without feeling any pain in his body. No one knows if the breathwork was what did it, but as he put it, "It sure didn't hurt."

This era is one in which people are finally giving themselves permission to feel good in natural ways. By the million they are catching on to the lifestyle changes necessary to promote organic good feeling. Early in this century Teddy Roosevelt said, "Three quarters of the work in this country is done by people who don't feel good." As one of our clients put it, "You have to breathe good to feel good." We could quibble over his grammar, but his sentiment could not be more accurate. When people breathe effectively, many systems in their body function better immediately. The skin, for example, is a direct beneficiary of Centered Breathing. In our breath-work seminars people frequently comment on how healthy their skin looks after even a few minutes of correct breathing. The fact is that approximately 70 percent of the toxins in the body are discharged through the breath. If breathing is effective, the other systems of detoxification (such as the skin, urinary tract, and colon) do not have to work overtime.

Centered Breathing directly enhances our ability to handle positive feelings. The body has approximately sixty thousand miles of capillaries. Regular exercise is known to actually add miles to the capillary system. So exercise not only promotes a feeling of well-being, it gives people more actual room to feel well-being. It is quite likely that the deep breathing afforded by exercise is what expands the "capillary mileage." Deep, relaxed breathing as demonstrated in chapter 10 appears directly to affect the body's ability to experience more feeling.

In our book *Conscious Loving*, we described the Upper Limits Problem, the tendency of human beings to set their positive feeling thermostats at a certain level and to bring themselves down in some way when this level is exceeded. They may start an argument to bring themselves down, or overeat to keep themselves from feeling good. Once we caught on to this problem in our own relationship, we saw that we tended to invoke the Upper Limits Problem after prolonged stints of feeling good. The obvious solution to this problem was to increase our ability to handle positive feeling. Over about a year, as we spotted more and more Upper Limits actions (criticizing, being sleepy, not listening, physically hurting ourselves), we gradually learned to avoid doing them. Soon we found ourselves living in a previously undreamed-of state: no conflict.

Now that we have become skilled at noticing the ways we bring ourselves down, we can catch them at the very beginning rather than after they have become full-blown. This skill has allowed us to go, for the better part of a decade now, with no conflict in our relationship. The energy that we had previously wasted through conflict we used to write books together, give several hundred lectures and workshops a year, and spend quality time with our family.

Breathwork has played a major role in our own ability, as well as that of many of our clients, to raise our positive feeling thermostats. If you catch an Upper Limits Problem soon enough, you can breathe right through it.

Gay once had such an eating problem that he weighed over three hundred pounds. Though he is still not sylphlike, he has kept his weight in the region of 195 for the past twenty years. On a six-foot-one frame, this amount of poundage makes him look more like an athlete than a pear. Even though most of the fat has been gone for a long time, the tendency to overeat as an Upper Limits Problem still remains. But now, more often than not, he can catch himself before he does it and breathes through it.

On one recent occasion Gay woke up feeling great. Following his usual schedule, he meditated for half an hour, showered, then wrote for two hours. The writing went well, and he felt even better afterward than he had when he awoke. Taking a break, he found himself in the kitchen, laying out a huge assortment of foods for breakfast. He unconsciously munched on a banana as he filled a cereal bowl and put two substantial pieces of whole-wheat bread in the toaster. Suddenly he "woke up." He realized that he was not really hungry. The banana alone took care of the actual stomach hunger he was feeling. He knew that he would feel bloated and stuffed if he loaded up with a bellyful of grains, and he suddenly saw that he was running an Upper Limits Problem. Instead of indulging it, Gay simply did about two minutes of full, relaxed belly breathing. The urge to eat passed, and he felt better than ever.

The potential for breathwork to reset the positive feeling thermostat cannot be overemphasized. Breathing is one of the few mechanisms in the human body that is sensitive both to the conscious and the unconscious mind. No matter what the unconscious has programmed a person for, a little bit of consciousness can change it. We have seen hundreds of people use Centered Breathing—sometimes even just a few seconds of it—to move through an Upper Limit and let themselves feel good longer and stronger.

MEETING THE TRANSCENDENTAL

In our own practice, about one out of every ten sessions of breathwork leads the client (and sometimes us) to a transcendental experience. Bliss, unity, and ecstasy are contagious, and when a client breaks into these realms, we often feel a resonance with them in our own beings. The client will be breathing along—perhaps wrestling with some troublesome feeling— when suddenly the tension will melt and the face will burst into a deeply rapturous smile. Frequently these moments are accompanied by realizations of a cosmic as well as personal nature.

The divine element of life is better experienced than talked about. In fact, we could all benefit from abstinence from talking about it for a few thousand years. Or at the very least, we should require people who talk about divinity to be actively in the grip of unity and ecstasy at the moment. One of my clients said he gave up on God at an early age because the concept never seemed to bring a smile to anyone's face. We have noticed in breathwork sessions that when someone experiences the divine, it always brings a certain look to the face: a combination of rapture, completion, and bliss.

The other remarkable thing we have noticed about transcendental experiences in breathwork is that they are always a byproduct: the people were not seeking it. Transcendental experiences always come out of an inquiry into something earthly, such as breathing into anger or fear. This point is extremely important, for it shows how body-centered psychotherapy can be a valid spiritual path.

One minister is a living example of this issue. When we first saw him as a client, he looked wracked with long-contained anger. His body was loaded with pain of various kinds: head, back, and joints. When we asked him about his anger, he got predictably defensive. He mounted a long critique of anger and how it had no place in his spiritual world. He said that he prayed daily to forgive those who had wronged him. After a great deal of careful work over half a dozen sessions, he finally allowed himself just to feel his anger. He was able to sit with it and pay attention to his anger sensations without judging them. In this final session, two bits of magic occurred. First, his pain went away: no more headaches or backaches. Second, he had an authentic experience of forgiveness. This forgiveness was not a concept, nothing he had prayed for. It was something he actually felt in his body. This was a turning point for him, because he learned that the path to the transcendental is found by a willingness to accept and go deeply into the earthly.

And the place to start is the absolutely obvious. The minister's anger was obvious to us, and we told him so. It was also obvious to him, judging from the way he defended against it, but all his energy was going into resisting it. We had a major factor on our side, though: He hurt, and the more he resisted his anger, the more he hurt. Some part of him had been wise enough to seek help, although he did not easily give in to it. The part of people that hurts is the part of them that most needs love. And this is the ultimate benefit of breathwork.

A WAY TO LOVE

Centered Breathing can enhance our ability to love ourselves and others, albeit not by focusing on love directly. Breathwork can clear a space in which a person can have the freedom to love himself or herself, often for the first time. And sometimes love spontaneously appears, much as forgiveness came spontaneously out of the anger in our friend the minister. Countless times in therapy we have watched in awe as people let themselves open up to and breathe with feelings like fear, grief, and anger, only to have those feelings effortlessly dissolve into love. It has made believers of a certain kind out of us. We now believe that everyone has freedom and universal love at their core. Although these organic absolutes are usually obscured by the difficulties of life, they are never, ever lost. When people are willing to be with themselves deeply enough, there is always a divine surprise at the end of their inquiry.

THE THREE FUNDAMENTAL BREATHING TECHNIQUES

Three Breathing Techniques that we have developed embrace most of the psychological or emotional issues that occur for most people in the course of daily living. We use these tools in our personal lives, and we have recommended them to thousands of people in our professional work. Their great benefit is that they are as useful at home as they are in the therapy office. For therapists, their applicability is broad. People from nearly every major school of therapy have gone through our trainings and found that they could adapt the three Fundamental Breathing Techniques to their work. Chapter 9 has given you a feel for how the techniques are used. In this chapter we will go through the specific instructions and give further examples of how they are applied. In addition, we present a Daily Breathing Program that we recommend you practice at home every day. It takes less than ten minutes to carry out, and it is designed to produce a relaxed, centered feeling while improving the breathing a little bit each day.

The first Breathing Technique is the procedure for Centered Breathing. It leaves the person feeling that combination of balance and relaxation best described by the word *centered*. We wholeheartedly recommend this technique to anyone who wants to feel good.

Before you begin any new program of psychophysiological activity, be sure to check with your medical practitioner if you have any health problems. All the activities in this chapter are designed to be done gently. But they do involve some physical movements and changes in breathing habits. If you are in treatment for heart or lung disease, glaucoma, arthritis, epilepsy, or any other disease, get your physician's permission before you do this or another new program. Chances are your health professional will be glad you are doing these kinds of activities, but it is always wise to be absolutely sure.

CENTERED BREATHING

It is easy to tell whether you need to learn Centered Breathing. If your breathing is up in your chest, and if it is shallow or rapid, you would certainly benefit from Centered Breathing. Another way to tell if this Breathing Technique would help you is to count your breathing rate sometime while you are sitting quietly. If you are breathing faster than fourteen times a minute, you would likely find Centered Breathing very helpful. Therapists will find that clients with the two major clinical problems—depression and anxiety—will always benefit from Centered Breathing unless the underlying problem is organic. If we think clients could benefit from it, we bring it up in the session in a straightforward way. The conversation, from our end, goes something like this:

> I notice several things about your breathing that are
> producing a lot of stress in your body. First, your breathing is
> largely up in your chest, rather than down in the center of
> your body where it belongs. When you're breathing up in your
> chest, it indicates that your fight-or-flight mechanism is
> activated. That alone will keep you not feeling as good as you
> could. The reason is that two-thirds of the blood circulation
> in your lungs is in the lower third of them. It's important to
> breathe down where the biggest share of the circulation is.
> Only half a teacup of blood circulates in your high chest every

minute, compared with over a quart down toward the center of your body. Second, your breathing is faster and shallower than is optimal. Breathing too fast keeps your body in a state of agitation. This problem is one that a lot of people have, and we have an effective way to remedy it. It's called Centered Breathing, and it takes about twenty minutes or so to learn. But you will need to practice it, preferably every day for a while, to master it. If we take the time here to teach it, will you agree to practice it every day on your own for five to ten minutes until you master it?

We also teach the Fundamental Breathing Techniques to groups, from as small as six people to as large as several hundred. Often we conduct breathwork groups into which we can put clients who want to learn the techniques. Teaching breathwork in groups has several advantages. It is clearly time-efficient from the therapist's point of view, and from the client's side, it is less expensive, since it does not tie up a lot of time in the individual therapy hour.

PART ONE: LYING DOWN

Centered Breathing is a direct approach; that is, it is a straightforward procedure designed to affect the breathing pattern. It certainly affects the emotions, but the object of the approach is the breathing mechanism itself. Here are the instructions, step by step.

BASIC INSTRUCTIONS

---

1. Lie down on your back. Bring your knees up so that your feet are flat on the floor. Set your feet a comfortable distance apart, about 12 to 18 inches, and a comfortable distance from your buttocks. Rest your arms on the floor, not on your chest or belly. Take half a minute or so to get

comfortable and let your body settle down. During all this breathe slowly and gently. Let all your movements be easy and gentle. This practice is designed to stay always in the comfort zone. If you start to feel any tension, pain, or dizziness, pause until it passes before you continue. Unless your nose is stuffy, always breathe through your nose. If your nose is obstructed, it is all right to breathe through your mouth temporarily.

2. Explore how the spine moves when you rock your pelvis slowly. This is important because ideally your spine and your pelvis move slightly with each breath. Coordinating your breathing with correct spinal movement is a secret ingredient to staying flexible as you get older. Here's how to do it. Gently press the lower part of your pelvis into the floor. Notice that doing this arches the small of your back slightly. Do it gently. Continue to press the pelvis into the floor, arching the back a little each time. Now begin to press the tailbone more into the floor. Notice that favoring the tailbone makes the back arch a little more. Do it very gently and slowly. Now slowly and gently flatten the small of your back into the floor. Notice that this tilts the bottom of your pelvis up. Slowly repeat this arching and flattening of the small of your back. Notice that doing so rocks your pelvis. Keep rocking your pelvis very slowly. Make it

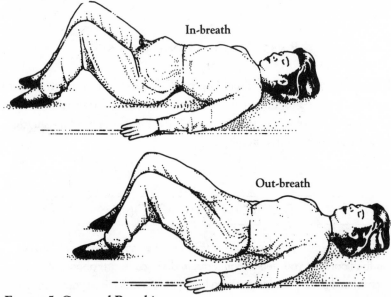

In-breath

Out-breath

FIGURE 5. Centered Breathing

a smooth motion. Arch the small of your back slightly, rocking the pelvis down toward the tailbone, then flatten the small of your back. Let it be a rolling motion, slow and easy. The movements can be very subtle. No one even needs to know you're doing them. Do this slowly for half a minute. (See figure 5.)

3. Now add your breathing to the movement this way. As you arch the small of your back, breathe in, filling your belly with breath. As you flatten the small of your back, breathe out. Don't strain. Just breathe fully in and fully out, deeply and easily. Breathe in as you arch the small of your back, filling your belly completely. Then breathe out as you flatten the small of your back, letting all the breath go. Roll the pelvis gently with each breath. The movement only needs to be slight, just an inch or two. Practice this now for a minute or so.

4. This combination of breath and movement is the fundamental thing you need to remember about Centered Breathing. Whenever you feel stressed or uncomfortable in any way, check your breathing. If you find it is not deep and full in your lower abdomen, and if you find that your spine is not moving slightly with the breath, shift immediately to Centered Breathing.

Continue practicing for as long as you like, then resume your normal activity.

PART TWO: SITTING AND STANDING

You will find it helpful to practice the technique sitting up and standing up as well. The same principles apply, but activating the muscles involved in being upright in gravity adds a different dimension to the technique.

SITTING INSTRUCTIONS

1. Sit comfortably upright in a straight-back chair. Begin slowly to arch and then flatten the small of your back against the back of the chair. Notice how doing this rocks your pelvis forward and back. Let it be a slow, smooth motion. Let it be easy and gentle. Practice for half a minute.

2. Add your breathing to the rocking of your pelvis. Breathe in as you

arch the small of your back. Breathe out as you flatten it against the back of the chair. Breathe your belly completely full in a relaxed way. Let the breath go down and in, filling your belly completely. Then as you breathe out, empty your belly completely and flatten your back against the chair.

STANDING INSTRUCTIONS

---

1. Stand with your back against a wall. Feel your back contacting the surface of the wall. Arch and flatten the small of your back against the wall. Do it very slowly and gently.

2. As you arch the small of your back, breathe down and in, filling your belly. See how full you can get your belly without straining. Then breathe out, flattening the small of the back against the wall. Practice for a minute or two, doing it very slowly and gently.

TWO SPECIALIZED INSTRUCTIONS

Sometimes people are not able to relax their abdominal muscles enough to get a significant amount of breath down into their centers. If you had trouble relaxing your belly muscles, or if you could not locate where to breathe down in the center of your body, the following instructions will be helpful. They are designed to help you relax the abdominal muscles. Oddly enough, we have found that it is easiest to learn to relax the belly muscles by tightening them first. These instructions are simply added to Step 3 of the basic instructions.

As you breathe out, tighten the muscles of your abdomen. These are the muscles you would use if you were blowing out the candles on a birthday cake. Then when you breathe in, relax these same muscles and fill the area with breath. On the out-breath, tighten the belly muscles again, expelling all the breath as if you were blowing out candles. Get all the breath squeezed out, then relax the belly muscles and fill the area with a big in-breath. Keep repeating this sequence, slowly and gently, for the next minute or so. Then go back to breathing normally.

This will give you increased discrimination over the muscles that need to stay relaxed in order for you to breathe correctly. Eventually the belly muscles should stay relaxed on the in- and the out-breath, but many clients have held their bellies tightly for so long that they have no idea how to relax them when they first begin.

The second additional instruction is designed to help people who have lost the ability to sense the difference between belly and chest. Some people have lost sensory contact with the front of their bodies—Moshe Feldenkrais called this problem Sensory-Motor Amnesia. These instructions may be added to Step 3 of the basic instructions if you need them.

Lying down on your back, place a book on your belly over the naval area. The book should have enough weight that you can clearly feel it. A hardcover book without the dust jacket is ideal; the rough binding helps keep the book from slipping off your stomach. Breathe slowly and deeply, making the book rise and fall with each breath. If you cannot make the book move, add more weight until you can clearly feel the area. Sometimes it takes people a few minutes to figure out where their belly is. Be patient. When you begin to get breath into your abdomen, take away the book. If you lose it, put the book back. Most people will get it within a few minutes of practice.

Very few people we work with can do these seemingly simple practices at first. Unhealthy breathing patterns are often strong, and they have usually been in place a long time. It is unrealistic to expect that only a few minutes of healthy breathing will correct the pattern permanently. Usually when people practice for a few weeks on a daily basis, they see enormous change. The practice does not take much discipline because it feels intrinsically good. Once people learn that they can shift their whole mood in only a few minutes of breathing, they are converted for life.

Once we learned what healthy breathing looks like, we were frankly dismayed at how seldom we saw it as we moved through the world. One colleague of ours mentioned that he spent a day demonstrating therapy techniques in the most regressed ward of a mental hospital. He saw right away that, in addition to their other problems, none of the fifteen patients were breathing correctly. Choosing one man to work with, our friend pointed out to the assembled staff that the man was moving his body exactly opposite to the correct pattern. In other words, the man tightened his belly as he breathed in, always holding his stomach muscles rigidly and forcing the breath up into the chest. The therapist had the staff try on the man's breathing pattern, and everyone got predictably agitated and disturbed within a couple of minutes. Then they adopted the ideal breathing pattern and were thoroughly amazed to feel how quickly a sense of well-being came over them. The man learned to breathe correctly over the next hour, and to make a long story short, within the month he was able to be discharged from the hospital for the first time in several years.

PRESENCING THROUGH BREATHING

Breathing is one place in the bodymind where conscious and unconscious meet. You can consciously take a breath and hold it at will. Or you can forget all about it for eight hours in a row, but you will still wake up in the morning, several thousand unconscious breaths later. Breathing therefore is an ideal place to notice any struggle going on between the conscious and the unconscious. Most people use their breathing to control or subdue their feelings. Children often hold their breath to keep themselves from crying. The adult equivalent of this pattern is subtler but is basically the same thing: By making adjustments in their breathing, humans learn to control the amount of sensation that gets to their awareness. The trouble is that it decreases aliveness and is followed by a predictable loss of well-being. As we worked with people, we found that if we asked them to make a subtle adjustment in the healthy direction—*breathing with their feelings rather than against them*—they would often feel better and have breakthrough realizations. Thus the second Fundamental Breathing Technique, Presencing Through Breathing, was developed.

The only way to learn this technique, since it is a "move" rather than a direct piece of instruction, is to see it in action several times. Here are excerpts from two therapy sessions in which the "move" was applied.

ALICE: I guess—I guess I feel like I've given up somehow.

US: It sounds like you're feeling discouraged and sad.

ALICE (*nods, jaw clenching, making small sniffing sounds through nose*): Yeah.

US: Notice that you aren't breathing deeply. Just little sniffs. Are you holding your breath to keep yourself together? Or from feeling sad?

ALICE: I guess. (*tries to take a deep breath, but it's labored and high up in the chest*)

US: Relax your belly, and breathe down into the sadness. Don't hold your breath against it.

(*Alice takes one deep breath, begins to cry, then holds breath again.*)

US: It's all right to feel that sadness. Breathe right with it. Breathe into where you feel it.

(*Alice takes two or three deep breaths and lets go. Her sobbing continues for a minute or two.*)

US: That's it. Breathe right through the middle of all those feelings.

(*Alice's breath is now coming full and deep. Her sobbing abates.*)

ALICE: Whew! I didn't realize there was all that in there.

US: Um-hm. How do you feel right now?

ALICE: Kind of cleaned out.

US: Great. Take some deep breaths into that cleaned-out feeling.

ALICE (*takes a few more deep breaths*): It's spreading out into my arms. (*stretches arms out*)

The following case is somewhat more complex.

HOWIE: Sometimes I wonder if my son really gives a damn about me as a person.

US: You're wondering if you are just a role to him? Someone who gives him money?

HOWIE: Yeah. I mean, he didn't even say thank you when I paid that bill he was about to get sued for.

US: It looks like you feel angry about that.

HOWIE: No, I'm not angry. I might be angry if I cared enough, but I've just about quit caring.

US: As you say that, your breathing is going fast and shallow up in your chest. Do that some more, and find out what that's saying about your feelings.

HOWIE: Sorry, I didn't realize that. (*makes a dramatic effort to breathe deeper*)

US: Notice how you apologized right after we called attention to your breath. What does that remind you of?

HOWIE: I don't know. (*his brow furrows, jaw clenches*)

US: Be with it for a moment. Think about it. Feel what you're feeling.

HOWIE (*pauses for about five seconds*): I guess I am angry, aren't I?

US: Looks like it. Take a few nice, deep breaths into where you feel you're angry.

HOWIE: It's out in my forearms. All over my back.

US: Yes. Breathe with it—be right with it.

HOWIE: I'm angry about being unappreciated.

US: Yes. Does that remind you of anything way back?

HOWIE: Boy, it sure does. My mom was sick all the time when I was a kid. And she was also real nasty to my dad. He could never do enough. Nobody could. She would just get this weary look on her face and say "Thanks, dear" whenever you brought her something. I hated to go into her room, and I felt guilty as hell about hating it.

US: So you have a strong background in how to be a martyr.

HOWIE (*flash of irritation passes over his face*): I hate martyrs! My mother was the ultimate martyr.

US: That's the sort of relationship you have with your son. You seem to do a lot for him, and then you feel unappreciated.

HOWIE: I never thought of it like that. Jesus, you mean I'm doing the same thing with my son that my mother did with me?

US: Think about it.

HOWIE: That's hard to swallow.

US: Notice that you're holding your breath.

HOWIE *(takes some deep breaths)*: I'm angry about that. I don't like the idea that I'm doing something myself that I hated when I was a kid!

US: Feel what's under that anger. It looks like you're also sad.

HOWIE *(takes several more deep breaths)*: Yeah, I am. I don't want it to be that way.

US: How do you want it?

HOWIE: I want to be appreciated.

US: Feel how much you wanted contact with your mother back then. She's been dead for a long time, but maybe you still want that deep down inside.

HOWIE *(beginning to cry)*: I guess I do.

US: And does that play a role in your relationship with your son?

HOWIE *(nodding)*: It's the same, really. He and I never really connect.

Under his Martyr persona, Howie had anger and sadness about a long-ago relationship. These feelings still lived in his body and in fact were programming his present-day relationships. The breathing flags reliably signaled to us when he was living in his persona. Noticing these flags enabled us to help him navigate fairly quickly down through his depths to the authentic self at the core.

Presencing Through Breathing is a way of going out to meet feelings with the breath. The traumas of life have often programmed us to use our breathing as a way of shrinking from our feelings. We hold them at bay through restricting the breathing. Presencing Through Breathing reverses this tendency. It shows us that we can use each breath as a celebration of expansion.

Although therapists are often first concerned with relieving a client's unpleasant feelings, it is also important to remember that breathwork can play a role in enhancing pleasant feelings as well. We were helping one client to work out a sexual problem: She had been nonorgasmic for a long time. We taught her how to breathe into the pleasurable feelings that emerged as she made love, and she was now beginning to experience more pleasure in lovemaking. One night she had a breakthrough into a new dimension of sexual pleasure, and she gave us this report when she came in: "When we first began to make love, I was not feeling much sensation. In fact, I was feeling sort of numb in my genitals. So I decided to breathe into the numbness. Within a few breaths the area began to wake up, and pretty soon the numbness was gone. I could feel some pleasure beginning. So I kept breathing into the good feelings. This made them spread down my inner thighs and up toward my stomach. It would come and go. Sometimes I would lose the sensation, then I would come back to the breathing and it would spread more. I found that I could control how much good feeling I felt with my breathing. When I wanted more, I just breathed deeper."

We felt like cheering when we heard her report. She had used her breathing to disperse numbness, an unpleasant sensation. But she hadn't stopped there. By breathing into her awakening sexual sensations, she was able to steer her way into deeper pleasure than she had felt in the past. Using breathwork to enhance pleasurable feelings is one of the best applications we can imagine.

MAGNIFICATION THROUGH BREATHING

If the second Fundamental Breathing Technique releases the parking brake from the breath, the third one presses on the accelerator. Magnification Through Breathing uses breathing to make feelings bigger. The principle can be stated simply: When you make an unpleasant feeling bigger, it has a tendency to disappear or reveal a more basic feeling underneath it. Breathing is the most direct method of magnifying any feeling. In later chapters we will explore the value of magnifying feelings, since the ability to make feelings and issues larger is a powerful healing skill.

Watch now as Magnification Through Breathing is applied. We will join a session in which a thirty-seven-year-old man, Chuck, is talking about tension in his chest.

US: So what are the exact sensations you are feeling in your chest right now?
CHUCK: There's kind of a band across my chest, like a belt.
US: From side to side?
CHUCK: Yes.

US: What else?

CHUCK: Pressure. Like a weight on my chest.

US: Okay, here's something a little bit strange we'd like you to do. Breathe into the pressure and the band. See if you can make them worse, make them bigger.

CHUCK: Uh, okay. I'm not sure quite how to do that.

US: Have the intention of making your feelings bigger. As if you could inflate them with your breath.

CHUCK (*takes several slow, deep breaths*): Okay, it's getting bigger.

US: That's it. Breathe some more, just like that. Make it even bigger.

CHUCK: Now it's turning into a burning more than a pressure or a band.

US: A burning. Okay, breathe to make the burning bigger.

CHUCK (*taking full, deep breaths*): Now it's kind of turning into more like a buzzing. It's weird. I haven't felt anything like that before. Like an electric current.

US: That's fine. It's perfectly normal. It's a sign that a lot of tension is letting go.

CHUCK: Okay. It doesn't feel bad or anything. In fact, it feels kind of good.

US: Go right into whatever you're feeling. Breathe into it, and make it bigger. See if you can magnify the good feeling, too.

When we use breathing to magnify a feeling, we are adding consciousness to an unconscious pattern. The unconscious has determined how much fear and anger you have. You didn't ask for it consciously. Once you know it, though, you can consciously magnify it. Paradoxically, magnifying it will either make it disappear, or reveal what else is underneath the surface feeling. It does not seem to work the other way around: Breathing to make something smaller does not seem to do the trick. If you knew how to make the feeling smaller, you probably would have already done so.

As therapists, we were extraordinarily grateful when we caught on to this technique. Most of our clients were people who wanted to be rid of various feelings. Our first hint of this technique was seeing Fritz Perls work with a young woman who expressed herself with very big, dramatic gestures. Perls did not zero in on the content of what she was saying but asked her to make her gestures even bigger. Shortly after, she had a breakthrough to feelings that had been concealed beneath her dramatic persona. It didn't take us long to apply the same idea to breathing. In fact, the next day we practically lassoed the first client who came in the door and had the person breathe to magnify his feelings. It worked, much to his astonishment and ours. (A more thorough explanation of why magnification works will be found in chapter 7.)

THE DAILY BREATHING PROGRAM

We recommend that you make this breathing program an ongoing part of your life. We do it ourselves every day, first thing in the morning, whether we are in Chicago or Calcutta. We do it as soon as we get out of bed in the morning, because it helps us begin the day in a state of clear energy that sets the standard for the rest of the day. We have come to love the centered, light feeling it gives us. We have shared the program with thousands of people, and we find that those who practice it daily make very rapid progress in reducing stress and feeling good. They report gains in several areas of their lives. First, they experience greater physical energy during the rest of the day when they do the program in the morning. Second, their moods become steadier, with fewer ups and downs. Third, their feelings of anxiety almost always decrease. Fourth, their mental clarity and feelings of transcendence increase.

The Daily Breathing Program, which takes only a few minutes, can be thought of as a reminder. Practicing it in the morning will remind your body and mind what correct diaphragmatic breathing feels like. Then you have a place for your breathing to come home to throughout the day.

The Daily Breathing Program consists of three elements. First is about two minutes of Centered Breathing. Second, the diaphragm is relaxed and toned through a unique activity that allows this crucial part of the anatomy to regain its full potential. Third is an easy stretch that promotes flexibility of all major joints. All three of these elements are best done lying on the back, although they can be done sitting up if that is necessary.

DAILY BREATHING PROGRAM

Step One • The purpose of this step is to establish correct diaphragmatic breathing, and to coordinate the movement of the breath with the movement of the spine.

Lie on your back. Bend your knees, placing your feet flat on the floor a comfortable width apart. As you breathe in, arch the small of your back gently and slightly. As you breathe out, flatten the small of your back against the floor. Breathe slowly and deeply, filling your belly full and gently arching the small of your back. Breathe out slowly, flattening the small of your back into the floor. Do this gently and slowly for about two minutes.

Step Two • The purpose of this step is to relax and tone your diaphragm, the large muscle in the center of your body that controls breathing.

Lie on your back. Bend your knees, with your feet flat on the floor a comfortable width apart. Relaxing your abdominal muscles, breathe fully in, expanding your belly as fully as you comfortably can. When it's full and expanded, hold your breath. Without letting any air out, contract your belly muscles, as if you were shooting the ball of air up into your chest. Then shoot it back into your belly. Do this rapidly, about once per second. Keep rocking it back and forth between belly and chest until you need to take another breath. Breathe normally for 15 to 20 seconds, then repeat the above process. Do the activity for about two minutes.

Step Three • The purpose of this step is to relax and enhance motion in the major joints of the body. Breathing is much freer and more effective when the joints are able to move easily in conjunction with the breath. This particular stretching activity is the most efficient way we have discovered to promote joint flexibility.

Lie on your back, knees up, feet flat on the floor. Stretch your arms straight out to your sides in a T position. Your arms should be straight out, not pointed up in a Y position. Begin by rolling one arm down the floor as the other one rolls up. Let the arms stay on the floor while you roll them up and down the floor. Do this a few times until you get a fluid motion. Now,

FIGURE 6. Step Three of the Daily Breathing Program

keeping the arms rolling, let your knees drop toward the side on which the arm is rolling down. Do this a few times until it becomes fluid and easy. Now, keeping the arms and legs going, begin turning your head in the direction opposite to the knees. Do this slowly and easily and gently for about two minutes. (See figure 6.)

With practice, the program becomes easy, producing reliable good feelings each time it's done. Even though we have done it thousands of times over the years, we never get tired of it.

A Simple Test of the Daily Breathing Program

We put the Daily Breathing Program to a test to find out if it worked as well as we thought it did. We recruited twenty-five people who reported that they felt tense and tired (they had put in a long day's work on an exacting project), and we taught half of them the Daily Breathing Program. We supervised them while they practiced it for ten minutes. The control group simply sat quietly and read about the program for the same length of time. The results, depicted on the charts in figures 7 and 8, are striking.

Although we use tension and tiredness as our target symptoms, the Daily Breathing Program doubtlessly works with numerous other symptoms. We look forward to more elaborate experiments by clinical researchers who can assess the effectiveness of the program in reducing other symptoms.

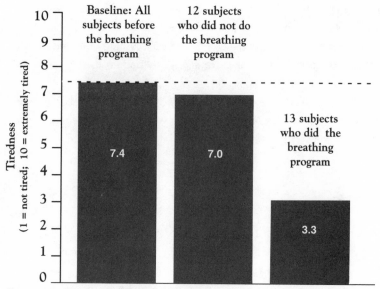

FIGURE 7. Effect of the Daily Breathing Program on Tiredness

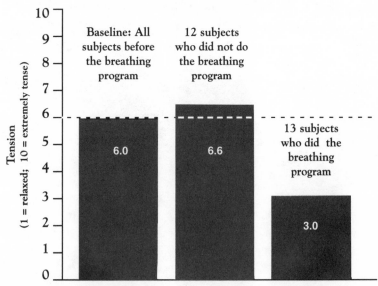

FIGURE 8. Effect of the Daily Breathing Program on Tension

THE MOVING PRINCIPLE: USING MOVEMENT IN THE HEALING PROCESS

All know that the drop merges into the ocean;
few know that the ocean merges into the drop.
—Kabir

Movement patterns precisely reflect emotions that need to be addressed. Movement indicates a client's degree of aliveness, and it is a bridge to the inner self. Attention to movement is a powerful door to discovery and transformation.

Movement is aliveness. If something is alive, it is in motion. In human beings the diaphragm expands and contracts, drawing air into the lungs. Blood flows, carrying nutrients even to the outposts of the toes. Digestion rides waves of motion through the intestines. Speech occurs through the vibrating dance of larynx, jaw, and mouth. We see because our eyes move. Our ears translate the motion of air into sound. Death occurs when brain waves stop.

Our personalities are made public through our movements. Our characters reveal themselves in the way we stand, walk, or start a conversation at a party. Each of us has our own life-dance, our way of moving through the world. More than we know another person's name, we know their movement signature. We recognize a friend down the street because of that particular walk or way of brushing hair off the forehead. We know before they speak if a close friend is unhappy or elated.

As children, we know the language of the body intimately and fluently. Recent research shows that fetuses have regular exercise periods, exploring the potentials of movement within the learning environment of the womb. The motions of the mother's breathing, digestive flow, and preferred walking rhythms surround the developing child for nine months, laying down the potential tracks for later movement styles. When a three-year-old discovers a bug, essence and body are one as she crouches and focuses every cell on that wonder. Expression is total, complete, and fluid. Emotions cross the face like clouds over the landscape, always changing, always shifting. The child moves forward into life wholeheartedly and whole-bodied—at least for a while.

Breaks and gaps in our initial embrace of life are always accompanied by contractions in movement. Kathlyn recalls the day our infant son Chris discovered the meaning of *hot* by crawling on an unprotected floor heater. He jerked his hand off the register as he yelled, momentarily freezing in pain. Emotional wounds freeze motion as effectively as physical ones do. We instinctively shrink from the sound of fighting, from the hand raised in threat, from the disapproving glance. In time we form our particular structure, pace, and style in response to where we flow and where we freeze.

Communication is also a function of movement. Upwards of 80 percent of our interactions with one another are nonverbal. We mean what we *do*, not what we *say*. As children, most of us soon noticed the difference between what people say and how they act. We learned to predict the future based on what occurred on a regular basis. The sound of pots and pans banging in the kitchen, for example, was followed by audible sighs and the shouted request for "someone" to come and help. The father's newspaper rattling meant "be quiet and stay out of the way"; a brother's particular smile preceded a teasing remark. We gradually learned to trust the body's voice and to note body expression before we talked. Moving also meant joy for many of us. Kathlyn's mother noted in her baby book, "She stands up in her crib and dances!" Kathlyn remembers that when dancing she felt whole and free, in touch with the essential rhythms of life. For her, it was her first connection with divinity.

Movement is the way we first experience ourselves. We play with our toes. We move forward into the unknown. We move backward into the past, the familiar. We expand with pleasure and excitement, and we contract to renew or protect ourselves. We lengthen with power, walking tall, and we shrink to disappear when we are in pain or fear. These life-rhythms are both universal and unique. We all share the same organic processes of locomotion and motion. In our response to each experience, we shape these potentials into the moving expression of who we are.

The Moving Principle can reveal a great deal in therapy. Donna, the busy director of a local mental health agency, noticed that she felt very uncomfortable when she leaned forward over the table in board meetings. In a therapy session, we used her simple awareness of discomfort to explore her relationship to advancing and retreating, the acts of moving forward and backing up. She stood and let herself take several steps forward while noticing her reaction. Then she moved backward a few steps and stopped to be aware of her thoughts and sensations. After repeating this sequence a few times, she looked up and said, "I've never felt comfortable being out there in the world. I'm afraid I'll be too much for people, that I'll intimidate them. When I back up, I feel as if I'm invisible. I know logically that's absurd, but I feel as if I can hide when I back up." Another client saw that her jerky pulsation between advancing and retreating reflected her ambivalence between seeing and being in the world in a straightforward way and shrinking into a helpless victim position.

Movement is a direct bridge to our inner life. Moving the way we feel, authentically, can actually build rich inner experience as well as uncover what is false to ourselves. We sometimes call the Moving Principle "inner movement" to distinguish it from calisthenics and locomotion. The purpose of inner movement is to reclaim both the wounded and the wonderful disowned parts of ourselves. Simply by focusing inward and moving with our genuine impulses, we retrace and erase the original map of withdrawal. In its place we create a new map of aliveness based on love and acceptance of the full range of human possibilities. Inner movement gives the mover choice. From our awareness of actual experience, we can own more and more of the range of feelings and actions.

When Kathlyn was in college dance classes, she recalls, she was a bit of a troublemaker. She wanted to know what was so valuable about a certain shape, an exact sequence of forms in duplication of the teacher's instruction. She knew there was something else about movement that made her feel joyous, and that it wasn't getting the arabesque just right. Finally the department head gave her the name of a class going on across campus. She walked into a scene that changed her life. A group of teachers, led by a dance therapist, was taking turns moving across the floor, gesturing and saying "No!" Their movement had a quality Kathlyn had not seen in any of her dance classes. The teachers moved from the inside, from their feelings. Their movements were not studied, but very intent; the inexpressible quality was surprising and electric. As they moved Kathlyn saw triumphant two-year-olds and defiant adolescents emerge from middle-age bodies. She felt those forgotten "no's" in her own body. She remembered the exhilaration of risking a new movement, stretching her mind through her body. She realized how far away from her body's truth she lived. "No!"—the beginning of self-definition—was also the beginning of her decision to become a dance/movement therapist.

Most of us have little experience in learning the language of the body. We spend hours in school dissecting, diagramming, and learning formulas. But how many times do you remember being taught to listen to your inner experience and to dialogue with the messages of your body? This inner blankness under most people's personas has a profound cost later in life. When children are grown and work goals are fulfilled, what vistas are left to explore? If we haven't devoted time and attention to inner movement, middle age and beyond can be very bleak. A large proportion of our clients come into therapy because they have run out of interesting personas. The prospect of continuing through the rest of life as an Ex-Cheerleader, Workaholic, or Computer Whiz suddenly becomes dismal. When these people are first asked, "What are you experiencing?" they often reply, "What do you mean?" Or, "I have no idea." Or most sadly: "Nothing. I feel blank."

The source of this blankness is their estrangement from their spontaneous body expression: the fear of looking stupid when moving. Most of us learned to use our bodies functionally, not expressively. We learned in school how to sit still except in certain structured circumstances like gym class, where we were usually told the appropriate ways to move. One of Kathlyn's earliest clients was stopped short in his session when he realized that he had never moved "for no reason at all." Most new clients feel extremely awkward at the prospect of moving expressively. They have had experiences that associate moving and dancing with embarrassment or rejection. Just think back to your school dances to remember your own and others' humiliations, feeling silly, stupid, or criticized. These responses were usually tied to even earlier experiences of being judged for natural expression. Children who are repeatedly told they are too fidgety, too loud, or too much trouble ingest those messages and store them. Over time, their natural movements become structured and ritualized. As people, they become divided. Instead of moving from the inside, they begin moving as they imagine will look good or appropriate. When their conformity reaches a certain level, the children enter school, where they receive the finishing touches through schedules, peer pressure, media norms, and focus on the intellect. They forget that they first learned through their body. Much later, movement therapy can help them reown these resources of the body.

Even after working as a movement therapist for twenty-plus years, Kathlyn is still amazed that the smallest gesture can be an accurate portrait of the whole person's problem. Focusing on movements that had emotional charge, she saw the larger patterns of which they were the nucleus. A woman's slight jaw-tightening and chin-thrusting were the core of a whole life-statement: "I won't play. Whatever you want me to do, I won't." A man glanced away when his wife spoke to him with feeling, just as he avoided direct contact with his boss's requests, his kids' emotional demands, or life's unpredictability. A woman in a recent session flitted around the room when she came in, smiling and chatting. When Kathlyn focused on that movement tone, she realized that flitting was the core of her mask, her Southern Belle persona. She breezed along the surface of life's difficulties and never risked attaching to anything that might be taken away, as her security had been taken away when her father remarried and abandoned her emotionally.

THE MOVING PRINCIPLE AND THERAPY

What can an awareness of the Moving Principle add to the quality of day-to-day life? In our clients' deepest explorations, certain themes recur.

The most predominant shift that occurs through the movement process is the growing ability to feel comfortable with the process of change. Most clients come in stuck in one or more positions about life and are looking for a secure niche for themselves in an ever-fluctuating world. Their position may be, "If I just try hard enough, I'll succeed." Or it may be the opposite; "Life is just a struggle." They are unaware of the power of making a paradigm shift, of being able to let go of old attitudes in order to adapt to and benefit from change. But once they learn to experience life as a process, they can literally become wind-surfers on the waves of change. They can spot coming changes and catch the moment of opportunity to ride safely on the flow of life.

One woman client, Leslie, initially expressed a common mind/body split this way: "I think about how I feel. Then I decide what action to take." The problem with this position is paralysis. Frequently Leslie's thoughts and feelings were conflicted. Her expression was often blank, her breathing shallow, and her movements flat. At the time, she was involved in her third extramarital affair in her long-term marriage. Some years after the second affair, she had told her husband about both episodes. He had been quite upset and said he "would never go through that again." So this time, Leslie hadn't told him, fearing that "it would pull the family apart." She said she really didn't want to be doing what she was doing. Consciously she wanted resolution; unconsciously her actions expressed the opposite impulse. Leslie saw herself as a decisive person, but for months (since the start of the affair) she had been frozen in indecision, not only about her marriage but in her business. She said she "just wanted it to be the way it used to be. I just don't know why I'm doing this. I figured if I understood *why* I was doing this I could stop." Kathlyn asked, "How did this work last time?" Leslie exclaimed. "I *swore* I would never do it again—everyone in my family, my parents, grandparents, were divorced, and that's what I knew growing up." We concluded that understanding and analysis hadn't worked very well to change her behavior. But that was the strategy she, like many people, tried first.

Many people approach healing and therapy as a philosophical exercise. If they can just make sense of a problem, they can decide what to do about it. Their world view is composed of little islands of safety called beliefs. These beliefs freeze their direct participation with the flow of feeling, sensation, and vitality. As Leslie began experiencing her feelings directly, she saw that as a child she had learned to lie in order to feel safe in an inconsistent world. As she breathed and moved with her feelings of frozenness, she recovered memories of having to take care of everything that her alcoholic mother and absent father had not. She had learned to contract and assess before risking any action. Safety and freezing became intertwined. Unwinding these frozen feelings is the heart of the Moving Principle.

BLOCKS TO IMPULSE EXPRESSION IN MOVEMENT

If no blocks to movement expression are present, movement occurs naturally. An impulse builds inside, takes form in a movement that expresses it fully, and congruently, then subsides in completion. When a person stubs a toe, for example, the emotional charge travels through the body, and the person hops, waves their hands, and shouts, "Ouch!" Reading a phrase in a book or hearing someone's voice on the phone can produce impulses that need expression. Emotions and sensations are flowing through the body continually, and the healthy person opens up to the full experience and expression of them in movement.

When blocks occur, the expression of an impulse usually takes one of two forms. Either it is incomplete, or it becomes polarized. We call incompletion the Arrow because the impulse never reaches full expression, its target. For example, a person may habitually leave sentences unfinished, while another withholds impulses to reach out. In incompletion blocks, clients are expressing only 50 or 60 percent of themselves.

When the expression of an impulse polarizes, we call it the Seesaw. In this block the person experiences life as an either-or proposition. The full range of expression is neither safe nor comfortable, and the person tends to swing back and forth between opposites. A client may describe daily life this way: "Either I'm really good and efficient, or I stay in bed all day and read romance novels." Such a person's movement style may oscillate wildly between extremes. One client's Seesaw began to show when he careened through our therapy office door wringing his hands and pacing frantically from one end of the room to the other. "I just can't seem to get through to these customers!" he exclaimed. "What do they want?!" After several minutes of frantic pacing, he collapsed on the couch and said, "I just give up. It's never going to work anyway!"

FUNDAMENTAL MOVEMENT TECHNIQUES IN BRIEF

For any person in any session, both of these blocks may occur. We have isolated their characteristics to allow therapists to work with Fundamental Movement Techniques that allow resolution of these two different styles. When a client becomes engaged in movement or has identified a block to the expression of an impulse, three techniques are useful. The *Moving Microscopic Truth* can help involve the client initially in the movement process. *Magnification Through Movement* is the technique of choice to complete an Arrow block. *The Polarity Process* is most useful for synthesizing new choices when a client is riding a Seesaw block. The central secret about movement in therapy is that *the process does the work*. Once a client uses the Moving Principle, the body knows exactly what to do. The therapist simply follows. Let's take a look at the first ten minutes of a recent session to introduce the three techniques; they will be described in more detail in the next chapter.

Maggie came in for an individual session during a week-long seminar Kathlyn was teaching. A vibrant, articulate young woman, she had volunteered for the first time slot.

MAGGIE *(striding forcefully into the studio)*: I knew I would be first.
KATHLYN: When did you know—where did that knowing come from?
MAGGIE *(laughs and runs both hands through her hair)*: I'm the first born, and I always do things first, kind of try them out.
KATHLYN: Let yourself take on the body posture that matches this experience of being first all the time.

This invitation initiates the first Fundamental Movement Technique, the Moving Microscopic Truth. We define *microscopic truth* as that which cannot be argued about. The microscopic truth verbally matches inner experience: thoughts, images, sensations, and emotions. The Moving Microscopic Truth adds to this the participation of the body.

(Maggie stands, laughs again, and takes a big breath as she stretches both arms out horizontally and decisively. Her breath doesn't quite fill her torso, and Kathlyn notices that she holds tension in the front of her shoulders.)

KATHLYN: Notice what is happening just under your collarbones.

MAGGIE: I feel happy—no, more than happy. Joy.

KATHLYN: How does that joy want to express itself? Let yourself tune in to how you can move with the joy.

(Maggie almost immediately begins rocking. Her hands tremble gently, and the trembling quickly spreads to her chest.)

KATHLYN: Go with that trembling. Let that happen more.

These words invite the second technique, Magnification Through Movement.

(Maggie continues trembling, and the quality of her movements becomes more jerky.)

KATHLYN: Notice anyplace in your body where you are stopping or con-trolling the trembling.

(Maggie pauses a moment, then points to the base of her throat and jaw. Her gesture has a prodding quality.)

KATHLYN: It looks as if you are poking yourself. Tune in to what you are experiencing now.

MAGGIE *(furrowing her brow and gritting her teeth)*: I'm mad. *(Snorts a laugh and coughs.)*

KATHLYN: Allow yourself to breathe up into your throat and jaw.

MAGGIE *(with clenched jaws)*: I don't want to do this.

KATHLYN: Say that again, and take a breath to see where you are experi-encing "I don't want to" in your body.

MAGGIE: I *don't want* to do this. *(Her hands sweep over her pelvis and the insides of her legs as she speaks. For a moment movement and breath are*

suspended.) But I really do want to do this. *(She stands up very straight and opens her hands, striking through the air like a sword.)*
KATHLYN: Let yourself go back and forth, Maggie, saying and moving "I want to" and "I don't want to" several times.
(Maggie does this intently for a few minutes, alternating between swaying with her head shaking, and stamping her feet and flailing her arms.)

These are responses to the third Fundamental Movement Technique, the Polarity Process. Sensations and experiences are often split for clients. The Polarity Process invites clients to allow the direct experience of opposites.

(Maggie's head flings back, and she stamps a third time. Then she spontaneously takes three large breaths and starts to cry from deep in her throat.)
KATHLYN: Be with yourself, Maggie. Whichever part wants to be seen.
MAGGIE: It's okay, it's okay. *(She sways again gently from side to side, wraps her arms around her shoulders, and rotates her whole body around in a slow rock.)* I just don't let myself be soft very often. To be first, I had to be pretty tough, take care of things, and put my feelings aside. It feels good to be with the "don't want to" part of me.

Ten minutes of careful attention to Maggie's process with the three movement techniques brought one of her fundamental issues to conscious awareness. Acknowledging and being with her true inner impulses allowed her more breath, more aliveness, and more choice. As the session progressed, we discovered a series of body splits and experiences that Maggie had previously disowned in order to maintain her persona of First.

THE POWER OF COMPLETIONS

People become frozen around unexperienced emotions, broken agreements, and unexpressed truth. Each time we do not tell the truth, hide our feelings, or break an agreement, our bodies store that information. Most of us are composed of layers of incompletion that armor us from directly experiencing life. People often choose to ignore their frozen bodies. They believe that if they do not let themselves see or experience the incompletions, no one else will. Clients are often amazed that body-centered therapists can so easily see what they think is secret. Seeing and stating the obvious—"Excuse me, but you have your head in the sand about this"—begins the thawing process.

In a recent training course, we suggested an activity that would immediately increase aliveness. Students put six circles on a page. In each circle they entered the name of a person with whom they had some incompletion about feelings, truth, or agreements. (Incompletions include regrets, resentments that have not been communicated, lies told, truths withheld, and apologies undelivered.) Then Gay asked, "How much more alive would you like to feel tomorrow morning?" People named a percentage, from zero to a hundred percent. Then the punchline was delivered. Gay said, "Okay. Complete with the people in your circles. To the extent you are committed to being more alive, feel your feelings, tell the truth, clear up broken agreements. If you want to feel a hundred percent more alive, complete a hundred percent of the incompletions in your circles." Uproar! Many students were outraged that the exercise had become real. One person said, "I thought this was just a game! I put down the deepest stuff of my life, and you're saying I *have to* clear it up by tomorrow!?" Invitations to aliveness often elicit deep resistance. We invited the students to look at their willingness to complete in a way that was totally friendly to them and everyone else concerned. Some students saw that they had confused willingness with previous demands from parents and other authority figures. Others made lists to complete over the next several weeks.

One woman who completed everything in her circles came back the next morning absolutely radiant. Her skin color was glowing, her voice melodious, and her movements were flowing and harmonious. She talked about altering her sense of time, feeling in harmony with life now, rather than trying to fit everything in to too few hours. She said, grinning, "I had time for everything. I did my completions, had some alone time just for me, and spent several delicious hours with my husband."

CONSCIOUS MOVING

In addition to increasing our ability to be more present moment-to-moment, conscious moving adds zest to daily life. As one client put it, "Gee, I can get high doing this!" Current aging research strongly suggests that activity is a major key both to longevity and to maximum quality in life. Consciously and unconsciously, most of us think that aging means less motion and more rigidity. In our practices we see a vivid truth every week: By engaging in moving as an exploration rather than as a chore, vitality increases. Some friends were present at an eightieth birthday celebration for Alexander Lowen, the pioneering bioenergetics therapist, held during a large psychotherapy conference. They remarked how much more vital this advocate of bodymind integration looked than traditional therapists half his age. He told the large audience, "I laugh every day, I cry every day, and I kick every day. And I feel *great!*" In our own lives we practice interrupting patterns and trying on new ways of moving on a daily basis.

As an experiment one day, you might explore doing your daily routines in a new way. For example, put your pants on the other leg first, brush your teeth with your nondominant hand, or have breakfast at dinnertime. With an attitude of exploration, daily life becomes fresh and inviting rather than repetitious and dull.

The ultimate Moving Principle is full participation with life. When we open to new moving possibilities and free the frozen places in our inner flow of movement, more participation and more responsiveness result. Our brain cells communicate intricate information by firing chemicals across synapses, or gaps between them. Movement can function in the same way to connect gaps in experience and to contact our deepest selves.

AN EXPERIMENT IN MOVEMENT THAT YOU CAN DO RIGHT NOW

DURING YOUR NORMAL ACTIVITIES ONE DAY, NOTICE:

• **how you move forward.** Do you cut through space directly, taking the shortest route? or do you prefer to meander a little, stopping to explore along the way? What shape does your body take when you advance: jutting, rounded, compact.

• **how you move backward.** When do you feel the impulse to retreat? Do you back up to make space for yourself (rather than moving forward and inviting someone else to accommodate you)? When you move backward, do you get smaller or larger inside? Do you feel safer?

• **how you get taller.** What is going on around you when you make yourself bigger? Are you with family or co-workers? Are you comfortable being as big as you are?

• **how you get shorter.** When do you have the impulse to "get small"? What makes you want to disappear?

• **how you flow through life.** Are you a speeder or a lingerer? When you move from one place to another, are you aware of the transition, or do you wake up again when you arrive at your destination.

LEARNING FROM TRANSITIONS

The realm of movement is an ideal way to study the transitions in our lives. The spaces between events reveal unconscious patterns very quickly. Most people are totally unaware of themselves as they move from one place to another: standing up, coming in the door, or putting on a coat. What people do when they don't think they're onstage (in other words, in an out-of-persona experience) reveals core patterns and attitudes very quickly. In therapy sessions we pay close attention to a client's style of entering the room and sitting down. Sometimes clients don't sit; they immediately pace or fling their possessions down and start talking the moment they come through the door. One person may come into the therapy room as if shot out of a cannon, revealing a hurry-up approach to life that needs to be balanced by slowing down. Another person steps through the door as if testing the water, revealing a tentativeness that is characteristic of many other areas of life. Some clients plop themselves down, while others poise on the edge of the couch waiting for instructions.

There are little transitions, such as getting into the car, and there are big transitions, such as getting up in the morning. The daily shift from the unconsciousness of sleep to the consciousness of waking life can evoke deep feelings of childhood or birth experiences. A change in normally orderly patterns can provoke the original transition issue.

Rosie, for example, a former client, came back in to work on a puzzling but disturbing issue with us. She had been feeling a lot of satisfaction with her family life and job over the previous year. But over the past few weeks she had noticed an experience of "digging in her heels" and feeling stonewalled with her husband, Tom.

US: What was going on when this feeling arose?
ROSIE (*after a moment's thought*): I see Tom going out the door, and I just feel so stuck, like crying all the time.

Tom had recently taken a new job, with lots of potential for growth and money. But the transition time required a temporary period of travel. He was in and out of the house a lot, often for short periods, before leaving again.

US: Say more about your experience of Tom leaving.
ROSIE: I just feel hopeless and all alone. (*Her hand flutters to her chest and she begins to cry.*)
US: Is that feeling familiar, Rosie?
ROSIE (*crying and gently rocking*): It's been there as long as I can remember. If I keep things under control, not too many surprises, I don't often feel it. But with all this upheaval, I just feel helpless.
US: Let yourself breathe and move with those feelings.

(Rosie rocks, cries, and moves her hands in clutching and shaking motions for
several minutes. The tears subside, and she looks up.)
ROSIE: I feel so sad about not feeling really connected to my mother.

Shortly after her birth, Rosie had been separated from her mother for
several days because her mother developed an infection. Now, the simple
act of Tom leaving the house, even for a brighter and more prosperous
future, powerfully echoed for Rosie her first transition into life. Although
this theme had arisen in previous sessions with us, she had failed to make
the connection between Tom's departures and her own birth. With the
core issue clear, we explored with Rosie her other choices in this current
transition. She saw clearly that she needed a little private time with Tom to
affirm their bond before he left.

EXPLORING MOVEMENT

If we can respond to the Moving Principle, we gain flexibility and choice
with our feelings and the events that occur in daily life. One client, Hank,
responded automatically and predictably to conflicts in relationships with a
succession of lovers. He was polarized in his reactions: He would either
explode with anger to assert his power, or he would collapse in helpless
sadness. His chest would puff out with rage or collapse with depression. In
either extreme he felt unable to hear his partner or to get his needs met. He
expressed tremendous frustration with his inability to find a middle ground.
In his therapy session, we first acknowledged the intense feelings of rage
and grief that he had experienced throughout much of his childhood. He
shook and sobbed with the pent-up emotions of years. Then we suggested
he do a movement posture that literally straddled these polarized feelings.
Standing like a sumo wrestler, Hank experimented with being a moving
mountain of energy. He pivoted and stamped, shaking the ground with
each vibrating step. His face lit up as he began to feel the flow of aliveness
from one side of his body to the other. "I feel waves of deep calm, and yet
power, moving like this," Hank said. "I can face the world directly." In his
interactions with his current partner he began to find a middle ground

where he could acknowledge his feelings, and to hear his partner's requests without swinging out of control.

Using the Moving Principle, we improvise explorations to identify what is keeping a client from full participation in life. Sometimes what is missing is simply aliveness, or juice, to fuel full aliveness. Most depressed clients, for example, generally breathe in a shallow style and move their bodies in a narrow range. They experience either a block to or lack of basic life energy. They just don't get other people's excitement about life. One client echoed the words to an old Peggy Lee song: "Is this all there is?" Other clients have so much juice that their body can't fully integrate the charge, and it short-circuits with illness, accidents, or fragmentation. Many enter therapy with limbs askew and a sense of being "all over the place." Still others live in their heads and have little if any acquaintance with the feelings and sensations of anything below the neck. And sometimes, as in Hank's situation, the flow of aliveness is split and polarized into opposites that have no bridge. Through movement exploration, clients directly extend the range of movement choices. Even inexperienced movers can easily learn to magnify a hand gesture until they discover the underlying feeling, or to tune in to and follow movement impulses. They shift from robotic responses to creative play. Many clients have been delighted to notice more spontaneity and more powerful inspiration at work, and a lot more fun from day to day.

One of a therapist's most essential skills is to use the Moving Principle as a vehicle to create and express empathy. To be accepted and deeply experienced in this creates trust and a bridge to deeper exploration. A therapist with movement skills can acknowledge the energy level, the posture, the pacing, and the feeling level of the client without either person saying a word. When Kathlyn came in to begin a session with Pam, for example, she found Pam hunched over on the couch, looking down at the floor with a black expression. Kathlyn quietly went over and sat next to Pam, touching her arm gently and breathing slowly and calmly. Pam began to cry softly. After a few minutes she said, "I have been so hard on myself this week. I wouldn't let myself be gentle because I haven't stayed on my diet, and I yelled at the kids. Until you sat next to me, I was in a kind of prison."

A clear indicator of the outcome of therapy is client involvement in the process. We have worked with clients who had been in more traditional "talk" therapy for many years without significant change. After a few sessions of moving, breathing, and being, their involvement becomes palpable. They are willing to do homework assignments and to study patterns that first emerge in the therapy session. Movement process is a collaboration, and clients quickly become engaged in inner exploration because they notice a difference in the quality of their life.

BODY IMAGE

Gaining comfort with moving also brings comfort with the body. For many people, accepting their bodies is a lifelong task. Body discomforts and body image problems are encouraged by the cultural standards into which we are born. *The New York Times* reported the research of Thomas F. Cash, a professor of psychology at Old Dominion University in Norfolk, Virginia, who with his colleagues has been studying the long-term effects of negative body image. They were most surprised to discover the tenacity of body image beliefs. When children are teased for looking different, the resulting negative self-assessment can last a lifetime. Cash suggests that the psychological effects of negative body image can influence a wide range of behavior, including eating disorders, psychological dysfunction, and desire for plastic surgery. In all our years as therapists, we have never encountered a woman who thought her body was just right! Men are apparently utilizing plastic surgery more now as well, although the tyranny of appearance has been mostly the inheritance of women.

Our body image changes when we shift our attention from how we look to how we feel, to how we *experience* moving and being. If we are repeatedly looked at with disapproval, criticism, or misunderstanding, we learn to see ourselves that way over time and to disown or deny our experience. Reclaiming the immediate experience of our body sensation can break the cycle of seeing ourselves through the distorted lens of others instead of experiencing an authentic sense of self.

One woman, Sophie, uncovered a central body image belief that had been imprinted when she was four years old. Up until that day her father had often picked her up after work and swung her high overhead. This gesture meant she was special and loved. On this day she ran to repeat the homecoming ritual, but her father said, "Oh, Sophie, honey, I can't pick you up anymore. You're too big." Sophie unconsciously internalized this fairly innocent remark. "Oh," she thought, "I'm too big. My body is too big. My needs are too much. I guess *I'm* too big." She quickly became plump— never fat, but always just a little "too big." In her relationships she either held back her desires and needs, or she dumped them in ways that her co-workers and lovers found overwhelming. Our therapy work together involved reowning her impulse to reach out and be fully received. We explored being "too big" with as many movements as we could invent and gradually dissolved the distorted mirror through which Sophie had formed her body image. She was dumbfounded when she realized that the root of her problem lay in her misinterpretation of her father's remark.

ENHANCED OPTIONS

The other common result that emerges in movement exploration is enhanced options. People find that their responsiveness and choices increase. One of the most common complaints that clients bring to therapy is the sense of routine and dullness in their day-to-day lives. They just don't see any options to their distress, and they often feel stuck in a limited repertoire of problem-solving strategies. Like Hank, new clients often experience themselves swinging from one extreme to another: "I either binge or starve myself," said Vicky, "until I can't stand it, then binge again, hate myself, starve." Another client, Susanna, despaired of ever being able to stop and enjoy a quiet activity without making the time by getting sick: "I just go, go, go until I drop and have to stop everything. Then I give myself a few days off and take the phone off the hook. Then it's back to full speed." After a time exploring movement process, a new synthesis occurred. We explored the contrast between the frantic pace of Susanna's activity and the pull toward stillness that she experienced in her upper back. As she shifted back and forth from speeding to stopping, a new pace emerged, almost a middle gear. "Oh, I can feel my breath as I'm moving," she said, "and I feel at home inside. When I'm speeding or dropping, I don't really experience myself! No wonder I hadn't been able to take care of myself. I was either out ahead of myself or totally shut down."

The middle range opens up where new possibilities and potentials emerge. Vicky, the binger/starver, discovered new ways to nurture herself, for example, with noon support groups at work. She discovered that her body loved bicycling, and she began to choose bicycling over binging. Susanna, the hard worker, discovered a new sense of pacing that she had never experienced. She began to explore the zone between zooming and collapsing. When that middle range became available, she realized that she had previously been slightly ahead of life, always looking to the next project. She literally discovered how to move at the right pace to "smell the roses," to experience life directly. Her exploration continues to uncover new creative possibilities both at work and with her family.

Because movement is the medium of our aliveness, increased movement ease and responsiveness brings greater freedom in all aspects of life. Some clients report that waiting in line changes from a personal insult to an opportunity to make up a new song. Confronting a problem at work has been transformed from pressure to possibility. One executive has learned to breathe and change his position when he recognizes stress building up. He calls it "getting a new perspective on things," and he reports that new solutions and combinations of ideas reliably occur shortly thereafter. One client has even developed a talent for finding things that are missing. She calls it "going into my finding place," an inner quietness where objects just appear. We think that bodymind unity makes people smarter. It certainly seems to make them happier and more satisfied.

A BODY-CENTERED MODEL

What does a healthy moving body look like? Most of our models in medicine and psychology are based on dis-ease, not on health or wellness. If professionals can eliminate the symptoms or diagnose and treat an illness, they tend to stop there and call that health. The body-centered model, in contrast, originates in a model of wholeness. Our viewpoint is grounded in the assumption that beneath persona and feelings, the essential person moves and breathes in integrity. Our task is to collaborate with the person to remove the blocks to wholeness.

Healthy people stand and move distinctively. Their gestures are economical and complete. Their eyes sparkle with vitality and presence; their skin color is radiant. Their standing body is balanced and fluid, with seemingly endless potential for spontaneous response to life's invitations. They express feelings fully and congruently; their communication matches their inner experience. They are inspiring to be around because they seem to magnify creative potential in everyone they contact. People feel better, lighter, happier around them. Perhaps the most distinctive feature of a healthy moving body is flow. Each movement impulse flows from its source through toned muscles to the periphery of the body in a little dance unique to the expression.

Healthy people are always inventing themselves. They tend not to get caught in mannerisms, and they have a large range of possible movements. Instead of the three- to four-hundred-gesture vocabulary of most people, they branch out closer to the three thousand possible movements we can make. As you read this, try to remember people you've met who seem to flow through life, creating ease and resolution with their presence. They stand out as models of what can be.

Kathlyn recalls that her high school dance teacher combined the strength of years of training with the spontaneity and immediacy of her willingness to explore and experience the whole range of feelings. She seemed to have endless energy and was intensely curious about life. She prodded her students daily to take the next step, to explore unfamiliar territory. She never hesitated to put unlikely elements together. For example, she would team the biggest linebacker and the tiniest girl to explore giving and receiving weight. She would orchestrate "chance dances," where the sections of movement would be rearranged each time, giving us the experience of literally changing our perspective and expectations. She was a leprechaun, teasing and tempting more life in her students from the spark of her loving presence.

Using the Moving Principle creates access to more vitality by shifting both the client's and the therapist's focus from "why" to "how." This perspective illuminates patterns very quickly and allows direct participation with feelings. Instead of getting lost in *content* we are noticing *context*, the movements and body attitudes that repeat. Clients begin to see that all the intricate details of the latest story are just flourishes on the same old thing. When we focus on that same old thing and invite a moving exploration, the old storyline can be completed to make way for immediacy and choice. Movement allows us to swim in the river of process and be bathed by the flow of life.

Gloria, who works in a big corporation, came to us complaining about the way her boss was treating her. She was feeling very anxious about her performance, as she was up for review and had heard some criticisms from her supervisor. She couldn't understand why she kept getting into conflicts with her boss. We asked her to describe her experience of anxiety in her body. She said, "I feel a gripping sensation in my lower ribs, with some hot shooting spikes up under my sternum. It all gets stuck in a ball in my throat." After a few minutes we invited her to move with the anxiety, to focus under the storyline to the actual sensations in that moment. As she shaped her hands in cascades of motion that looked like someone rapidly playing a harp, Gloria felt the sensation of anxiety rush up from her chest to her head. We encouraged her to continue expressing exactly what she was experiencing, and within a few minutes the anxiety had dissolved and she felt energetic and clear-headed. Most surprising to Gloria, she realized that this pattern of anxiety most often turned into headaches that would influence her work performance.

GLORIA: Gosh, you mean I could just feel what I'm feeling and not have to turn it into a drama and confrontation?!

KATHLYN: You have a choice now when those feelings come up.

GLORIA: But they're so strong; I feel so pulled by them, as if I'm really going to get in trouble.

KATHLYN: How is that experience familiar?

GLORIA (*after a pause*): Oh—I remember being really nervous when I would bring my report card home. It seemed as if I could never be good enough. If I brought home A's and B's, my father would say, "Why the B's?"

Gloria cried for a few minutes, remembering how much she had wanted her father to see her specialness, not just her performance. She saw that she had now projected this family pattern onto her current boss. A few weeks later, she came in again. "I was amazed how comfortable I felt in my review," she said. "I heard what my supervisor said as feedback, not criticism. It was incredible to actually hear things differently!" "How did you do?" we asked. "Oh, yeah"—she laughed—"just fine. I'm getting some new assignments with more responsibility."

Movement exploration examines the language of the body that is both universal and at the same time unique to each person. It allows the therapist to meet and acknowledge the client. More important, it draws forth the meaning of movement from the client. The process of discovery is exhilarating and creative. Those moments of connection empower the client far more than the therapist's interpretations or advice, accurate as they may be. When we uncover the source of a pattern or remember a lost part of our past, we become more whole, more unified. Most new clients mistrust, misinterpret, or misuse information from the body. In the process of being with, matching, and moving from internal impulse, clients can discern the meaning of repetitive or common gestures. Take, for example, fingernail-picking. As people have explored this simple and seemingly trivial movement, they have discovered a world of meaning in it. Here are some of these meanings, culled from a half-dozen sessions with different people.

- "I hate my hands. They're too big and gawky."
- "I do this when I'm nervous. It kind of calms me."
- "If I don't pick my nails, I'll say something awful and get in trouble."
- "I'm really angry at my parents. I'd like to scratch them."
- "My grandmother always picked on me. And she thought short fingernails were extremely common. I guess I do that to get back at her."

- "If I pick on my nails, I don't seem to try to control everything as much."

Movement patterns *are* life patterns. Once the therapist learns to see the context rather than the story, the pattern in the fabric of the client's life becomes vividly bright. Movement is a major key to the inner mystery. In the next chapter we will take a close look at the three Fundamental Movement Techniques and how to implement them.

THE THREE FUNDAMENTAL MOVEMENT TECHNIQUES

In this chapter we will explore the three Fundamental Movement Techniques in detail. Each of them is designed to draw clients easily into direct participation with their issues. Each gives the therapist a tool to be with the client's experience, to bring more choices to the client's life. Each technique—Magnification Through Movement, the Moving Microscopic Truth, and the Polarity Process—is closely interwoven in a typical session. The examples we will use to illustrate these techniques will often include more than one movement skill, although we will focus on each separately.

MOVEMENT FLAGS

The movement techniques build on a knowledge of movement flags, which were introduced in chapter 4. Basically, a movement flag is a gesture or larger movement that is inconsistent in some way with the client's communication, a gap or bulge in the surface flow of interaction. Movement flags are the semaphores of the unconscious. They signal us to "Pay attention to this!" When a young woman named Bobbie sat on her hands as she was describing a recent supervision meeting, we asked her to notice what that movement might be saying. She laughed and said, "I didn't realize how nervous I was about appearing too forward. I guess I can't do much of anything if I'm sitting on my hands, can I?" Very simply, a movement flag is a movement that does not fit. It does not quite make sense in the overall context. The therapist can learn to notice gestures and movements that stick out, and to bring the power of presencing to illuminate their meaning.

Because movement flags are rich diagnostic guides, we will look at several examples of them. These feeling leaks are easy to spot with a little practice. They are so useful because they are often, along with breath flags, the most obvious signals from the unconscious. A movement flag tells the therapist that a break in awareness is present and signals an opportunity for exploration. Movement flags usually involve the extremities: hands, feet and head. Less frequently do they emerge from the torso or other parts of the body.

It is important to remember that movement flags are idiomatic to the mover. Each of us has the same basic emotions but a private language for expressing them. Our study of movement flags and movement techniques is designed to provide an outline for exploration, not a dictionary of body language. If we point out a ring-twisting motion to a client, she may ask, "So what does *that* mean?" If we give her an interpretation, we are not respecting the years of nonverbal learning that have resulted in that particular gesture. We may have some ideas based on our years of engaging with clients, but the most effective and empowering interventions are those that direct clients inward to their own knowing. Even if you never intend to become a therapist, the study of movement flags can open rich areas of exploration and deeper inner experience for you.

Given that disclaimer, the following common movement flags may be fruitful areas to begin noticing:

- FACIAL TICS: These include grimacing, pouting, or screwing up a part of the face.
- SCRATCHING: This interesting movement flag often signals irritation. The therapist can look like a magician by asking the scratching client: "Were you irritated about that?"

- PICKING: This flag has several subcategories. Clients may pick their fingernails, cuticles, face or other body areas, lint from clothes, or debris from the couch or rug, to name a few common patterns.

- SMOOTHING: Smoothing also occurs in several domains: hair or face, clothes, and the area directly around the client. One particularly useful gesture to notice is smoothing the rug in a wiping pattern. One client recently identified her unconscious attempt to "smooth things over" in her marriage when this flag emerged.

- HOLDING MOVEMENTS: Clients often hold their neck or arm in a way that carries some emotional charge. One hand may hold or restrain the other repeatedly. Clients may cross their arms as they hold themselves. Any part of the body may be held during a session when material arises that involves that area. One man, Lou, held his knee from underneath as he was talking about his relationship with his father. When we brought his attention to this movement flag and asked him to magnify it a little, he remembered several times in junior high and high school when he had wanted his father's support in the track meets that he competed in. His father had one reason after another for not being able to attend, and Lou felt "cut off at the knees" by this lack of support.

- BRUSHING MOTIONS: Clients may brush off an arm, brush a hand through the hair, brush imaginary crumbs off the front of the body, or make a brushing-off motion that repeats during conversation.

- ROCKING: This often-subtle movement flag is frequently a signal that the client is experiencing feelings and sensations from early in life. Clients have found rocking movements to be a way of comforting, grounding, reassuring, protecting, and isolating themselves. Rocking is easy to magnify, and it connects the clients directly to early caregiving issues.

- SELF-TOUCHING: This movement flag occurs frequently, and it often underscores the issue being discussed. Clients often feel that touching reassures them that they are present, stops feelings, or grounds them. Some have noticed touching themselves in the ways they were touched as children. One woman touched her chest as if she were pinning herself down while talking about her work week. When we invited her to breathe and be present for the message of that touch, she realized that she immobilized her upper body and expression when she pinned herself. She was afraid her exuberance would be "too much" for the conservative firm and so would give herself an unconscious signal to tone it down.

• THE "HINGE-CRINGE": When clients are fearful or avoiding, they frequently contract in a cringelike movement, especially at the joints of the body. As their body shrinks, the clients also report feeling smaller inside. We notice that overweight people often make space for themselves by backing up and shrinking rather than by asserting their personal space by moving forward.

Before the therapist can use any of the Movement Techniques, the primary obstacle to them must be confronted: Most people have grown so alienated from the natural expression of the body that movement is the last thing they think of to help solve a problem. We have heard countless times, "You mean you want me to move around, like dance or something? What does that have to do with anything?" Some simple but effective skills can be used to engage the client in the movement process. Let's take a look at several examples of engaging in movement.

MAKING THE TRANSITION FROM TALKING TO MOVING

Important material may arise from the Five Flags. Repetition might be a verbal flag, for example: "I just wish I *knew* what to do. My father always *knew*; in fact, he thought he *knew* everything." The therapist may make the transition to moving in this case by asking, "How are you experiencing that issue in your body?" As the person is talking, the words might have an emotional charge: For example, "I *won't* do that again!" Using the Magnification Principle, the therapist might ask the client to repeat that word or phrase louder, magnifying the tone of voice. Or the words might be accompanied by a movement flag: "I'm a little nervous about this date tonight," the client might say, tugging at his collar. The therapist might ask the client to tug more strongly at his collar while repeating, "I'm a little nervous."

Body sensations provide another entry into movement exploration. An experience such as nausea, headache, pressure, pain, or tension may be presented by the client. The quickest and most powerful tool to use with body sensations is the Moving Microscopic Truth. Even reluctant movers seem to respond easily to an invitation such as "Let your hands paint or sculpt that sensation. Move your hands to match the quality of nausea." Dozens of times we've taught students to use this tool, which can easily be inserted into many kinds of therapeutic and educational settings. At home, when we're confused about an issue, we'll often take a few minutes to let our fingers do the walking. As hands and sometimes more of the body match the internal experience, a resolution or clarity quickly emerges.

In the realm of movement itself the most useful material is often contained in movement flags such as finger-picking, facial tics, or toe-tapping. Magnification Through Movement quickly opens up the material underlying the flag. If a client crosses her arms with a defended quality, the therapist might ask her to close up quickly and emphatically. Lack of movement is as important a flag as repeated movement. If the shoulders are immobile or the person's chin is firmly tucked under, that is a valuable starting place. One possible intervention is: "As you're talking, I notice that your chin doesn't move at all."

With this background, let us now explore the three Fundamental Movement Techniques. These techniques are useful regardless of the therapist's orientation and background. They can be combined with massage, physical therapy, and a broad range of psychotherapeutic approaches.

THE MOVING MICROSCOPIC TRUTH

For most of us, the despair of separation from self begins with denying or overriding inner experience. When we acknowledge and meet our inner experience with movement, the gap is closed and we come home again to the experience of unity. Each time we express the truth without embellishment the cord of life pulses more strongly.

The Moving Microscopic Truth, the first Movement Technique, is the Presencing Principle in action. This way of moving allows a bridge between inner experience and outer experience. Essentially, it is movement that matches feeling, sensation, or thought. The client is asked to be with and allow the movement that wants to occur. While personas freeze the flow of aliveness through the bodymind, the Moving Microscopic Truth frees inner movement and essence.

WORKING WITH AN ATTITUDE FLAG

The Moving Microscopic Truth can evolve from any of the Five Flags: verbal, movement, attitude, postural, or breathing. The following example involves an attitude flag. Dana came into the room for her second session hesitantly and quietly. Her attitude was strikingly fearful. She looked like a kewpie doll trapped in a horror movie. Dana is tall, blond, and very wide-eyed. When we asked her how she had experienced her relaxation homework, she pursed her naturally puckered lips. She held her breath and hesitated, picked her sleeve, glanced around the room, and sighed. "I don't think I did it right," she said. This waterfall of flags was almost overwhelming, but Dana seemed to summarize the attitude flag accurately. Many clients are almost paralyzed in life by their fear of making mistakes.

We engaged Dana in the Moving Microscopic Truth by asking her to walk around the room, trying very hard to do it right. (Clients are generally comfortable with the familiar act of walking. The therapist can encourage different attitudes and emphasize different aspects of walking to quickly involve a client in the Moving Microscopic Truth.) Dana got up stiffly and began moving slowly around the room. Her spine was rigid and her upper back was held behind her pelvis, as if she were walking into a strong wind. She looked absolutely straight ahead as she spoke of feeling tension in her back and holding in her toes.

DANA: Of course, I have to watch where I'm stepping to make sure I step in the right place.

US: How do you know that you're stepping in the right place when you're not looking where you're going?

DANA: Oh, well, I guess maybe I don't know where I'm going.

US: You look as if you're scanning the horizon, looking ahead.

DANA: Yes, I guess that's what I do. I'm looking so far out there in front that I don't see the next step.

US: Take a moment to notice if there is any other place in your life where you do that same thing—look out in front rather than at the next step.

DANA (laughing after a pause): Yes, when I'm hiking. I'll stumble over a twig because I'm looking so far up the trail, I don't see where I'm going.

Dana's Trying to Do It Right persona melted as she gained this awareness. The sharp angles of her jutting chin and thrusting elbows softened as she slowed down and looked around the room, noticing and asking about a wall hanging for the first time. She made a further connection as she ambled about the room. She had spent years learning to be a physical therapist because she had been told that it would be a good living for a woman. She had never slowed down to consider her actual experience of working with people in that way. She had set her sights on the goal, not the process. After a year of practice she realized she hated physical therapy.

The Moving Microscopic Truth allows clients to explore their inner experience. It is a process of discovery, in which surprise is common. The mover explores the inner world by noticing sensory experience and following the feeling with congruent movement. The initial point of departure may be vague or very specific. The Moving Microscopic Truth weaves increased aliveness from each thread of awareness.

SCULPTING INNER SPACE

Teresa, a student in one of our movement classes, started her discovery process by identifying a familiar empty space in her middle. Using the

Moving Microscopic Truth, we invited her to move her hands in a way that matched this empty feeling in her body. As she moved her hands to sculpt this empty space, she looked as if she were shaping a large box. Teresa described it as a solid, granitelike place around her heart area. She saw it as black with red spots in it. As she focused inward while continuing to move her hands, she appeared to be turning the box over, shaking and prying at its corners. She said she couldn't see into it, but she knew there was something alive in it. She felt cracks in it, full of electricity. We invited her to continue sculpting this image as it changed, acknowledging it and giving permission for it to express itself. She continued moving and feeling the electrical quality during the session, and she agreed to explore at home as well.

When Teresa came in for her next session, she excitedly reported her odyssey. "I first discovered that this part of me is really mad at me," she said. "It feels like I have two people inside, each mad at the other. The first couple of days we were at a standoff, kind of toe-to-toe and head-to-head. Then it disappeared for a day or two, and I couldn't feel that granitelike part at all. I backed off and didn't push to find out; I just rested and gave it some space. Moving with it on the fourth day, I suddenly realized that that's where I hold my neglected feelings. When I let myself feel the sadness, I noticed my breath move into that place for the first time. It seems like there's so much garbage in there. It actually felt as if it were my personal trash bag. If I neglect myself and don't pay attention to my heart area, the black trash bag balloons and crackles. When I notice and dialogue with it in movement, it actually shrinks. But the most interesting thing is, I saw that this movement experience is connected to a dream I've had repeatedly over the last three weeks. In it, devils are chasing me, and they are black with red eyes. Since I've been moving with myself, the dreams have stopped."

THE MOVING MICROSCOPIC TRUTH IN PRACTICE

We use the Moving Microscopic Truth in nearly every session because of its power to connect clients with issues quickly. It can be used for a five-minute exploration of a stomach sensation or nagging thought, and it can develop into longer movement sequences. The healing move is to match experience with expression.

In one therapy session, Jean came in wanting to address her habit of poking, picking, and squeezing pimples on her face and upper chest. She had noticed an acceleration of this old pattern over the last few days, and it bothered her. We began moving before Jean had even sat down.

KATHLYN: Jean, let yourself take the picking motion you do and pick the space in front of you, rather than your face.

(Jean closes her eyes to focus more closely and makes small, sharply picking motions with her fingers.)

JEAN: I feel really embarrassed doing this openly.

KATHLYN: Let yourself be embarrassed. How does your body want to express embarrassed?

JEAN *(bent into a shuffled, head-down, pulled-back position)*: I really want to turn away from you.

KATHLYN: Go ahead, let yourself do that.

(Jean turns away with a tucking, shrinking movement.)

KATHLYN: It looks as if you are trying to hide.

JEAN: Yes, I don't know why, but I am.

KATHLYN: Don't worry about why right now. Let yourself explore hiding. See how your body wants to express hiding.

(Jean abruptly stretches up and thrusts her chin forward with a defiant gesture, not allowing any conscious hiding movements.)

KATHLYN: It looks as if it's difficult for you to allow yourself to hide.

JEAN *(with tears welling)*: People aren't supposed to notice that I'm hiding. I'm ashamed of hiding. I'm supposed to be tough, and hiding is weak.

KATHLYN: Jean, let both of those impulses speak. Let them dialogue with each other as much or as little as you want. Hiding, then standing up to it, being tough.

(Jean spends several minutes alternating quickly between hiding and opening up, contracting and expanding. As the intensity of this Polarity Process lessens, Jean's hands start to move again. Her hands appear to be tentatively seeking each other in a shy and very poignant movement.)

KATHLYN: Your hands seem to want to make contact with each other.

Often the therapist's most effective intervention is to reflect back the quality of movement to the client.

(*In that moment Jean's face changes, and she turns into a young child. Her mouth puckers and trembles.*)

KATHLYN: Notice both your mouth and your hands, Jean. Let yourself move with those feelings.

(*Jean's face has a held-back quality, as if she wants to say something but won't. As she is poised, suspended in that feeling, her hands move slowly into fists. With the fists comes a trembling in Jean's chin and a flush of color through her cheeks.*)

KATHLYN: What are you experiencing as you move now?

JEAN: Ummm, I feel—resentful, angry.

KATHLYN: How does that resentment want to communicate? Is there anything you want to say?

(*Jean's face and body undulate in a tense, push-pull dance between talking and holding back.*)

JEAN: I really want to say "Momma." (*She breaks into big, gulping cries. Her hands flutter around her face, then reach out just a few inches from her. Her sobbing continues for several minutes.*)

KATHLYN: Let your hands move where they're wanting to go.

(*Jean reaches out, then quickly pulls back into a tuck, then hesitantly reaches out again.*)

KATHLYN: What did you want to say to your mother?

JEAN: I want to say, "Momma, don't go!"

(*Jean takes Kathlyn's hands and continues to cry more deeply. After a moment she hugs Kathlyn tightly.*)

JEAN: I really wanted to say "I love you."

Kathlyn and Jean continued softly talking as the session concluded. Jean realized that her unspoken feelings were being unconsciously communicated through her picking habit. She saw that her deepest impulse was to reach out, to contact both her mother and the world. When that didn't work, she had turned the reaching impulse against herself, where it had grown over time into a picking habit. We gave her the homework assignment of noticing and following her desire to reach out.

The therapist can support the Moving Microscopic Truth both verbally and nonverbally by matching the client's experience. Here are some phrases that we have found useful:

- "Let yourself move your hands (or feet, or face) to match that sensation you're experiencing right now."
- "Let yourself paint that quality in the space in front of you."
- "Notice just the way it is right now. Move to match that."
- "Allow your hands to sculpt the shape of that feeling."
- "Let yourself open up to just what you're experiencing right now."
- "I notice your hands picking your sleeve. Be aware of what you're feeling as you do that."
- "Let that movement be as intense (big, sharp, full, etc.) as you feel inside."
- "Let your stomach speak directly through your hands."
- "Say yes to that feeling in your body."
- "Take on that character in your walk. Walk the way that feels inside."

In the Moving Microscopic Truth we often ask clients to move their hands first. Moving expressively is such a foreign language for most of us that clients sometimes interpret the request to "let your body move with that" as an invitation to shut down totally. But most clients feel safe and comfortable using their hands, which contact the world in thousands of ways every day. It is a new experience to use the hands creatively rather than functionally, but most clients quickly become interested in the discoveries they make.

The therapist can also utilize the Moving Microscopic Truth internally. He or she can practice the Loop of Awareness by matching the client's breathing and simply being present to the feeling and attitude flags the client presents. Trying on the client's posture internally often creates an emphatic feeling connection that gives the client permission to investigate little-known areas.

Helping a client to match breathing and moving is a powerful aspect of the Moving Microscopic Truth. We create gaps in our experience by holding our breath when we are moving, or by breathing and moving in disharmony. Frozen movement is usually accompanied by frozen breath. In other words, breathing flags and movement flags often occur together. We notice that when tension is present, the breath is usually absent. A sore back is usually a stiffly unbreathing back. A simple and effective direction in a movement session is "Let your breathing match your movement." Or "Let your movement match your breath." When breath and movement flow together congruently, energy is released for healing and transformation. When one client, Robin, mentioned a phone conversation with her sister, her chin began to tremble. She simultaneously inhaled sharply and swallowed. We invited her to let her breath match the feeling in her chin. She began trembling and exhaling more forcefully. Quickly she realized that she was angry at her sister and usually swallowed it rather than confront her.

MAGNIFICATION THROUGH MOVEMENT

The basic direction of Magnification Through Movement, the second Movement Technique, is "Do more of what you are doing." When a movement flag occurs in therapy, magnification is often the simplest and most effective intervention. It is especially powerful with movement flags because the small, idiosyncratic movements we all display are the tips of the icebergs of memory, incomplete interactions, and unfulfilled potential. For example, a shrug may magnify into throwing off an old burden. A squint may magnify into the memory of being disciplined by grandfather and retreating from his disapproving look. Magnification Through Movement allows the client to discover the personal meaning of gestures and habitual patterns. We find that it helps clients bring long-standing, unconscious patterns into the light of awareness. It is an engaging process that clients find intriguing and empowering. To really know that you are the best expert on your experience is an exhilarating moment for any of us who risk stepping beyond the control of our personas.

Magnification Through Movement can be used effectively with verbal phrases that are underscored by movements. A verbal flag can be magnified by asking the client to repeat it louder, or with more emphasis on the words that have an emotional charge. The intention here is to bring words and movement into relationship with each other. For example:

CLIENT (*slumps, with a sigh*): I feel this *flatness*.

THERAPIST: Say that again, making *flatness* louder and even more intense in your whole body.

CLIENT: I feel this FLATNESS. (*She collapses like a deflated balloon.*) Oh, I really squash myself when I'm scared.

The following are phrases we have used to invite magnification. As an awareness experiment at home, identify one of your own common gestures and move through the following directions.

- "Let yourself do ——— more."
- "Continue ——— and make it bigger."
- "Make that ——— even more intense."
- "Exaggerate your ——— and notice what else happens in your body."
- "Let more of your body express that ——— feeling."
- "Take that ——— all the way."
- "Breathe into that ——— feeling more deeply, and move with that ——— sensation."

Let's take a look at a therapy session where Magnification Through Movement was useful. At the beginning of the session, Janice was talking about her troubled relationship. She repeatedly brushed her hair off her forehead with her left hand, sighing and looking blank. We asked her to magnify the brushing movement and the intensity of the sigh. After she moved for a few minutes, she said, "I'm stuck. I should be able to get out of this." Her hand pressed her forehead as she said this, and her eyes scrunched toward her nose. We asked her to continue magnifying the pressing motion, and some tears began to flow as she said, "I need to feel that my efforts have a result—I wasn't noticed." Her hand shifted to rubbing her forehead at this point, which we encouraged. She rubbed for a new moments, with her whole face scrunching up now. Her left side began to shift and shrink, pulling back. When we asked Janice to magnify the way her left side wanted to move, she said, "My left side doesn't know. It's blank, hidden." We asked her to keep noticing her impulses to move as she breathed a little more deeply. Suddenly she noticed that her right side felt more vibrant and was moving completely differently from the way her left side was moving. We encouraged her to let each side move independently of the other, magnifying the impulse of each. She quickly noticed that her right side "wants to figure things out." This information had come spontaneously from her participation with her inner movement impulse. She was visibly surprised at the words that emerged.

As she continued to magnify the withdrawal of her left side and the control of her right, she began to have thoughts about her fundamental split in life. As she moved her left side with a floating, exploratory quality, she heard a critical voice saying, "There's not enough time for this nonsense!" When she moved her right side in measured, quick tones, she had an image of her father hunched over his newspaper, not even glancing at her journalism article. Her right side had developed a Protector persona that kept her focused on external tasks rather than her inner self and feelings. Her right side carried the belief that she wasn't creative and couldn't write—she'd always wanted to be a writer. Over time, she had stopped being present to the impulses from her creative left side.

We asked Janice to let the right and left sides communicate with each other, to just listen to the other's viewpoint. Now her exploration flowed into the dialogue of the Polarity Process, a technique that we'll discuss shortly. As she alternated between soft and angular arms, flowing and percussive feet, luxuriously slow and frantically hurried turns around the room, she began to experience more space inside her. She described a middle kind of space inside where she felt "more" and was "aware that conflict is not all there is." She had discovered that she was more than the polarity of hiding and confronting. Her face broke into a radiant smile, and she looked up clear-eyed for the first time in the session. Her spontaneous centered breathing let us know that Janice had integrated new information.

THE POLARITY PROCESS

The third Fundamental Movement Technique, the Polarity Process, builds a connection between the either-or experiences that many people have. One woman said, "Either I can't get out of bed in the morning, or I don't stop for a minute all day. I can't seem to find a middle ground." An older man reflected, "All my adult life I've been superresponsible. The only way I seem to let myself rest is to get sick." These polarities, which are often persona strategies, can be united in a new synthesis that fits the person's essence more accurately. The Polarity Process changes "either-or" to "both-and." Clients may explore a new middle ground, as explained in chapter 9, or extend their range into opposites that haven't been fully owned and experienced.

The directions for the Polarity Process are often very simple. Some questions we have used are:

- "What is the opposite of the sensation?"
- "What's the other side of this issue?"
- "If you didn't (strike out), what would happen?"
- "Let yourself become the (good boy), then the (bad boy), back and forth several times. See what happens as these two parts dialogue."
- "Let both those impulses move at the same time."

Polarities frequently occur as left/right body splits. People tend to store certain moods and qualities in one side of the body or the other, often with little or no communication through the middle. In one woman, her left side carried her collapsing, Give Up persona, while her right side stored her sharp, biting impulses. A man discovered that his lowered left side expressed his reluctance about entering into new experiences. Its basic refrain was "I don't want to. Do I have to?" In contrast, his right side, with its wider chest and higher shoulder, was a militant cheerleader. It blared, "You *have* to be strong, in control at all times."

In one of our recent trainings, a student, Jessie, was very stuck at a point in her session where she was lying down. Her facilitator asked her to allow her conflicting feelings to occur at the same time. She had noticed that the left side of her body felt very sad, while the right side was fidgety and restless. She had been paralyzed trying to just experience one or the other. Her persona had been built around doing everything perfectly and in a linear fashion, one thing at a time. Her facilitator said, "Let each side of you express what is really going on. Don't worry if they're not the same." Within a couple of minutes of both sad and fidgety moving at the same time, Jessie began writhing authentically and powerfully in snakelike arcs that mesmerized the whole training group. After several minutes of spontaneous flailing, Jessie sat up and said, "Oh, I can breathe into my middle for the first time. It feels delicious!"

She later connected her split experience to her internalization of her parents' opposing basic attitudes. Her mother's basic world view was, "Why bother?" Her father's, in contrast, was "Hey! Let's *do* something!" Jessie said she had often felt paralyzed in making a decision because she couldn't get directions from just one internal voice. She had embodied her parents' basic conflict and continued to act it out unconsciously until she worked through the Polarity Process and found a new middle ground.

The Polarity Process allows clients to own a fuller range of their experience. For example, if we imagine that effectiveness and rage are opposites, a continuum of possible feelings and sensations might look like this:

EFFECTIVE COPING STYMIED FRUSTRATED ANNOYED RESENTFUL ANGRY RAGING

$\longleftarrow\!\longrightarrow$

A client may shift from being effective to raging without any awareness of the stages in between or of the internal clues that a feeling of anger is building. Or the client may repeatedly respond from the resentful end of the continuum whenever something stressful occurs at work, with no access to effective action. In the Polarity Process we invite clients to own what is missing in the full range of their responses.

In most cases the Polarity Process evolves from one of the other Fundamental Movement Techniques, but sometimes it is the most effective first intervention. We were beginning our second session with Norm, a freelance journalist, when we noticed a polarized movement flag. As he was describing his issues, he held his head very straightforward, with rigid lines of tension in his neck. Whenever we asked him a question about his experience, he shifted his head to a three-quarter angle, glancing suspiciously out of the corners of his eyes. After several exchanges we realized that this rigid-suspicious oscillation was a pattern. We then asked Norm to consciously move from one position to the other, focusing on his sensations and other body feelings as he alternated between rigidly straightforward and three-quarter view. After several alternations, Norm's face flushed. We suspected this movement flag signaled some shift in the pattern.

US: What are you experiencing right now?
NORM: I just had a flash of anger. I realized that I'm angry with you.

This is the moment therapists get paid for, and we were excited that Norm could feel and express his anger.

US: Let yourself have your anger. Go ahead and breathe into it. Be with it.
(Norm breathes a little more deeply, clears his throat, and shrugs his shoulders and head. He looks as if he were shaking off a heavy burden.)
NORM: I can feel how I've had to be really watchful all my life. My father was always looking for an opportunity to catch me off guard. He'd kind of tap the side of my head if I wasn't paying attention. When you kept asking me to notice what I'm doing, pay attention, it sounded like my father. I thought you were going to get me, you know.

When a client feels safe enough to experience and express the truth, the Polarity Process can move very rapidly. The actual movement flag may be subtle and small. Mel was a delightful client who was willing to dive into his experience and was deeply committed to his full aliveness. In the following session he was talking about a feeling of "deadness" that kept surfacing, despite his successful business and family life. In that moment his face split into radically different expressions. His left eye and face looked as if they were melting, while his right eye brightened with a wary alertness. Mel continued simply describing his sensations until he realized his left side had become quite numb. The more numb the left side became, the more animated and intense his right side appeared. We could see the moment the light bulb came on. Mel looked startled, and a shiver moved through his body. Body enthusiasts will note his reference to vision, which was where the initial movement flag appeared.

MEL: I see. All this focus I put into having the largest store and the happiest kids has been my way of avoiding this core deadness inside. I've been running from just being with it. Whew!

US: Let yourself be with that deadness, Mel. Befriend that feeling.

MEL (sighing, then crying): Ooh, it's so deep. I am just so sad. I've been sad for so long.

Mel's mother had died suddenly when Mel was two. He had developed a go-get'em persona to outrun his intense grief and feelings of abandonment. Interestingly, his sadness had lodged to the left side of his body, where many clients experience their more feminine aspects. Over the years of denying and overriding his sadness, the left side of his body had become more and more numb until it radiated signals that Mel couldn't ignore. His willingness to be present to his true feelings eventually mended the gap and allowed him to access all the love and tenderness that his left side also stored.

The Fundamental Movement Techniques bridge the conscious and unconscious self. They bring patterns to awareness, allow clients to express creatively, and provide paths to freedom and choice. Through movement, each of us can rediscover our internal dancer and the unique dance we can bring to life. We have found that these three techniques are the first steps in beginning this life-dance.

THE COMMUNICATION PRINCIPLE: HOW TRUTH CAN HEAL

*Truth is a river that is always splitting up into arms that reunite.
Islanded between the arms, the inhabitants argue for a
lifetime as to which is the main river.*
—Cyril Connolly

A problem will persist until someone tells a fundamental level of truth about it. When the truth is expressed, there is room for the problem to transform in a healing direction. The truth is defined as that which cannot be argued about.

Over the years as our work deepened, we made a discovery that transformed our own lives as well as sped up our therapy with others. We learned how to discern the truth, and we learned how to harness the power of truth for rapid change.

BEGINNING THE INQUIRY INTO TRUTH

Each of us can recall as children trying to figure out what is true. We recall seeing people express what they thought was true, often heatedly, and seeing what destruction was wrought by distortions of the truth. We put a great deal of energy into trying to figure out whose version of truth was correct. Gay recalls that he was often the courier between his warring grandparents. They were both bright and loving people out of each other's

---

AN EXPERIMENT IN COMMUNICATION
YOU CAN PERFORM RIGHT NOW

Participants in our workshops find this experiment very valuable. You can do it with a partner or by yourself. For two minutes, say as many sentences as you possibly can that meet the following criterion: Each statement must be something that no one could argue with. They can be either simple or profound, from "I have a tie on" to "My father moved out of the house when I was five" to "My mouth is dry." Say as many things as you can that are so true that they cannot produce argument.

If you are like our workshop participants, you will find that communicating the truth for two minutes is harder than it sounds.

---

presence, but when they were in the same room with each other, it was as if they would undergo a personality transplant. They would become bitter, snide, and quarrelsome; characteristics that would dissipate the moment they were out of each other's presence. It was mystifying to Gay how they could change so quickly. His grandfather would communicate the "truth" to him that his grandmother was impossible to deal with. She would say something very similar about his grandfather. Gay could see that each of them was telling a distorted version of the truth based on their own agenda. As a young child Gay alternated between withdrawing from them and choosing sides. One day he would think his grandfather was the victim, while next day he was the persecutor and the grandmother was the victim. As Gay matured, he saw that both of them were hiding their true deeper feelings inside and engaging in their outer struggle partly to keep from having to confront these deeper feelings within themselves. Both of them were disappointed with the choices they had made, by the creative impulses they had stifled. Rather than confront these painful issues, they blamed each other.

Later, when we began to practice psychotherapy, we often found ourselves in similar situations. We would be working with a couple as they righteously espoused their positions, making each other wrong in the process. Sometimes a couple would tell us that they had been having the same argument for decades. For a long time we put energy into trying to decide who was right and who was wrong. Then we had a revelation: If a given communication continues to produce conflict, it means that there is a deeper level of truth that needs to be communicated. We call this the Communication Principle.

This principle is vitally important for all of us to understand. As human beings, we need to discover what the truth is under all our distortions of it. As therapists, we must listen to our clients with a laserlike empathy. Empathy is important and necessary: We all need someone to listen carefully to our stories. Without a hearing, people will not easily let go of their position. They have taken the position as a safety move to deal with fear, so they must feel some level of trust and comfort before they can let it go. But the skilled therapist will go beyond empathy. The therapist's job is to help people focus the laser beam of consciousness on themselves so that they will find the truth beneath their stories, the true safety beneath all positions. Without the Communication Principle, the unskilled therapist will often keep the person trapped in their story longer than necessary, because he or she does not trust and know intimately the ocean of consciousness that lies beneath the surface ripple of the story.

Here is where the Five Flags become crucial. They signal to the therapist when the client is ready to go to the next deeper level. The flags are unconscious signals from clients that they are ready to go beneath the story to the unarguable reality underneath the surface. If you try to get clients to give up their stories too soon, before they have developed trust in you and in the deeper source in themselves, you will get instant feedback. They will get upset or miss their next appointment, letting you know you need to use more empathy and less laser for a while.

OUR WORKING DEFINITION OF THE TRUTH

After decades of inquiry, we developed a working definition of the truth. By "working definition" we mean one that works. It works by stopping conflict inside people and between them. It works by restoring harmony where there has been trouble. The truth is what cannot be argued about. The truth, when it is revealed, resolves arguments both within ourselves and between ourselves and others. In the quotation from Cyril Connolly that opens this chapter, the inhabitants will argue until they all acknowledge the truth: "We are on an island." As long as they think their version of the truth is right, no progress will be made.

Tension in the body is caused by the body arguing with itself over the truth. The ulcer is the hole burned by not being whole. In clients' relationships, we discovered, when they told a type of truth that could not be argued about, their arguments stopped. In our own relationship, prior to our breakthrough to the truth, we would say things like "You're trying to control me!" and "You're going to leave me!" We thought we were expressing the truth when we said those things, but what we were really doing was perpetuating arguments. We began to get underneath the level of conflict and find ways to express the unarguable: "I'm afraid you'll leave me," "I'm scared of being engulfed." We developed a process definition of the truth: If it produced an argument, it was not a deep enough level of truth. We would keep communicating at deeper levels until all disagreement ceased.

One day Kathlyn was to speak about our work before a large, enthusiastic crowd in Santa Barbara. The man who introduced her made a racket behind her on the podium as she began to speak. He moved things about, straightening papers and dragging chairs, so completely oblivious to the noise that people in the front row were chuckling about his insensitivity. Kathlyn felt angry at the noise, but she was so caught up in beginning her talk that she didn't think to say anything about it. It lasted only twenty seconds or so, but when the man left the stage, she noticed that she had the beginnings of a sore throat. At the time she did not connect her unexpressed anger with her throat problem. In fact, in the back of her mind she chalked it up to southern California smog. After the lecture she mentioned her irritation about the man's noise to her mother, a resident of Santa Barbara who had attended. Instantly Kathlyn's sore throat went away, and only then did she see the connection between withholding her anger and the pain in her throat.

If we think of truth as a river, the withholding of truth is like a dam. We all know what happens when a river meets a dam: The dam lets go, the river backs up, or the river splits and heads in other directions. In our practice of therapy we see examples of all three possibilities. A couple comes in to work on their troubled relationship. Using the Five Flags, it becomes obvious to us that there are secrets between them. If there is one thing that several decades of practice have taught us, it is this: Secrets make people sick. So we ask, Where are the secrets here? If the couple is cooperative and we are sufficiently skilled, the dam will let go and the truth will be told. The river flows again. Sometimes secrets are revealed in a first session of therapy that go back to the earliest days of life. But the dam does not always let go easily. Often, people will continue to withhold the truth, even in the face of powerful feedback that this strategy is deadening to them. On many painful occasions we have seen people sacrifice a long marriage because they were afraid to reveal a truth. Withholding became more important to them than the relationship itself.

The truth does not always bring people together. We have worked with approximately fifteen hundred couples as of this writing. In about one-fifth of these relationships, the people chose to part ways after opening up to their deeper truths. There are many people who simply do not belong together; for them, facing the truth is a prelude to a separation. In the same way, many people have changed jobs after acknowledging some unarguable truth about their work. Sometimes people fall in love again with a job after acknowledging something they are angry or hurt about, but it often works the other way too. The truth is an energizer, much as opening the dam makes for a stronger flow. How this energy will be used cannot be predicted.

When the river backs up, problems occur. In addition to the psychological problems, many physical problems clear up when a fundamental level of truth is told. And these problems are not trivial; they include ulcers, cancer, colitis, and chronic headaches. Among the couples we have worked with, several hundred suffered from secrets when they first came to us. A common secret is that one person—and sometimes both—has consummated a sexual affair. When this secret is withheld, there is a predictable loss of vibrancy in the couple's relationship. It took us many years of working with people to find out that people are a lot more telepathic than they think they are. Frequently they sense intuitively that something is wrong. When they ask "What's wrong?" their partner says "Nothing," and then they start to feel crazy. We have worked with many people who lived in this state of secrets and feeling crazy for years, sacrificing health and creativity in the meanwhile. The person who is holding the secret has his or her own share of strain accumulating inside. It often leads to an illness, feeling tired, or setting up to get caught.

The dammed river of truth may split up into tributaries that run in random directions before they find their positive forward flow again. We observe this in people who seek outlets in trivial pursuits for the frantic energy of fragmentation, without probing into its source. Few things make human beings more frantic than withheld truth.

As we often tell our clients, there are only three rules for making life and relationships work: Feel your feelings, tell the truth, and keep your agreements.

Each of these three rules involves communicating the truth. When we do not allow ourselves to experience our feelings, we are lying to ourselves. When we do not tell others our truth, we are lying to them, even when we are not actually expressing something false. When we break an agreement, only the truth will fix it. Apologies are only a short-term fix and can be used as addictively as any drug. That is, apologies are often a substitute for looking at the truth. By making oneself wrong—"I'm sorry"—one often can escape inquiring into what is actually going on.

New research by psychologist James Pennebaker offers some fascinating insights into the healing power of truth. Now at Southern Methodist University in Dallas, Pennebaker has authored dozens of interesting research papers, most of which are summarized in a recent book called *Opening Up* (New York: William Morrow, 1990). In one classic experiment, he asked people to write about their most traumatic experience for fifteen minutes a day for four days. From a clinical perspective this would hardly seem enough to scratch the surface of such a trauma. But the results were profound. Following the writing process, people had measurably stronger immune systems, and their visits to medical doctors decreased over the next six months. Other studies have demonstrated the powerful effect of truth-telling (or truth-writing, in this case) on the health and physiology of human beings.

Another relevant area of Pennebaker's research is the lie-detector confession. Experienced polygraph operators know how to zero in on the "hot-spots" in a person's interview. If a suspected embezzler has a blip on the machine when he talks about his desk, for example, the operator may direct further questions to him about the contents of the desk. Under skilled interrogation, the person sometimes breaks down and confesses. At this point, two profoundly interesting things inevitably happen. The first is that the person's physiology resolves itself: blood pressure comes down, sweat production drops, and muscles relax. The second fact, of great interest to the therapist, is that the person is often extraordinarily grateful to the polygraph operator. Pennebaker mentions one case in which the subject was so grateful that he still sends the operator Christmas cards from prison. The irony here is remarkable: Outwardly, the subject's life changed drastically for the worse, but inwardly there was relief and relaxation. Outwardly, the polygraph operator was the agent of ruination, but inwardly the person feels enormous gratitude to the operator.

Let's explore two examples from our practice of how truth is a healing agent of the first order. We were working with Meg, a woman who had been sexually abused by her stepfather. We had helped her inquire into her feelings at the time of abuse (she had been eight years old) and the personas she had adopted to deal with the trauma. Her feelings were fear, hurt, and shame, plus a great deal of guilt because there was a part of her that had been sexually aroused by the incident. She had sealed these feelings off, burying them under a rigid, rule-oriented Tough Girl persona. Finally we invited her to describe exactly what happened, eliciting a detailed description of the incident. As she spoke during the hour, she began to feel better and better. She felt considerably less anxious, and a foggy sense of depression began to lift. Still, she did not seem complete. There was a worry line on her forehead and a tightness around her mouth. We join the session at this point:

US: Meg, you seemed unresolved, as if there's something more.
MEG: Yes, I don't know what, but I don't feel quite together yet.

US: Is there something more, something maybe you still need to feel or say?

MEG: Um, I don't know.

US: You look as if you feel sad, and the corners of your mouth are twitching. Let yourself feel that.

MEG *(begins to cry)*: God, I just had a horrible thought.

US: Something that feels awful to think about.

MEG *(sobbing hard)*: I—I never thought of this before, but there was part of me that liked it.

US: You liked your stepfather touching you?

MEG *(nods)*: Yeah.

US: Liked the feel of it? Or the attention?

MEG: Both. I mean, it felt good, just the body part of it. The rest of it felt awful, but I liked the feel of it. And yes, I liked the attention. I liked getting back at my mother, too. I was so mad at her for throwing my dad out and bringing this new man in, I think I liked getting revenge on her by getting him diverted to me. Then it got to feeling too awful and I made him stop, but there for a while I felt real powerful, having this big guy interested in me.

Moments such as this—when we face something squarely that we have previously shunned—are powerfully healing. Following this conversation, two health problems (yeast infections and a mild hearing loss) that had plagued Meg for years cleared up permanently. In addition, she found that the unresolved issues from this earlier time in her life had been getting in the way of intimacy in her current relationship. After expressing the truth of her early feelings, her wall against intimacy disappeared, bringing her much closer to her mate.

In couples therapy, we learned after much trial and error that when people express a deep enough level of truth, they stop arguing with each other. Over the years we have refined the process so that couples can move from arguing to a healing level of the truth in relatively few interactions.

An excerpt from a session will illustrate this process in action. Peter and Amy were in their second session, and in Peter's words, "We're more stuck than we were before we first came in." This news is not exactly what a therapist likes to hear, but at least Peter was being honest. The first twenty minutes of the session was spent in jabs and skirmishes by both partners. Finally we make a move that ultimately will lead toward resolution.

US: I hear, Amy, that you have a bunch of things you're upset at Peter about. (*Amy snorts in derision, as if to say "You don't know the half of it!"*) I also get how angry you are at Amy, Peter. You're both mad. And you both think you're right. And I want you to know that being right is going to keep you stuck. I'd like you to separate being angry from being right, just for a moment.

PETER: What do you mean?

US: Well, you're angry, right?

PETER: I guess.

US: Well, try it on.

PETER: Yeah, I'm angry.

US: Okay, Amy, do you have any problems with that?

AMY: With whether he's angry or not?

US: Right.

AMY: Nope—he's angry.

US: But notice, Peter, that if you said you're right, Amy wouldn't agree with that.

PETER: Okay, but—

US: Hold on a second. Just let yourself be angry. Tell Amy that you're angry.

PETER: I'm angry.

AMY (*releases a big sigh*): Okay. Me, too.

US: Notice how you are experiencing the anger in your body. What are you feeling?

AMY: Tight—constricted in my throat.

PETER: I'm all right.

US: Yes. What are your anger sensations?

PETER: Oh, yeah. I'm hot all over. Tense in my back, down in that place my back always hurts.

US: What else are you both feeling? Under the anger. Other places in your body.

AMY: Bone tired.

US: And you, Peter.

PETER: I'm afraid it's always going to be this way. Fighting all the time.

US: And way back in your life, where were you when you first felt afraid there would be fighting all the time?

PETER (surprised): Oh, Jesus. That was the story of my childhood.

AMY (suddenly having a "light bulb" go on): We're just replaying his mother and father's battles.

US: Looks like it.

There was more, of course, but here you see communication in action. Peter and Amy moved from arguing to healing the moment there was a breakthrough to the truth. When both of them gave up being right and simply tuned in to their anger, their argument stopped. The opportunity then opened up to both of them for a realization of deeper feelings and insight that they were replaying a past family pattern. In Peter and Amy's case the process went exceptionally smoothly. There are dozens of things that can derail the process and prevent it from coming to completion. That's why good therapists are those who can both think and feel on their feet.

LEARNING THE LANGUAGE OF TRUTH

Learning to speak the kind of truth that heals has been compared by many of our clients to learning a new language. In our view it is actually harder. In learning to speak Portuguese, for example, you are not confronted every moment by an overwhelming emotional pull to speak English. There is the force of habit, of course, but most people are less emotionally invested in speaking the old language then they are in protecting themselves from the truth. Most people would not feel compelled to stop in the middle of a Portuguese lesson to mount a righteous defense of English. But that is exactly what they do in learning to speak the language of truth.

There are many ways of defending against the truth. Listen in on a few minutes of a therapy session, in which a novice therapist slowly gets bamboozled by the client's strong repertoire of defenses.

THERAPIST: What are you feeling in your body right now?
CLIENT: It's all her fault. I'm not kidding. She just would not stop criticizing me. Finally I just walked out and spent the night at my brother's.
THERAPIST: It sounds like you're angry, real angry.
CLIENT: Oh, hell, no. I ought to be, but I'm not.
THERAPIST: So what are you feeling right now in your body?
CLIENT: Great, just fine. No problems. Now that I've got her off my back for a while, I feel just great.
THERAPIST: Um, well—
CLIENT: Sure, I know what you're looking for. You want me to cry or something, but I don't feel like it.
THERAPIST: Well, not exactly like that. I mean—
CLIENT: Now my headache is beginning to come back.

It all began with a fairly simple request. The question—"What are you feeling in your body?"—would not seem on the surface to deserve such a stonewall of resistance, denial, and hostility. Basically all it requires is for a person to feel and report. With an uncomplicated response like "I feel a tightness in my neck and a heavy pressure on my chest." But these two moves—tuning in to what is going on inside and reporting it out with nothing added—are extraordinarily difficult for many people. And the defenses against these simple moves are very seductive.

A more experienced therapist would have probably gone in one of two different directions. He or she could have simply listened to this highly agitated client for a while longer until he had blown off some steam. Then, a body-centered invitation to tune in to feelings in the body might have been more readily received. Or, the therapist might have mounted a more forceful confrontation when the client ignored the very first question: "I notice that when I invited you to tune in to what you were feeling, you started blaming your wife instead."

When people are asked to tell the truth, they tend to do one of two things. The first response would be to talk about *what actually is*. If we ask a man what he is feeling at a given moment and he says "I'm scared," this statement has a high likelihood of being true; at least, it is hard to argue with it. The second response would be to offer *concepts about what is*. His story may be factual or not, entertaining or not, helpful or not. But one thing is for sure: It can be argued about. If the man says, "I'm scared because my wife is threatening to leave me," he is now in the realm of concepts. His wife may say, "No, you're really afraid because your mother left you when you were three and this reminds you of it." Who is to say which story is more accurate? The one and only important thing to remember about concepts is that they are capable of producing disagreement. If the person says "I'm scared you're going to leave me" and it produces argument, find a deeper level truth that produces harmony.

A great deal of human misery stems from hopelessly confusing concepts with truth. In training therapists we sometimes show a videotape of ten-second interactions between two people. After running it once, we ask what happened. Nobody ever gives the correct answer, even though the interactions are simple and these are highly intelligent graduate students. Every single student responds with a different story, often wildly embellished with the student's projections. One of the segments we use simply shows two people sitting in chairs facing each other. One person asks "How are you feeling?" and the other responds with a shrug. Pretty basic. But the stories the students project upon the interaction are wonderfully imaginative. One student said, "He's deeply afraid that the counselor is going to abandon him." Guess who is afraid of being abandoned? Another student thought that "there is an underlying sexually seductive tone." Guess whose interactions have an underlying sexually seductive tone? Finally, after we run the segment a dozen or so times, asking "What happened?" after each, some brave soul sticks up his or her hand: "What happened was that the counselor said 'How are you feeling?' and the client shrugged."

There is always a stunned silence in the class, followed by a collective jaw-dropping realization as they get the point. Then, fiendishly, we always ask: "What makes you think it's a client and a counselor?" In fact, it is just two friends, one of whom is dressed a little better than the other, but no student to date has failed to project "client and counselor" onto them.

THE MAIN DEFENSES AGAINST SEEING
AND SAYING THE TRUTH

Every week in therapy we watch people struggle with seeing and saying the truth. Here are some of the most commonly encountered ways of avoiding dealing with what actually is.

- DENIAL. Some people simply refuse to look at the truth. They find more security in denial, looking the other way. They show all signs of being angry—clenched jaws and terse words—but when asked about it they say "No, there's nothing wrong."

- ILLUSION. Others pretend the truth is something other than what it is. They may chant affirmations or put on a happy face to pretend their anger doesn't exist. Their security comes through clinging to their illusion.

- DISTORTION. Still others distort the truth. Their "I'm angry" becomes "All you therapists are alike, always ganging up on me."

- EXECUTING THE MESSENGER. One of the most troublesome habits we see in therapy is when people get mad at the person who brings them the truth. Some clients even shun their families and friendship networks because everybody seemed bent on delivering the same message, something like "You're ruining your life by drinking too much."

- DRAMATIZATION. Some people dramatize the truth, seizing upon a small grain of reality and blowing it up into a soap opera or fuel for the gossip mill.

- NOT KNOWING HOW TO ACCESS TRUTH. Another difficult problem is that many people have had their truth defined for them by others for so long that they have no idea what is real and what is not. Someone else's concepts have been superimposed on the truth, and the two have become indistinguishable.

Most defenses can be divided into two broad categories: those that are directed toward other people, and those that take place inside ourselves. In the first category are projection, aggression, and passive aggression. In *projection* someone else is made wrong, blamed for the issue that really lies inside the person. *Aggression* may take the form of actively striking out at another person, through verbal, emotional, or physical intimidation. It may also be expressed through self-destructive behavior, like drinking or drugs, that inconveniences other people. *Passive aggression* attempts to control others through being unresponsive, as in the prototypical uncommunicative and sullen teenager.

The defenses that operate inside ourselves, accounting for much drained energy, include repression, dissociation, overintellectualizing, overcompensation, and displacement. If we repress our "I'm scared," we act as if it did not exist. *Repression* allows us to edit out uncomfortable feelings and thoughts, either forgetting that they existed in the past or acting as if they were not happening in the present. If we use *dissociation*, we might escape into fantasy or into a succession of new jobs and new relationships. For an illustration of *overintellectualizing*, consider this response, made by an engineer, to the question "What are you feeling right now?" He said: "Fundamentally there's a possibility that under some circumstances I have in the past felt some semblance of nervousness when confronted by situations where it is not easy nor perhaps possible to predict the outcome." In plainer language he was saying something like "I'm scared I'm losing control." In *overcompensation*, a person with anger and sexuality problems goes to the opposite extreme and joins a monastery where celibacy and silence are the rules. If we were to use the *displacement* defense, we would choose some other channel to express the energy missing from the true source. One couple avoided looking at the deep conflicts in their relationship for many years by putting all their energy into their children and horses.

A third category of defenses are sometimes referred to in professional literature as "mature," because these defenses are generally not troublesome to self or others. These defenses include altruistic sublimation, hope, suppression, and humor. In *altruistic sublimation*, we take our minds off our own issues by helping other people or by performing some kind of useful work. When we use *hope* as a defense, we deal with a difficult present by keeping our attention focused on future possibilities. A healthy person might use *suppression* to develop a stiff-upper-lip attitude. The biggest psychological best-seller of all time—M. Scott Peck's *The Road Less Traveled*—begins with the line, "Life is difficult." This attitude "Let's face the facts" is helpful to many people because it enables them to accept things as they are rather than to escape them. On the other hand, many if not most adults use *humor* to deal with difficult feelings and painful times. Anyone who has seen a Woody Allen movie has seen the past master of turning garden-variety adult angst into laughter.

As your awareness increases, however, you may want to notice whether your use of the mature defenses is costing you intimacy or productivity. Gay recalls that humor was a much-needed survival tool in his family, and he carried this over into a Class Clown persona in school. Although many people say his sense of humor is his most likable characteristic, he noticed as he moved into adulthood that he overused it in intimate situations where it blocked his ability to get close to others. Kathlyn would give him a compliment, for example, and he would make a self-deprecating joke about it. As he grew in maturity he had to take a closer look at his "mature" defenses. He discovered that some of them blocked authentic feelings, such as fear and hurt, that he needed to be straight about.

Defenses such as denial and distortion are found in healthy children up to about the time they go to elementary school, while the other-directed defenses such as illness, aggression, passive aggression, and projection often last in healthy young people nearly through high school. After midadolescence, however, all of these defenses begin to cost the person love and success. The inside-the-self defenses such as intellectualization and repression are quite commonly found even in successful adults, as are the "mature" defenses like humor and hope.

WHAT COMMUNICATING THE TRUTH LOOKS AND SOUNDS LIKE

We know we are hearing the truth when we hear statements of primary feeling, with no blame or justification implied.

There are several primary feelings that people get to in therapy when they reach the "bottom line": fear, anger, and sadness. There are other feelings, of course, such as shame, guilt, and excitement. But we have come to regard fear, anger, and sadness as the big three because they have the power to stop symptoms and arguments. In other words, when people express these basic feelings in straightforward ways, their problems often begin to clear up. It is important for people to express these feelings cleanly, however, and especially not in a way that blames or justifies. If a person says "I'm angry" or "I'm scared" with no blame or righteousness, the healing process is often accelerated. But if it comes out as "I'm angry because you've ruined my life" or "I'm scared because I've finally seen the extent to which you're a jerk," there is little likelihood that the problem will clear up. Here the person is confusing truth with concepts and using it as a blunt instrument. Similarly, others may communicate "I'm angry" with an unemotional flatness; this often means that there is deep feeling underneath that is being carefully controlled. Only clean, clear statements of feeling are ultimately healing.

We know we are hearing the truth when we hear statements about the quality of feeling.

Healing is accelerated when the person learns to distinguish qualities of feeling, and to be able to communicate those qualities. For example, "I'm feeling sad, and it feels like a heavy band across my chest."

Listen in on a session in which the quality of a feeling is being discussed.

THERAPIST: What does the anger feel like in your body?
CLIENT: Umm, it's hot, and I feel like—like I'm going to explode.
THERAPIST: Hot and like you're going to explode. Notice where you feel that sensation of being about to explode.
CLIENT: My chest. I'm afraid if I let myself get angry, I'm going to blow.
THERAPIST: And that reminds you of—
CLIENT: Oh, jeez, my father. When *he* exploded we all suffered.

We know we are hearing the truth when we hear statements about the exact nature of sensations.

Many people are amazed to discover that sensations change or disappear the moment they describe them exactly. Obviously there are limitations to this idea: If someone with stiletto heels is standing on your toe, describing your sensations won't change them much. But many sensations are signals, and when you get the message, the phone stops ringing. This finding was a happy surprise to us as therapists. People would come in with painful symptoms—perhaps a headache or stomachache—and we would invite them to describe the sensations as precisely as they could. Often, the symptom would disappear and a deeper level of the problem would emerge. Underneath the headache would be a hidden cache of anger; the stomachache might reveal frozen fear that had not been acknowledged.

One of the most remarkable discoveries that we have made in couples counseling is this: Underneath the battle there is often shared feeling. Two people may be stuck in polarized positions, each thinking the other wrong. But upon deeper inquiry, they often discover that they are both scared or sad or angry. We have seen this moment of realization many times, but is always deeply moving.

In our therapy work we often focus on sensations in the body as a place to begin the truthtelling. Few people mount an argument when the other person says "My neck is tight." Unarguability is but one of the values of focusing on sensations. An important part of healing takes place when the client is able to pinpoint the problem in time and space. A headache patient, for example, invariably is aimed toward healing when he or she is able to recognize that "I'm angry" is connected to "My shoulders and neck are tight and pulled back." Prior to this awareness, the source of the headache is thought to be "out there somewhere." Over the years, we have seen such clients attribute their headaches to bad weather, spouses, bosses, nutritional deficiencies, faulty appliances, and even, in one memorable case, the paper boy. These attributions did nothing to alleviate the symptoms, however, which disappeared only when the understanding dawned that the headaches were caused by their own reaction to the paper boy, not by any of his intrinsic properties.

GROUNDING AND MANIFESTATION: THE ART OF TURNING INSIGHT INTO ACTION

Give me a place to stand and I will move the world.
—Archimedes

Therapy ends with a beginning. The end-point of any effective therapy comes when people are able to stand their ground in the face of the roller-coaster that is life, to translate their learnings into real-life action, and to manifest what they truly want rather than what their past has programmed them to want. When therapy works, the client owns the principles needed to lead an effective life. Every therapy session is a microcosm of the entire process. Every session can, with skill on the part of the therapist, end with a sense of groundedness and a plan for action, or manifestation. These are the next two of the nine strategies in body-centered therapy.

GROUNDING

In our work, *grounding* as a strategy has several levels of meaning. The first is purely physical. When a therapy session ends, clients should feel they have their feet on the ground; they should feel connected to the earth. They should also feel grounded in their ability to make contact with other people and the world around them. This point is important because body-centered therapy often produces an altered state of consciousness—in colloquial terms, the person feels high. It is essential that he or she be grounded enough to get around in the physical world after the session: to walk, to drive, to honor stop signs and other rules of the material world. It is irresponsible for the therapist to let people leave the office without making sure they are processing information clearly on the physical level. Generally, this is accomplished by having the person stand up, converse, and make eye contact with the therapist until a satisfying sense of grounding has been attained.

Grounding has a second meaning for the therapist: Has the client connected the learnings from therapy to the real world? Unless insight is translated into action in the real world, it is usually of little ultimate value. Some clients, in fact, are insight addicts, using therapy as a substitute for living effectively in the real world. With these clients it is especially important to press for connecting the breakthroughs in therapy to new plans of action.

A third meaning of grounding is more metaphorical. Ultimately, grounding depends on a balance of experience and expression. Human beings become ungrounded when they either experience more than they have expressed, or express more than they have experienced. In daily life most of us experience much more than we can express. We are beset by overwhelming feelings that we cannot possibly express effectively at the time they are besetting us. The boss calls us in and yells at us about something we did or did not do. The appropriate response, from the point of view of our primitive nervous systems, would be, say, to lie down on the floor in his office and scream until we felt good again. While the boss chewed us out, fear, hurt, and anger probably assaulted our nervous systems. To restore our internal balance and harmony, it would be ideal to discharge all these pent-up feelings by expressing them. But our mind keeps us in check because it knows that to do so might jeopardize the next paycheck. So we creep out of the boss's office, awash in unexpressed feeling, a study in ungroundedness.

In the second form of ungroundedness, we express more than we experience. Several TV evangelists have recently come to grief through this

AN EXPERIMENT IN GROUNDING
YOU CAN DO NOW

Sometimes, if the person has gone on an extended excursion to the inner and outer realms, we use a technique we call the Fundamental Grounding Technique. In this technique you walk in place rapidly, crossing the midline of your body with your arms and legs. Specifically, you alternate touching your right hand to your left knee and your left hand to your right knee. This technique causes your brain to process information rapidly from right to left hemisphere, bringing about a state of integration. Most people feel a noticeable shift in positive feeling within ten or twenty seconds. We encourage you to look at figure 9 and take a few moments to experiment with this simple but powerful technique.

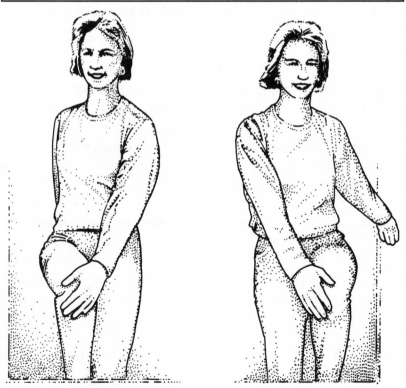

FIGURE 9. Fundamental Grounding Technique

form of ungroundedness. They place great emphasis on the expression of piety, the benefits of their path, and the need for financial support. Something is missing at the core, however; a lack of integrity gives their expression a hollow sound. Their lack of grounding in practicing what they preach catches up with them sooner or later, much to the glee of their detractors and competitors.

This is of great relevance to therapists, because it is absolutely essential that we practice what we preach. If we are not living up to the standards we advocate for our clients, we are setting ourselves up for trouble. By placing ourselves in a teaching role, we set ourselves up to overspend our reserves. In our own personal lives, we see over a thousand individual clients a year, and we work with thousands more in workshops. That is a lot of time to spend in a teaching role, and several times a year we find ourselves "all teached out." Then we take some space for ourselves to recharge our batteries. Many of our vacations are opportunities for us to practice a lot of breathing and moving and communicating with each other. Having such extended periods of time to practice what we preach allows us to get grounded again.

Both these forms of ungroundedness can be seen in poorly conducted therapy. In verbal therapy, people often talk too much and experience too little. They may talk about their feelings and their issues, but they do not actually touch into the feeling level where the issues live in their bodies. This type of therapy often leads to an overload of insight and a lack of real change in daily life. In body-centered therapy, it is often the other form of ungroundedness that the therapist must look out for. Often clients experience their feelings so deeply that they are not able to express them enough to catch up. Unless the therapist is careful, clients may leave the office still processing so much on their inner level that they are not in balance.

Listen in on a session that was particularly deep for the client. Liz began the session by discussing some sadness she was feeling about the breakup of a relationship. As we guided her into the sadness, she used her breathing to connect with it. This led to an even deeper sadness. Memories came up from the time in her childhood when her father died. She sobbed deeply for quite a while, curled up into a ball on a mat on the floor. When we join the session, the sobbing has subsided, but she is still engaged on the inner planes.

KATHLYN: Liz, it's time to start coming back. We've got about ten minutes left. How are you feeling?

LIZ: Ummm. (*Long pause.*)

KATHLYN: Still feeling a lot of sadness?

LIZ (*no reply for about twenty seconds*): Umm-hmm. No, I guess I don't really feel the sadness anymore. I feel really cleaned out. I'm just buzzing all over. (*In our work it is typical after a deep emotional release for the client to feel tingles and buzzes in the body. These are normal signs of a body awakening to more aliveness.*)

KATHLYN: As soon as you're feeling like it, come back up to a sitting position, then back to your feet.

(*Liz sits up, rests there a minute or so with her eyes closed, then opens her eyes and stands up gingerly.*)

KATHLYN: Great, stand your ground—get your feet firmly on the ground. Feel your feet, where they make contact with the earth.

LIZ: Whew, I'm really still flying!

KATHLYN: Enjoy the feeling. Let yourself feel it while you're making eye contact with me. Let yourself know that you can feel your feelings deeply and be in total contact with the world.

This last statement is really the summary of what grounding is all about. Most of us need to learn that we can both have our feelings and be in touch with others around us. Often life teaches us the opposite—that we can't have our feelings, and if we do, we need to keep them sealed privately inside ourselves.

MANIFESTATION

Manifestation is the act of turning dreams and desires into reality. Long before we begin to practice manifestation consciously, we have all had years of practice in turning vision into reality. Imagine that you are sitting at home reading a good book. An image appears in your mind of a warm brownie with vanilla ice cream melting over it. You try this image on in your body, and it generates a resounding internal "yum." You go to the kitchen and assemble the final product. Soon, you are savoring the crunchy, soft creamy-sweetness of the concoction. That is manifestation in action: You have turned an internal desire into measurable physical reality. It is wise to harness this skill and use it consciously, so that you can take advantage of this remarkable human capability.

AN EXPERIMENT IN MANIFESTATION YOU CAN PERFORM RIGHT NOW

Pause for a moment.

Ask yourself: What do I really want?

Consider three areas first: Relationship, Health, Material Goods.

Come up with one item you would like in each of those areas that you presently do not have.

Effective therapy results in people being able to generate what they want more rapidly and effectively. The Latin root of manifestation (*manifestus*) meant "plain, clear and evident." The current meaning, according to Webster's, reflects the original Latin: "clearly visible to the eye; not obscure or difficult to be seen or understood." This meaning, in fact, is crucial to manifestation as a strategy in body-centered therapy. We believe that the ultimate test of any method of change is physical reality. And like it or not, the ultimate test of physical reality is that it can be weighed, measured, or counted. Unless clients' inner changes show up in the real world of their daily lives, more work needs to be done.

THE SOURCE OF MANIFESTATION PROBLEMS

The underlying source of people's inability to manifest what they want is that early in life they lose touch with essence. They develop a split between who they really are and what they have to see, think, and do to survive. When they are out of touch with essence, they have no choice about what they want. Unless they are grounded in essence, their wants come from their programming: They want what they have been programmed to want. When people begin to touch into essence, their wants take on a higher quality and a greater power.

This process can be studied intensely during a fast. Several times we have benefited enormously from fasting for three days to a week. When a fast intensifies on the second and third days, it is common for us to experience all our toxic cravings: chocolate, ice cream, rich sauces. But as we regain touch with our innate body consciousness, there is a deepening that has requests of its own. It does not want chocolate or ice cream. It wants food that refines and enhances consciousness. After the toxic cravings clear out, we always find that at the deepest level we want pure water, juices, fruit, vegetables, and simple grains. It is a joy to come off the fast after a week and treat our bodies to these essence-level desires. On several occasions, on the day of breaking a fast, we have taken an hour or so to eat an apple.

The same process holds true for manifesting wants and needs. In touch with essence, human beings want things that are healthy and helpful to themselves and others. Operating from the level of persona, however, they often want things that create disharmony in their bodies as well as in their relationships.

BARRIERS TO MANIFESTATION

There are three barriers that we frequently encounter in therapy that prevent people from manifesting what they want. The first is that what they want is not *really* what they really want. Because of our unmet childhood needs and the traumas of life, many of us want things that are unattainable or that would be outright toxic to us. For example, one client had desperately wanted contact with her distant and aloof father when she was growing up. We met her at forty-one years of age, when her third marriage was falling apart. As she explored the reasons why she had not been able to manifest a workable relationship with a man, she found that she was a walking cauldron of old anger combined with an insatiable demand for contact. Her husbands could never satisfy her, because what she really wanted was something that she had missed a lifetime ago. She had not realized until her work with us that she had confused two realms in her mind: the realm of her relationship with her father and the realm of her relationships with her husbands.

We work with many people who crave something toxic, something that is harmful to them. Often this craving is so strong that they prefer it to love, connection, and attention from the real people in their lives. Cravings for drugs, tobacco, food, and alcohol are common, but there are other addictions as well. Some people, for example, abuse exercise, using it as a defense against recognizing relationship problems or against contacting their strong feelings. A major key to healing addictions is finding out what authentic need the addiction is covering up. Alcohol or drugs may be a cheap (but ultimately very costly) substitute for handling a specific feeling like fear or grief. What such addicted people really want is not alcohol or drugs but a way to deal with their feelings. A great deal of work is often required for them to find out what they really want, the things that would truly serve them.

A second barrier to manifestation is that most of us think in terms of what we do not want rather than in terms of what we want. In one experiment we conducted, we found that normal adults were able to name roughly three times as many things they *did not want* in a relationship as those they *did want*. In a second experiment, we simply asked several hundred adults, "What do you want in a close relationship?" Approximately half of them responded only with a list of things they did *not* want. Many of us are running away from something so quickly that we haven't figured out which way we really want to go.

A third barrier to manifestation is that people often cannot get past where they are because they have not loved themselves for being there. If you want to lose ten pounds, it is essential first to love yourself for weighing whatever you currently weigh. If you start out hating where you are or being afraid, your entire manifestation process is contaminated with hate and fear. Usually people find a way to sabotage manifestation projects that come from hate and fear.

The best place to start any process of change is from a space of love. "Love it just the way it is" is a phrase that we frequently use in counseling sessions. It may sound simple, but people find it extraordinarily difficult to give themselves the moment of self-love that it takes to begin the process. Listen in on a session in which Gay is introducing this concept to a client, Thomas. The problem Thomas brought in was overwhelming anxiety, which he wanted to be free of. We enter the session about halfway through.

GAY: Notice where you're feeling all that fear. Where do you feel it in your body?

THOMAS: Well, I feel it just about everywhere. All over.

GAY: Notice where the actual sensations are.

THOMAS: Hm, I feel them in my inner thighs. All the way up the front of my body. Real strong in my thighs, then up and down in my belly and chest. They stop about my throat.

GAY: Yes, that's good. Thomas, feel those feelings. Just be with them, let them be.

THOMAS: Unh-hnh.

GAY: And now just love them the way they are.

THOMAS: Love what?

GAY: The fear, the sensations.

THOMAS: I'm not sure . . .

GAY: It's different. You probably haven't done it before.

(Thomas laughs nervously.)

GAY: Here, try this out: Is there someone or something that you know you absolutely for sure love?

THOMAS (pause): I love my daughter.

GAY: Her name is—

THOMAS: Julie.

GAY: Okay, think of the feeling of love you have for Julie. (Thomas nods his head.) Now love your fear just the way you love Julie.

THOMAS: Ahh. *(He turns his attention inward.)* Hmm. That's hard, loving fear the way I love Julie. I mean, fear . . . *(He makes a face, as if disgusted.)*

GAY: That's it, though. You deserve the exact same love that you give to Julie. I'm sure Julie would want you to love yourself the same way you love her.

THOMAS: I never looked at it that way.

GAY: What happens to the fear sensations when you give 'em that Julie-love?

THOMAS: It's strange—they disappear.

GAY: Very good. That's because they need your love and attention. As soon as they get it, they quit bothering you.

Often, in fact, the only move that needs to be made is to love something just the way it is. In other words, the act of doing this seemingly simple thing produces a process of positive, organic change with no other effort on the client's part.

BASIC STEPS TO MANIFESTATION

We have found that the most important step in getting what you want in life is stating what you want in a positive way. If there is one principle of which we have to remind our clients (and ourselves) most often it is this one. Most people are so conditioned to think in terms of what they do not want that to turn it around is a very difficult task. In the following example you will see Kathlyn working hard to get a client to think positively. Susan has just recited a long list of complaints about her husband.

SUSAN: . . . but the thing that really griped me was that he just walked in the house and went down into the basement without even saying hi.

KATHLYN: In that situation, how would you like it to be?

SUSAN: It wouldn't matter. He's totally uninterested in anything but himself. He doesn't think of anybody else—me, the kids, anything.

KATHLYN: I can hear how angry you are. But, for example, when he walks in the door after work, what do you actually *want* him to do?

SUSAN: Well, I sure don't want him to just ignore me and go right downstairs, as if I don't exist.

KATHLYN: Right, but what I'm wondering is exactly how would you like it to be.

SUSAN: What good does it do to think about that?

KATHLYN: Well, try it out. Take a moment to put your energy into thinking up what you'd like rather than what you don't want. What do you want?

SUSAN (*long pause*): I don't know.

KATHLYN: Suppose you could dream it up any way you wanted. What would you like him to do?

SUSAN: I guess kiss me. Act interested in my day.

KATHLYN: So he would come in the door, kiss you, and ask you about your day.

SUSAN: Yeah. (*A slight smile sneaks onto her face, the first she's displayed in the session.*)

KATHLYN: How about asking him for that? Tell him how you'd like it to be.

SUSAN: I don't know if he would be open to that.

KATHLYN: What does that remind you of? Having a man not be willing to pay you attention?

SUSAN: Oh, well, with four girls my father never had enough time to spend with any of us. Or interest, really. He saw us as my mother's job. And he had his job to do—making enough money.

KATHLYN: So your background is wanting affection from him and not getting it.

SUSAN: My father or Richard?

KATHLYN: Probably both of them. Does that sound accurate to you?

SUSAN: I guess so.

KATHLYN: We're getting toward the end of our time. I wonder if you'd be willing to ask Richard for exactly what you want between now and next session. Treat it like an experiment. Just see what happens. Probably the worst is that it won't make a difference. But maybe it will. Okay?

SUSAN: Yeah, I'll do it.

Learning to turn our complaints into statements of what we want has transformed our own personal lives. It worked for things we complained about inside ourselves—like our weight and feelings we didn't like—and for complaints outside ourselves, like things in each of us that irritated the other. Both of us come from families of ardent pessimists. Some of the family slogans were "Yeah, sure, things are going great now, but just wait!" and "There's many a slip 'twixt the cup and the lip." The prevailing mood was that something bad was waiting around the next corner. An awesome ability to see the worst possibility in every situation was passed down to both of us with great care. In our twenties we both independently woke up to the very real possibility that our prevailing negative worldview was actually keeping good things from happening and causing bad things to proliferate. This realization will not be new to anyone who has strayed near the self-help section of a bookshop in the past twenty years, but it came as a profound insight to us back in the pre–self-help-book days of the sixties. Now when we "catch" ourselves issuing forth a stream of negative thoughts, we routinely turn those around into a positive statement of what we want. As a result we have learned to invite our clients to turn their complaints into positive statements, too.

A PLAN OF ACTION

One of the most important grounding and manifestation techniques we use is to get the client to develop and commit to a plan of action. The plan of action is designed to connect the client's learnings from the session to the postsession world of their daily life. Requesting action on the client's part turns his or her attention toward the outside world.

While writing this section, we decided to look over the past week's sessions for examples of action plans that clients had agreed to carry out. One client, a medical doctor, was so busy that he routinely overlooked self-nurturing activities like exercise, proper diet, and time for cultivation of an inner life. In his session we homed in on the source of his lack of self-nurturing, which stemmed from a childhood that had programmed him to serve others. To bring these insights into the real world, we asked him to form a plan of self-nurturing for the following week. He assigned a realistic time value to three areas: exercise, eating, and meditation. We sat with his calendar for a few minutes and helped him pencil in specific times for those three activities.

Another plan for action was developed in the final three or four minutes of a session with an ethereal twenty-eight-year-old woman who makes her living as an artist. Her plan was much less concrete. In the session we had explored several different personas that seemed to be interfering in her relationship with a new man in her life. Noting her interest in dreams, we invited her to begin a dream journal so that she could track the work of therapy in the metaphorical world of the night. We showed her some ways that other clients had found useful in recording and remembering dreams, and we invited her to bring her journal into the next session.

Another session was that of a chiropractor in her late thirties who had gained twenty pounds since the birth of her baby. She was panicked that the weight was not coming off as it had when her earlier child was born. This issue, coupled with some relationship problems, had brought her to our office. We noticed in her second session that when she talked about food and dieting, she held her breath. There was a connection for her (as there is for many people) between breathing and eating. Physiologically, the hypothalamus is involved in both feeling and eating; and as you will recall, breathing is often used to control feelings. We also noticed that even when she was not holding her breath, she did not take deep in-breaths. Her out-breath was deep, but her in-breath was shallow. Toward the end of the session, we spent a few minutes working directly on her breath, attempting to get a balance between in- and out-breaths. When we were able to get her breathing in balance, she immediately felt better, so we invited her to put this new awareness to work in a plan of action for her eating. She agreed to use her meals as "breathing meditations," focusing on breathing correctly while she was eating and also noticing when she held her breath during meals.

In still another session a couple was struggling with the issue of commit-ment in their relationship. Their pattern was one that therapists commonly see: She knew she wanted the relationship, but he wasn't sure he did. It was their first session, and after listening to them tell the history of the struggle, which went back over a year, we worked with them on getting under the surface to the feelings below. It turned out that each of them had been traumatized by rageful parents, but they had adapted to their parents' unpredictability in completely opposite ways. He had withdrawn and become distant, while she had grown needy and clingy. This drama was being played out over and over in their present relationship, though neither of them had ever realized the archaic underpinnings of the issue. At the end of the session we asked them for a plan of action to put this powerful insight into operation right away in the relationship. They came up with an idea that we certainly would not have thought of. They decided to monitor their main symptoms (his withdrawing and her clinging) on a daily basis. They would review these at the end of the day and discuss the feelings that were under the symptoms. They decided to give ten minutes to this activity at a certain time each evening. If they had not seen the symptoms, they would spend the ten minutes giving each other back rubs. If the discussion took place, they would give each other a shorter back rub afterward to reward themselves for dealing with the issue in a straightforward manner rather than using it as a mud-slinging exercise.

SUMMARY OF GROUNDING AND MANIFESTATION STRATEGIES

Whenever you feel ungrounded, you have a spectrum of options, from the simple to the subtle, from which to choose. On the simple end of the spectrum, you can do the Fundamental Grounding Technique until your body feels balanced and your mind is clear. We use this technique week in and week out in therapy, particularly after deep sessions, and we have never seen it fail to help the client feel more grounded. Another simple grounding technique is to tell the truth while making eye contact with someone. This balances you with regard to experiencing and expressing. Expressing the truth is very grounding in itself; doing so while looking into another person's eyes seems to bring about a rapid state of balance.

More complex is the manifestation technique of making a plan of action. A plan of action can be immediate, such as how to spend the rest of the day or how to translate a therapy learning into a phone call to a parent. Or it can be more comprehensive, such as plotting a new life direction. A plan of action grounds you because you acknowledge exactly where you are—"I'm feeling lonely"—then commit yourself to a specific way of getting what you want: "I want to make some new friends, so I'm going to go to the party tonight."

Figuring out what you want, as opposed to what you don't want, is both a grounding and a manifestation technique. It grounds you because you have to look deeply inside yourself to get the information. It has manifestation power because the positive images of our desires have the greatest likelihood of producing positive results. If you know you want a red car, you are probably more likely to be satisfied than if you only know that you do not want a purple one.

One of the reasons body-centered therapy is so powerful is that its every technique tends to deepen contact with the inner self and with essence. It produces rapid change even as it simultaneously grounds us. Many types of therapy produce rapid change, but that is not enough. What is ultimately important is growing with balance, so that the ordinary processes of daily life are not disrupted.

Loving ourselves exactly where we are is ultimately the most powerful way of grounding ourselves and opening the space for creative manifestation to occur. We have seen hundreds of clients who were ungrounded because of a deep emotion they were feeling. Regardless of how agitated or spacy they were, when they presenced the feelings, such as fear, and loved themselves for feeling it, the feeling disappeared. Body-centered techniques operate from this principle: The rapid path to somewhere else begins with being and loving right where you are. Deeply experiencing ourselves grounds us, opening the possibility for manifesting what we most want.

LOVE AND RESPONSIBILITY: THE ALPHA AND OMEGA STRATEGIES OF MIND/BODY HEALING

In the last chapter we touched on the concepts of love and responsibility, both of which are essential to effective living. Now it is time to take a more detailed look at how these concepts are used in self-change. In this chapter we will discuss the two final strategies of body-centered therapy, love and responsibility, then demonstrate how the body-centered therapist puts them into action. Love and responsibility belong together in our conceptual framework because they are often the two things that clients most need in order to be happy. As therapists, we have seen a poor grasp of these strategies contribute to a great deal of unhappiness. By the same token, we have been blessed to be present when thousands of people made shifts in love and responsibility, resulting in powerful changes in their life circumstances.

HOW LOVE AND RESPONSIBILITY WORK

At its best, human action begins in love and culminates in responsibility. Most of us would like our actions to be conceived in love and carried to

AN EXPERIMENT IN LOVE AND RESPONSIBILITY THAT YOU CAN DO NOW

Think of something you have struggled with in yourself—perhaps it's your weight or your fear of speaking in public. Let your mind settle on this one thing so that you are clear about what it is. Now think of someone or something that you know for sure that you love. Perhaps it's a certain loved one or an action like riding your bike in the country on a sunny day. The only requirement is that you have reliably felt love in the presence of this person or thing. Let yourself feel that love in your body and mind right now. Now take a leap: Love that thing you have struggled with just as you love the person or thing that you know for sure you love. You may say, "But I hate it." All right, then love yourself for hating. Then love it. Greet it with loving acceptance.

Now for the responsibility part of the experiment. Acknowledge yourself as the source and creator of the problem you have been focusing on. Let's say you are focusing on your weight. Even if you come from thirteen generations of overweight ancestors, you can choose to take responsibility for your weight now. Responsibility begins the moment you take it. You don't have to wait for anything to happen before you take responsibility.

completion in ways that have integrity. Body-centered therapy uses love and responsibility in a way that renders these often-elusive ideals practical and relevant to every moment of life.

First, let's look carefully at what love and responsibility actually are. We have found by practical experience that a major barrier for most people is lack of a good working definition of love and responsibility. When they are defined in a new and more practical way, they can begin to serve us better in the change process.

What Is Love?

Philosophers have argued about love for centuries, but for people who wish to change their lives, this is the best definition we have found: *Love is the action of being happy in the same space as someone or something else.* If you can be happy in the presence of your fear, your fear will not bother you, because it rests in love. This definition of love reminds us that love is an action, and that it is something that we can learn to steer. It is essential to view love this way because there is a great deal of programming that would have us believe that love is capricious and outside ourselves. If we want to harness the power of love for self-change, we have to take responsibility for carrying the source of it within us.

Love involves being happy with no as well as yes. In our own lives as well as in our clients', we have found that love is made up of equal parts of acceptance and limits. It is essential to feel good about both. If you are good at saying yes but not at saying no, you will suffer from many boundary problems. People will take advantage of you, you will enable their bad habits, and you will end up alienating the very people you so much want to love you. On the other hand, many people live in a state of "no" inside themselves, rejecting and denigrating themselves and others, so that they do not get to taste the sweet feeling of acceptance that comes from taking life as it is.

Love is about happiness within ourselves and a willingness to go to great lengths to support other people's quests for happiness. Our definition implies that *we always have the power to be happy if we so choose*, even though we may not be able to predict or control the situations that we find ourselves in. This insight gives us a great deal of power to become loving in situations that may have triggered less pleasant emotions in the past. In therapy, our definition of love has great practical value. We have watched people's lives change dramatically when they learned to love and be happy in situations that they greeted with contraction, denial, and distaste in the past.

Our client Gina experienced such a transformation. Gina had suffered for years from a number of paralyzing fears that had reduced her freedom.

She had stopped leaving her house unaccompanied, operating a motor vehicle, going to restaurants even with her husband, and shopping by herself. She had experienced panic attacks in her car and in a shopping mall, both of which had resulted in the police having to bring her home. Her case was interesting to us because her treatment took only one session, and we never learned why she was afraid of all those things. Sometimes the therapist's curiosity goes unsatisfied if the client gets better quickly. (We are always more than happy to forgo our curiosity on these occasions.) Gina's treatment consisted of making one major shift in her consciousness.

After her husband brought her to the office and departed, we talked with Gina for a while to get acquainted. Then we invited her to identify the sensations she felt, using the presencing and communication techniques we have described. She identified dizziness, sweeping tingly sensations up and down her body, crushing pressure on her rib cage, and a strong desire to vomit. When she had described exactly what her fear sensations felt like, we invited her to love and be happy with all those sensations. Her jaw dropped, and she spun off a flurry of reasons why she could never do this in a million years. After all, the fears had ruined her life—and now we were asking her to love and be happy with them! We pointed out that hating her fears had done nothing for her, so why not try something completely different? There was a long pause, during which we could almost see the mental cogs turning. Suddenly Gina howled with laughter. Tears streamed down her face as she laughed. "You mean, just be happy with my fears? Just love them? Not try to make them go away?" Yes, we replied.

We spent the rest of the session fine-tuning this new idea in Gina's mind and body. We role-played several scenes where her fears were likely to come up. Now she had two options: Get scared and flee from the fear, or get scared and be happy with it. Twice we invited her to go out onto the street by herself to practice. Sure enough, the fear came up each time, but each time she took the action of loving and being happy with it instead of resisting it and running from it. Then we sent Gina on her way with the homework assignment of loving and being happy with her fear whenever she felt it. A followup call a week later revealed that this new strategy had enabled her to shop, drive, eat in public, and all the other things she had resisted in the past. Whenever the fear presented itself, she felt it and loved it. A second followup six months later resulted in even better news: Most of Gina's fears had dissolved. In fact, when we asked her about one of the fears she had complained about in the first session—dining in public—she couldn't remember ever having experienced it!

This remarkable story is the only one-session treatment of such a paralyzing symptom that we can remember. If we could produce this type of result reliably, it would be even harder than it already is to find a parking place in our neighborhood!

Love—the action of being happy in the same space as something else—has a great deal of power. So does responsibility. Many of us are hampered with a poor understanding of responsibility, as we are with love.

WHAT IS RESPONSIBILITY?

Responsibility is being fully accountable for your actions. It is also the act of claiming that you are the source for whatever is occurring. When we are responsible, we are accountable for what we do and we identify with the cause of it. True responsibility, then, connects us to the heart of the universe because with it we are allying ourselves with the source of creation. This definition of responsibility is distinct from concepts like fault, blame, and burden, which are frequently confused with it. Both of these actions—love and responsibility—have so much power to transform us that many of us will go to the ends of the earth to avoid them.

Our friend Paul traveled the globe in search of the perfect guru. He had recently returned from a long sojourn in India, Nepal, and Tibet. While he was there, he had been blessed by Sai Baba, danced with dervishes, and chanted with the Dalai Lama, and he had had numerous other spiritual adventures. But he was still unsatisfied. When we explored the issues of love and responsibility with him, he discovered that his search had been motivated by a quest for love. He wanted to experience a type of pure love from a guru, and he felt that if he experienced it, he would be free. We pointed out to him the main problem with this: If we believe the source of love is outside ourselves, we are doomed. We are locked into a consumer rather than a producer mode. The only satisfaction comes from the act of acknowledging the source of love inside ourselves. Thinking you need love from somewhere else presumes you don't have it.

Paul had projected divinity and the source of love onto others, and he was waiting to get it from them. But the main point of his journey seemed obvious to us: It was time for him to claim for himself the source of love and holiness. This problem is closely related to responsibility. At some point in our spiritual quest, if it is to be successful, we must realize that we are one with the source. We must align ourselves with the source of divinity, own it completely, and begin acting from the awareness that we are made of the same stuff as the universe. This act has the power to change all of life. Our friend Paul had never made this move: He wanted someone to bestow oneness on him. This was a fatal flaw in his way of thinking. When we do not claim responsibility for the source of divinity, we hold it at arm's length, thus splitting ourselves in two. It's us against the universe, and as Frank Zappa once said, "In the fight between you and the world, back the world."

Paul resolved both these problems at once. We invited him to presence all the places in his body where he felt dissatisfied and unlovable. Then we asked him to think of someone or something he absolutely knew he loved. In other words, we asked him to presence the feeling of love in his body. Then we assisted him in experiencing his own love toward those places in himself that he felt were unlovable. We continued with this process until he felt thoroughly lovable. He experienced a perceptible shift—a relaxation of his facial muscles—the moment he really began to love himself. There was no further need for searching for love; he could give it to himself. He could enjoy being with gurus or not, but it would make no difference in whether he was lovable.

We also invited him to take responsibility for being the source of divinity in the universe. We asked him to close his eyes and get a picture in his mind of the holiest thing he could think of. He visualized the smile of the Dalai Lama. We asked him to feel in his body how this image felt. He experienced a warm sense of open space in his chest. Then we pointed out that it was the innate, natural holiness in himself that enabled him to perceive holiness in the Dalai Lama. To a hungry shark, the Dalai Lama might look simply like protein; it would not see the holiness. To a mosquito the Dalai Lama might look like an expanse of tasty skin. We quoted an old Sufi saying: "When a pickpocket sees a saint, all he sees is pockets." We were trying to get Paul to recognize that only his own divinity could recognize divinity outside himself. A slow smile spread over his face as he began to claim his own natural holiness. By making this move, he could become a producer and a distributor rather than a consumer. In short, he took full responsibility for being a source in the areas of love and divinity.

BARRIERS TO LOVE

There are several kinds of resistances or barriers that people maintain that keep them from loving themselves. Some of these barriers are in the mental realm, in the beliefs and opinions about ourselves and the world that most of us consider to be real. Other barriers are in the realm of the emotions—the feelings that stop us from acting effectively. As body-centered therapists, we have found resistances that have been overlooked by cognitive therapists: resistances that are found in the body, in the form of tension, dead zones, and energy blocks. Often all three types of barriers occur at the same time with regard to a specific issue. A person may have had an emotional experience of discouragement or failure at age five. Out of this experience the person may have developed a belief that "nothing I do will ever work." This belief may be accompanied by feelings like sadness, anger, and fear. It may be locked into place by tight shoulders, a rigid belly, and a tendency toward headaches. When a therapist invites the person to inquire into this issue, barriers from each of these areas—mental, emotional, physical—may need to be addressed.

MENTAL BARRIERS

Let us consider the mental level first. Human beings have an astonishing ability to construct logical supports for even the most ridiculous beliefs.

One of our first learnings as therapists was that our clients' beliefs—even their most distorted ones—were supported by a coherent logical structure. In other words, even their most unhappy-making beliefs made perfect sense to them. They were so in the grip of these sincere delusions that they had never questioned them. When we came along and questioned beliefs that had been making them miserable for years, they mounted arguments in defense of them! We learned to ask about clients' beliefs in a certain way, so that we could unearth the structure that supported the delusion. We would ask: What are you afraid would happen if you didn't believe————? If a client believed she was doomed always to be fat and depressed, we would ask her what she was afraid would happen if she were not fat and depressed. Frequently we would find that such beliefs are anchored in a fear of something cataclysmic, even of death. At an early age, in a state of absolute vulnerability, the person would make an unconscious decision to be fat and depressed. The belief had become associated with survival—with life itself—so that to let it go would be tantamount to letting go of life itself.

Sometimes a belief is anchored to approval. In other words, the person feels that if he let go of the belief, it would cost him the approval of someone important. Other beliefs are anchored to control. We fear that if we let the belief go, we will lose control. One man had difficulty letting go of his belief that he should stifle his sexual urges. When we invited him to love his sexuality rather than numbing it, he initially could not accept the possibility that his sexuality was lovable. He felt that if he did not keep it hidden, he would run wild, becoming "like a monkey in the jungle," in his words.

Confusion is one of the main types of mental resistance that people display when we ask them to love themselves. Sometimes their confusion is about what love feels like. They have gotten love mixed up with other feelings like acceptance, concern, and worry. Many of us grew up in circumstances where people's love for us was blended in a puree of other feelings. Later, when we began to love ourselves, we were not sure how to give ourselves pure love.

Another type of confusion comes when we are not sure we have ever felt love. Dozens of times in therapy we have invited people to love themselves, only to have them burst into tears and say something like, "I don't know if I've ever felt love." Sometimes this turns out to be true, and sometimes not.

On deeper inquiry, many of them find that they have blocked out love that was actually there, because they were resisting some other feeling like anger, shame, or sadness. But even after considerable work on themselves, some people find that they actually do not know what love feels like. In these cases they simply have to make it up for themselves. They have to design a feeling inside themselves that they can call love.

EMOTIONAL BARRIERS

There are many emotional barriers to love. Because the people who love us are so often in the grip of some conflicting emotion, we receive their love along with a barrage of other feelings. Thousands of people have sorted out love from fear, anger, shame, unwantedness, guilt, and sadness in therapy. The quickest way to discover your emotional barriers to love is to love yourself, and notice what feelings bubble to the surface immediately thereafter. If your self-love has no emotional barriers, you will simply feel loving toward yourself. If blocks are there, feelings may come to the surface that you have used to resist love in the past.

BODY BARRIERS

Body barriers to love are harder to discover without outside help. People who are tense, for example, usually do not think they are. They have lived with tension for so long, they think that is the way life is. Usually it is only when symptoms appear that they begin to inquire into their tension. One of our clients, Barbara, had a collapsed chest that gave her a discouraged look; she also had a tendency toward respiratory problems. She had never connected her body posture and her respiratory symptoms until she picked up a book on mind/body integration in the library one day. As we worked with her to help her clear up this issue, she showed us a series of family photos. Her mother had had exactly the same posture! As a little girl, Barbara had not had the posture, but by the seventh grade she had adopted it. Now, at midlife herself, she was still holding on to it. As she released the tension in her chest, however, she came up out of herself and found that she could stand up straight. She actually gained an inch and a half in height. Her respiratory problems also cleared up over the space of about six months.

Simply put, people are usually too tight or too loose—just right is hard to come by. Both excess tension and slackness result in body amnesia. People forget how to feel in given areas of their bodies, but years of body amnesia result in the loss of life's meaning and richness. One of our clients wrote us a year after finishing therapy: "When I first came in, I felt nothing. I didn't exactly feel bad—I just felt nothing. It took us months just to get past all the numbness and years of not paying attention to my inner self. Then I uncovered all the bad feelings I had hidden away. For a while I wondered whether I had done the right thing. Wouldn't it have been better to stay numb? But there was another part of me that wasn't ever going to be happy unless I could recover my potential.

"I remember the day my body woke up. I was sitting at home watching TV while I was doing the breathing activity you had given me. Suddenly it was as if a veil were lifted, and I could feel the inside of my body again! I could feel where I was scared and where I was angry and where I was holding on to hurt. Underneath all my emotions there was this new world of body energy to feel. It was like the first time I snorkeled and discovered the sea-world I'd never known about. It's amazing to me that one moment I was one kind of person, then the next moment I felt completely different. I would not have believed that it was possible to change that quickly."

BARRIERS TO RESPONSIBILITY

People go to great lengths to avoid responsibility—look at our bulging prisons. Some time ago, California officials conducted a survey in which they asked thousands of prisoners, "Why are you in prison?" Only a tiny percentage of the prisoners said it had anything to do with them or their actions. Most of them blamed their lawyers, unhappy childhoods, and societal problems. Many of them blamed wives and children who had betrayed them by turning them in. This is incontrovertible evidence that people will avoid the power of personal responsibility right up until they are caged.

When we first began to work as therapists in the late 1960s, Gay worked for a treatment facility for juvenile delinquents, and Kathlyn worked for a mental health center. In these centers we saw people who took no responsibility for their lives, to such an extent that society had to step in and do it for them. Some actually wanted to take responsibility but did not know how or had been so wounded that they could not muster the energy to do so. These people were great challenges to work with, but they provided endless satisfaction. When they moved into greater power over their lives, it was a joy to behold. Other people, however, had no interest in taking responsibility. They were convinced—some terminally, it seemed—that their problems were somebody else's fault, and that their job was to get even with those who had wronged them. No one in the mental health field has demonstrated any reliable method of treating such clients. The penal system does not have much luck with them, either, as current recidivism rates run in excess of 80 percent.

Nowadays, since we are both in private practice, we seldom see the latter type of client. Most of our clients are very much interested, at least on the conscious level, in taking responsibility for their lives. Either they just don't know how, or they have unconscious resistances to it that make it harder for them to learn. Their major barrier to taking responsibility is that they do not know what true responsibility is. From their early childhood, their concept of responsibility has been contaminated by blame, shame, and fault-finding. By adulthood, the issue of responsibility has become so corrupted for them that it is painful to consider. A lot of our work with these people goes into straightening out their notion of what responsibility actually is.

UNFAMILIAR MENTAL LEAPS

True responsibility involves making mental leaps that most of us are unaccustomed to making. The first leap is simply to see connections between events. For example, you may notice that you get a sore throat before you give a speech. If you are taking no responsibility, you may look outside yourself for the culprit—perhaps an offending microbe. Practically everyone you meet will be happy to give you their opinion of this subject: "There's a lot of it going around!" But how many of your friends will point out the connection to you by asking, "What is it about you or what's happening in your life that contributed to the sore throat?" A responsible answer might be: "I didn't want to give the speech, and my unconscious must have picked up the message before I did and made me sick." But if you are like some of our clients, you will get mad at the people who ask you such a question. People have been known to fire friends who dared imply that they had some responsibility for the events of their lives. Some go further to develop support networks of friends who reward them for taking no responsibility.

A second unfamiliar mental leap is to notice a connection between events without adding any excess emotional baggage to it. The suggestion that their emotions might have something to do with their sore throat, for example, immediately makes some people feel guilty. There is something about admitting responsibility that triggers guilt in some people, as if they should have known better. Others get hostile when asked to look at the connections between events in their lives. In our counseling classes at the University of Colorado, we teach a module on helping people take responsibility for their illnesses. Even among the counselors, who would presumably be more committed than most to this enterprise, this inquiry sometimes triggers outrage, denial, and shame. Typically, about a third of the graduate students react with hostility and irritation when we ask them what was going on just before their last few illnesses. Another third react with shame or guilt. The remaining third get excited by the powerful possibilities for change that the inquiry opens up. Because they have a good working definition of responsibility, they can experience excitement in a situation that brings forth only fear and anger in the others.

One time in the mid-1970s, when our understanding of responsibility was only just beginning to take shape, we happened to be waiting in the wings to give a talk at a conference. We struck up a conversation with a pleasant, soft-spoken man who had been on the dais earlier that morning. It was Carl Simonton, who would later gain fame as a cancer physician who worked with people's attitudes as part of their treatment. He mentioned something that we found quite amazing. He said that half his patients had quit his program when they found out that they would have to play some role in their own healing. Given that all of them had terminal diagnoses, one would think that they would be highly motivated. Not so—half would presumably rather die than take responsibility.

FOCUS ON THE PAST

Another major kind of barrier to taking responsibility is that many of us are still stuck in replaying situations in which we were in fact victimized decades in the past. When the opportunity arises for us to take responsibility for something in the present, our minds and bodies immediately return to the past, to when we were authentically victims. Our grown-up consciousness recedes, and trapped in the mind and body of a child—often an infant or even a fetus—we are unable to seize the reins of power over our present lives.

People who are anchored to past incidents and traumas find it hard if not impossible to take responsibility in the present. When we bring this issue up at seminars, several hands usually shoot up in the audience. The question the person asks is roughly the same, whether we are in Auckland, Oshkosh, or Austria: "Do you mean to say that a three-year-old is responsible for her daddy coming home drunk and beating her up?" Or: "Do you mean to say that the Jews were responsible for being persecuted by the Nazis?" Of course not, we reply. We are saying just the opposite. There was very likely a time when the person was *authentically* victimized, powerless in the face of the persecutor. Because that experience was not completed emotionally and psychologically, a pattern was set in place that may be affecting how their lives and relationships go now.

But here is the clincher: Regardless of the past, it is essential for us to take responsibility now. Now is the only time that matters. There is no need to explore how we might have been responsible at three years old or even yesterday. We should do this only if it will not delay our taking responsibility today. Some people get bogged down in trying to figure out how they might have created situations far in the past, an inquiry that consumes energy that they could be using for taking responsibility now. One of the worst aspects of New Age thinking is that normally bright people get fascinated by concepts like reincarnation—in their attempt to explain why they repeat certain patterns—rather than throwing their whole energy into transforming their patterns right now. In fact, unless all energy is focused on the now, the responsibility-taking enterprise usually fails.

People construct their view of the world in large part through the language they use. Some people keep themselves locked into impoverished roles in the world through the choice of language that does not claim responsibility. Many of them say they "have to" run an errand, or that so-and-so "made" them angry. "Gotta run," they say. "No time right now." In our body-centered therapy sessions, we have heard thousands of clients complain of "stress," as if stress were an entity outside themselves that was applying pressure to them. In fact, people do not "have to" do much of anything; nobody can "make" us angry, and there is no such thing as stress in our bodies. Certainly there is tension, and this tension is our response to certain external events. But only by taking full responsibility for our responses can we do something effective about that tension. Once we identify the trigger—perhaps a ringing telephone—and the response—further tightening of overburdened shoulders—we can turn off the phone or learn to relax our shoulders.

Responsibility often comes into our lives with pain or threat attached. "Who's responsible for this mess?" the angry parent demands, and the child who volunteers is punished. Because responsibility is linked with pain early in our lives, we often resist taking responsibility as adults. Responsibility becomes a burden instead of what it could be—a celebration.

After searching for many years, we have come to an understanding of responsibility that gives maximum empowerment to the individual. We believe that everyone has the power and freedom to change how they perceive the world. We believe that everyone can change the way they feel about anything. All of us come equipped with an ability to sense our connection to infinite being, and to identify with the source of the issues that face us. Only by claiming our connection with the source of the problems in our lives can we claim connection to the power and glory that awaits us if we take full responsibility. Very few of us have the self-esteem necessary to embrace this level of responsibility. We shrink from claiming contact with the source, thinking that we are made from some other substance than the rest of the universe. By separating ourselves, we dwindle to a shadow of our former selves. Then our existence becomes impoverished, life a shadow show.

Think of the alternative, though. What if we could stand up and claim our connection with all the universe? What if we could always stand at the ready to look for our part in our problems instead of seeing the source outside ourselves? These seemingly simple moves would transform every moment of life. As therapists, we have seen the results of such shifts in perception a thousand times or more. When people own their connection to the source, they light up with a type of aliveness that is not often seen in the real world. Taking this level of responsibility gives us a fresh burst of energy that we can devote to making the changes we need to make in life.

To understand how a new definition of responsibility might look, consider this moment from one of our relationship workshops, where we do a lot of work with participants on how to take a "clean" form of responsibility that is not contaminated by burden or blame. When the participants reassembled after a break, Gay stood in front of them and held a dollar bill aloft. With a flourish he attached it to a clothespin that Kathlyn was holding up. "Who is responsible for this dollar bill being here?" he asked. Obviously you are, said the crowd. "Why?" he asked. One person after another took the microphone and gave a version of the same basic point: Gay is responsible because he put it there. We wrote this definition of responsibility on the board.

The game continued. We asked the question "Who's responsible?" awhile longer. Finally someone said that Kathlyn was responsible, because the clothespin would not be there if it weren't for her. After much confusion, everybody got this definition of responsibility: that we can be responsible even if we are a bystander-participant.

But we did not stop there. We continued to ask "Who's responsible?" Some people got frustrated and annoyed, while others were genuinely mystified by what we were getting at. Finally, after about twenty minutes, someone had a breakthrough. A woman stood up, beaming from ear to ear. "I'm responsible," she said. "Why?" we asked. "Because I *take* responsibility for the dollar bill being there." "Show us," we said. She walked to the front of the room and whipped the dollar bill out of the clothespin. She handed it to Gay, who returned it to her, by tucking it into her coat pocket. "People who take responsibility should be rewarded," he said. The participants, after a moment of stunned silence, erupted into applause.

An excited discussion ensued, with people understanding that they could take responsibility simply by taking it. You don't have to worry about the past or who did what: You can just take responsibility because you want to. Besides the dollar bill, there is another major payoff to this move: People feel truly secure only when they are taking this level of responsibility. When we are denying our connection with source in any way, we are basing our lives on a flimsy foundation. We are saying: The rest of the universe may work in a certain way, but I'm an exception. Taking this point of view can mean big trouble. Just ask the 97 percent of the prisoners surveyed in California who still did not see any connection between their actions and why they were in prison. Life was trying to teach them that they were no exception to how the rest of the universe worked. They still were not getting it.

LOVE AND RESPONSIBILITY IN THERAPY

With an understanding of how love and responsibility are best defined, let's enter the realm of therapy to find how they can be put to use. The first dialogue comes from our work with a young father, Jesse, who is dealing with a sensitive issue, one that only the courageous will speak about.

KATHLYN: What can we work on with you today?

JESSE: Well, it's something that I've hesitated to talk about—it's something I haven't even mentioned to my wife.

GAY: Yes?

JESSE (rubbing his eyes, looking shamefaced): Sometimes when I'm holding my daughter (his daughter is eight months old), maybe giving her a bottle while my wife is sleeping or something, I'll get sexually aroused. Just a twinge of an erection. But I definitely know it's a sexual feeling I'm having. I'm certainly not going to act on it in any way or anything, but it bothers me. I feel love for her, a tremendous amount, more than I've ever felt before. Then this thing will happen, and it bothers me a lot.

KATHLYN: What is it exactly that bothers you?

JESSE (*looking surprised*): Well, I think it would bother anybody.

KATHLYN: Maybe yes, maybe no. But what about it bothers *you*?

JESSE: I feel guilty. I feel as if my wife would be upset if I told her.

GAY: One thing to know, Jesse, is that those feelings are really pretty normal. The standard explanation for them is that we were all erotically involved with our mothers when we were being fed and being close to them. So now when you're with your daughter, feeding her and being close to her, it brings up those same feelings.

JESSE: Hunh. That's interesting. I don't know, though. . . .

KATHLYN: It sounds as if something else about it bothers you.

JESSE: Yeah, well, I guess the part that really bothers me is not wanting to tell my wife about it. Normally I'm pretty truthful with her. I can't really think of anything else that I'm not willing to tell her.

GAY: So it sounds like two different things—feeling guilty about the feelings themselves, and also feeling something wrong with not telling your wife about them.

JESSE: Yeah, as if it would drive her away if I told her.

GAY: Take a moment and tune in to that feeling you're experiencing right now.

(*Jesse looks down, adopting the shamefaced look again.*)

KATHLYN: Let yourself feel it wherever in your body you can.

JESSE: It's kind of a heavy feeling in my chest, as if I'm going to cry.

GAY: Just being with that—love that feeling.

JESSE (*surprised*): I'm not sure how to do that.

GAY: Think of someone you know for sure that you love. Like your daughter.

JESSE (*smiles*): Okay.

GAY: Now, love your feeling just like you love your daughter.

JESSE: That's hard.

GAY: What stops you?

JESSE: I don't love that part of me.

GAY: Think of how you love your daughter. Love yourself with that same feeling.

(*Jesse relaxes somewhat as he begins to love himself. Then a pained look flickers across his face.*)

KATHLYN: What just crossed your mind?

JESSE: I remember once being caught masturbating.

KATHLYN: By your mother?

JESSE (*nods*): She walked into my room without knocking. I was so humiliated. There was this secret part of me that had been violated.

GAY: What happened?

JESSE: Oh, she was about as freaked out as I was. I don't think it had registered on her that I was growing up. She was pretty uptight about sex, anyway. I don't remember what really happened, whether she punished me or anything.

GAY: But something about it reminds you of now.

JESSE: Yeah.

GAY: Tune in and feel the connection.

JESSE: Oh, okay. I get it. I don't think I ever really had the same kind of relationship with my mother after that. Before that day, she and I were like . . . buddies. Then we weren't anymore. (*Jesse starts to cry.*) I missed that.

KATHLYN: Sure. And now it sounds as if you're afraid you will lose that special something with your wife, if you let on about your sexual feelings with your daughter.

JESSE: Yeah, that's right. You know, it's funny, too. Lately I've been criticizing my wife a lot for withdrawing from me.

GAY: It's been looking like she's pulling away from you?

JESSE: And this fits in, doesn't it?

GAY: How do you see it fitting in?

JESSE: Well, I'm setting it up so that it looks as if *she's* pulling away, when it's really *me* that's the cause of it.

KATHLYN: So your old pattern with your mother is causing you to see your wife doing the same thing your mother did.

JESSE: That's amazing, isn't it?

GAY: Amazing that you can see it so clearly. Congratulations! Now, what's one action that's most important for you to take out of all this?

JESSE: Well, I think the big thing is to talk to my wife. Tell her about the whole thing—my feelings, the old pattern, everything.

KATHLYN: Sounds good to me. When?

JESSE (*laughing*): Not going to let me off the hook, are you? Tonight.

GAY: Great. Let us know what happens.

Here, Jesse dealt with both love and responsibility in a clear, straightforward way. We chose his example first because it was one in which neither the client nor the therapist hit any snags. But often the enterprise does not unfold quite so smoothly. Resistance comes up, or some transference reaction, or something that slows down the process. When resistance or transference occurs, we simply have to handle it. That's the way life—and therapy—works.

Notice the key moment when we helped Jesse invoke the love he felt for his daughter to assist him in loving something in himself. At first he didn't know how. He didn't like this aspect of himself, let alone love it. But he knew how to love his daughter, and he was able to use this fine feeling to help him go into the unknown.

Notice, too, the key moment when he takes responsibility. He had seen his wife as the one who was "withdrawing." It looked as if she were pulling away from him. But this was because he was seeing her actions from within his own projections. The moment he shifted to a position of responsibility, he could see that he was a rejection waiting to happen. This view of the way life works has a great deal of power. It leads us to think first of changing ourselves from within, using how the world treats us as feedback.

Let's listen in on another session in which love and responsibility helped the client make an important shift. We encountered some choppy water with Cindy before the sailing got smooth. Hers is probably a more typical therapy session than the one with Jesse. The following interchange took place about twenty minutes into the first session with Cindy, who is a teenage girl.

KATHLYN: Okay, so it sounds like you've been saying that your mother is being unreasonable, that she's on your case all the time, and this is causing you to be discouraged. Do you feel like that summarizes what you've told us so far?

CINDY: Yeah. I didn't exactly say discouraged, but that's close enough. I said I was depressed. That's what Dr. ——— (*her family doctor*) said I was, anyway.

GAY: You were sleeping a lot more than usual?

CINDY: Yeah.

GAY: And you weren't studying for school, I think you said.

CINDY: Yeah.

KATHLYN: I'd like you to take a moment and do something kind of different that we've found really helps people feel better. Tune in to the sensations you're feeling in your body right now.

CINDY: I don't know what you mean.

KATHLYN: Okay, turn your attention on what you're feeling down in your body.

CINDY: Like, think about it, or what?

GAY: More like, let yourself feel what you're feeling inside. Like, are you feeling that depressed or discouraged feeling right now?

CINDY: Kinda.

GAY: Okay, be with it for a moment—let yourself sit with it. Feel the sensations.

CINDY: Okay. Now what?

KATHLYN: Tell us about the sensations. What are they?

CINDY (*pause*): Like a heavy feeling.

GAY: I notice you touch your chest. Is that where you mostly feel it?

CINDY: Yeah.

GAY: Can you tell us more about it?

CINDY: Well, it's kind of a dull feeling. Like it would be hard to breathe. It makes me not want to do anything.

KATHLYN: So part of the sensation sounds like tiredness.

CINDY: Yeah, like I want to sleep and sleep. But when I wake up in the morning, it's still there.

GAY: So there's something else going besides needing sleep.

CINDY: I guess.

GAY: That's a really good start, Cindy. See if you can feel more of what is going on in there.

CINDY: You know, there's also like an irritated feeling in my arms.

KATHLYN: Under the skin?

CINDY: Uh, sort of. All along my arms, from the shoulders down into my fingers.

GAY: Hunh, that's interesting. So, dull heaviness in your chest and irritated feelings in your arms?

CINDY: Unh-hunh.

KATHLYN: Take a few deep breaths, Cindy, and notice what happens to the sensations when you breathe that way.

CINDY (*takes three big breaths*): I'm not sure.

KATHLYN: See if it makes them bigger or smaller.

CINDY: Oh. (*She takes a few more big breaths.*) My chest gets heavier—and yeah, the arm thing feels more irritated, too.

GAY: Good.

CINDY (*sarcastically*): Good, hunh?

GAY (*laughing sheepishly*): I don't mean good like that. I mean, that helps us understand what's going on.

CINDY: Oh, I see what you mean.

Usually, if a few deep breaths increase or decrease the sensation right away, this is a good sign that the symptom can be readily treated with our body-centered therapy techniques.

KATHLYN: Do you feel that people, your mother especially, treat you like you're still immature?

CINDY: Yeah, right.

KATHLYN: What if I had a way that you could get her to treat you like someone who is absolutely responsible, like a grown-up? Would you be interested in learning it?

CINDY: Sure, I guess so.

KATHLYN: Let's see—does that mean that you're "sure" or more like "I guess so?" The reason I ask is that I don't want to take the time to explain it to you unless you're really interested. It's too powerful an idea to play around with.

CINDY: Uh, okay. I mean—sure, I'd like to learn that.

KATHLYN: Okay, take total responsibility for this situation that's going on right now.

CINDY: What do you mean?

KATHLYN: Take complete responsibility for the conflict with your mother, and for all the feelings you're feeling. Claim full ownership of it.

CINDY (*gets mad*): Like it's all my fault?

GAY: Absolutely not!

CINDY: I'm confused. If it's not my fault, it's her fault, right?

GAY: Try looking at it a whole different way. Suppose you are a hundred percent responsible for it, and your mother is a hundred percent responsible, too.

CINDY: Jeez, I don't know.

KATHLYN: That gives you full power, and it gives your mother power, too. Then you can solve the problem like two grown-ups.

CINDY: Hunh, that's interesting.

GAY: So, why do you think you're creating this whole situation?

CINDY: God, I don't know.

GAY: That's a start. Keep thinking, keep looking.

CINDY: Well, I've been dreaming of my father some nights. My real father, I mean.

KATHLYN: Your real father is where?

CINDY: Well, he lives down in (*a southern state*). At least, I think he still does.

KATHLYN: You haven't seen him in a while?

CINDY (*snorts*): No.

GAY: Sounds like you're angry at him.

CINDY: Not really. I don't give a shit about him.

GAY: It sounds like you're angry and hurt, but you're trying to cover it up with not caring.

CINDY (*bursts into tears*): He hasn't even sent me a card on my birthday now for three years. Since I was eleven.

KATHLYN: That must really hurt.

CINDY (*nodding and crying*): Yeah.

GAY: Stay with that hurt down in your body. Breathe it on through.

(*Cindy cries for another minute or so.*)

CINDY: You think that's why I've been such a pain in the butt? Because I'm feelin' all this on the inside and haven't known what's bothering me?

KATHLYN: What do you think?

CINDY: I guess so. Kinda stupid, hunh?

GAY: Can you love yourself for all that right now?

CINDY: What do you mean?

GAY: Well, you were judging yourself pretty hard—saying it was kinda stupid—and that's not treating yourself very well. I'd like you to love yourself instead of being hard on yourself.

CINDY: I don't know what you mean.

GAY: Well, have you ever felt love?

CINDY: Uh, well, I love my mom. And I love my little sister, when she's not being a pain.

GAY: Tune in to that love you feel for your mom and your sister. Can you feel it in your body?

CINDY: Umm-humm. Kind of a warmth.

GAY: Yeah. Give that same feeling to yourself. Right now. Love yourself, even for being a pain.

CINDY: Wow. I never thought of that.

KATHLYN: You lit up. It looks good on you.

CINDY: Yeah, I feel good.

GAY: Great. Let's leave things there, then.

Teenagers are notorious for blaming their ills on other people. People have been complaining about this aspect of adolescent behavior since ancient times. But as Cindy's example indicates, it is possible even for adolescents to embrace the principles of love and responsibility. A colleague of ours once spent a week working intensively with a group of a hundred or so teenagers. When he was asked what he had learned from the experience, he said: "The good news is that they are human, too. The bad news is that we're all still teenagers inside at some level." He is right. Nearly all of us, no matter our age, are still working out the issues of love and responsibility.

In our own lives, we still confront these issues every day, even after working with them for so many years. There are still places in ourselves that we find difficult to love. There are still aspects of our lives where we still get stuck in learning how to take responsibility. Perhaps these issues will never recede fully. It may be that the best we can expect of ourselves is that we will continue to work with love and responsibility consciously, seeing life as an unfolding series of opportunities to grow. For the therapist, the only true security comes from seeing small increments of daily growth in ourselves as well as in our clients. If we can see life as a learning opportunity, with love and responsibility as major parts of the curriculum, the mere act of waking up in the morning can be an unparalleled thrill.

CHOOSING INTEGRITY

There are three things a therapist needs to be successful: integrity, effective strategies, and love. The strategies in this book are the most effective we have found in our twenty-plus years in the healing profession. But no strategies, no matter how powerful, will produce reliably good results unless the person who practices them is grounded in integrity and love. That is why, in our professional training programs, we spend as much time working on love and integrity as we do on practicing the techniques in the nine strategies. In fact, because the techniques are so powerful, the people who practice them must be masters in the area of love and integrity.

Neither love nor integrity is easy to understand, much less master. Therapists in general are much more capable of expressing tender love than tough love, we have found, although a balance of both is crucial to success in healing. Tender love can understand, accept, and embrace; tough love can draw lines, set limits, say no, and mean it. Before we can effectively express these qualities as therapists, we must be able to express them to ourselves. And as we all know, most of us have considerable trouble embracing ourselves completely while at the same time setting healthy limits within ourselves. Those of us who can say yes to ourselves often say no, and those of us who can readily say no to ourselves cannot say yes. But both yes and no are essential: The former opens the door, and the latter allows us to walk through it without bumping ourselves.

In therapy every week we are called upon to say yes. Clients, one after the other, come in with something that needs accepting. They may be struggling to embrace a feeling or to come to terms with something they hate about themselves. We help them say yes to it, to welcome it into the totality of themselves. We are also called upon to say no. We look them in the eye and say "Do not start drinking again" or "Do not kill yourself" or "Do not go back to that abusive relationship." Those therapists who cannot say yes, due to rigidity or too much unexamined territory in themselves, do not last long in the profession. Those who cannot say no, due to blurred boundaries within or a lack of discipline, burn out even more quickly. Only a harmonious balance of tough and tender love will do, both in our own evolution and in the successful practice of therapy.

As to integrity, many books have been written on the need for scrupulous ethics in the helping professions. Each year, Gay teaches a graduate course at the University of Colorado on ethics in the helping professions. In nearly two decades of teaching at the university level, he says he has seen the focus on ethics go from practically nonexistent to nearly obsessive—and for good reason. Malpractice insurance fees in the same time period have gone up twelve hundred percent, largely due to the alarming statistic that approximately one out of ten therapists engages in sex with clients. Sex, fraud, and breaches of confidentiality are currently the main areas in which suits are brought, but there are at least a dozen other ethical issues in which judgments have been made against therapists. Now we devote as much time to ethics in the profession as to teaching clinical technique, because we have found that it is not lack of technique that causes burnout of therapists and injuries to clients; it is lack of integrity.

Integrity has three main components, the first two of which are straightforward: We do what we say we will do. We do not do what we say we will not do. Both are important to therapists, so important that laws have now been established in most states requiring that therapists discuss certain issues in initial sessions. In Colorado, for example, a law now requires therapists to communicate several pieces of information to every new client: (1) that sexual intimacy is never appropriate and should be reported to the state board; (2) that a second opinion is always an option; (3) the fees and duration of therapy, if known; (4) the techniques that are likely to be used; (5) that information is legally confidential except in certain situations (danger to self or others, for example); and (6) that one can terminate therapy at any time.

None of those items are there just because they are good ideas. They have all been learned the hard way by therapists who were sued for breaching them. There is no doubt that subsequent refinements of the law will require further information-giving by therapists in initial sessions. Personally, we are highly in favor of these laws, because we have seen that they work. As this book is being written, we are treating several mental health professionals who have come for therapy because they felt themselves slipping toward an ethical breach. Five years ago, we had several professionals in therapy because they had already slipped. We believe that today's stringent laws are keeping therapists more on the ethical straight and narrow.

A third component of integrity may hold the key to the first two components. The original Latin root of the word *integrity* refers to a quality of wholeness or soundness. It is this meaning that we are speaking of here. Integrity is the extent to which we are aligned within ourselves. How well is the fit between our intentions and our actions? Are our feelings in agreement with our thoughts, so that there is a quality of unbroken wholeness in ourselves? To what extent do we tell the truth about what is going on inside ourselves? Without inner alignment, there will be no ultimate integrity.

Laws may scare people into behaving less unethically, but we would like to see all people taste a more fundamental ethical shift. Many of us know the negative side of ethics: When we mess up, we get punished. But fewer of us really know the positive side: When we have integrity, we get to feel more alive. Not keeping agreements costs aliveness. In our classes we certainly point out the unpleasant things that can happen to people who are unethical. In fact, we often have therapists who have breached various ethical standards and been punished for it come in for guest lectures. But we also take care to emphasize the heights of energy and creativity that integrity allows people to attain. Early on in our own marriage, for example, we found that not keeping agreements cost us intimacy. If one of us did not do what he or she had agreed to do (and it was usually something simple or trivial), we had to waste potential intimacy-time repairing the damage. Soon it became apparent that living in a state of integrity allowed us to be closer and to express more creativity together. As we came to value this type of aliveness, we found ourselves choosing integrity for its positive benefits rather than to escape the pain of breaking agreements.

We would like all human beings to taste the degree of aliveness that is possible when love, integrity, and effective techniques are applied as a harmonious whole. There is truly nothing like it we have experienced in the realm of healing. The payoff for clients is that they get to move as quickly as they are able toward their chosen goals. And we therapists get to experience the unique and priceless feeling of complete aliveness and service in each moment of our work.

As therapists and as members of the human family, we feel blessed and privileged to spend our hours and days in this exalted state, moving at the speed of life.

HOW WE BECAME
BODY-CENTERED THERAPISTS

There are many streams of body therapy, going back over several generations of development. Since our work springs from a unique combination of sources, we would like to give you a detailed description of where it comes from.

GAY'S STORY

I was originally trained as a traditional psychologist and only later gravitated toward a body-centered approach by noticing what worked and did not work with my clients. Many of my earliest learnings in body-centered therapy came through trial and error. Sometimes I wish I had been blessed with a mentor or had been trained formally from the beginning in some method of body therapy, but on the other hand I am glad I had the opportunity to start fresh without seeing the world through someone else's filter. I may have reinvented a few wheels along the way, but at least I can be sure now that what I do is based on experimentation and not on faith.

I may have been predestined toward breathwork and the body as a path to transcendence by two factors of my childhood. My mother was a heavy smoker and remained so throughout her life until her addiction finally killed her. I have vivid memories of her sitting at her desk, surrounded by a blue haze of Camel smoke, typing furiously to meet a deadline. She was a journalist and writer, and she often said that coffee and cigarettes were the two indispensable *accoutrements* of the author's trade. Smoking was a major means of rebellion against her mother, who lived next door her whole life. My grandmother absolutely hated tobacco, so naturally her husband and all her children smoked heavily. My grandfather puffed away on the foulest-smelling cigars imaginable, and when he was given the ultimatum of giving up cigars or moving out of my grandmother's bedroom, he chose cigars. He moved into a screened-in back porch (this was in the tropics of central Florida) and spent the last thirty years of his life sleeping by himself. I think it is an exquisite irony that a family of such committed smokers should produce a specialist in the use of breathing for healing in the next generation.

The second factor was my being fat as a child. My father died during my mother's pregnancy with me, causing her to stop eating and rely even more heavily on coffee and cigarettes. This event may have reset my hunger thermostat, because I was apparently insatiable as soon as I came out. By the end of my first year I was a butterball, and I stayed fat throughout my childhood. It became a huge issue for my mother, a symbol to her of her bad mothering. Perhaps I learned that, since my body could be a source of such difficulty, it could also be a vehicle of great pleasure. Interestingly, I never handled my weight problem until I moved away from home. Finally in my twenties I did some therapy work and changed my eating and exercise habits. I became one of those medical rarities, a person who lost a great deal of weight and kept it off. Now I exercise an hour a day, eat healthy food, and as a result my body is a source of streaming pleasure for me all the time.

A dramatic event when I was twenty-four gave me a flash of insight into the future of the approach that we describe in this book. I was walking along a snow-covered country road in New England in 1968. It was a winter of bitter discontent for me. I was still overweight, in a job I hated, and in a marriage that was a nearly constant battleground. The only two sources of happiness for me at the time were my relationship with my daughter, just then beginning to walk, and the new field I was beginning to study at the

University of New Hampshire. I had begun work on my master's degree in counseling on a part-time basis the year before. The focus on human potential in the program contrasted sharply with the stultifying sense of stuckness I felt in my daily life. My unconscious would soon arrange a learning experience for me that would change everything.

As I trudged along the road thinking about my seemingly overwhelming problems, I stepped on a patch of ice that was hidden by snow. My feet shot out from under me, and I landed on the back of my head (where today I can still feel the knot). In cartoons characters see stars when they are knocked out. I can testify personally that this actually happens. But I did not black out completely, or if I did it was not for long. The next thing I was aware of was being in a clear, serene open space in my mind and body, a state of consciousness I had never been in before. I could feel an enormous space of peace all around me. All the phenomena of my mind and body—my thoughts, feelings, and body tensions—occurred within this space, but the space was bigger and deeper than any of these things. It was my first taste since childhood of what in this book we call *essence*.

As I floated in this space, I could see down through all the layers of distortion in myself. I could feel the mass of my fat and the terribly tense muscles under it. I could see how I'd blocked off my creativity to conform to the strictures of the middle-class life and marriage I had entered two years or so before. I could even see why I had gotten married to the person who still seemed like such a stranger to me. When I met her, I was still in shock and grief over my grandmother's recent death. My grandmother had always been my main love connection in the world, and I had rushed headlong into the relationship to get away from the void my grandmother's death had left. No wonder the marriage wasn't working. I was placing a demand on her that she could never fulfill. I could see how on her part the issue was the same. She was attempting to deal with the loss of her father by projecting everything she never got from him onto me.

As I began to leave the peaceful essence-space and come back into the pain of my shivering body, I framed the question "Why?" Why had I created it all like this? In a flash I saw that I was unconsciously replaying my father's script. He had been fat, in an unhappy marriage, and died young. I was going down the same path. Then the experience was over, and I got painfully to my feet. But when I got up off the ground, I was a different person. Things unfolded seemingly magically from that moment. A week later, I was in a supermarket and saw two books that spoke to me. One was a diet book, *The Doctor's Quick Weight Loss Diet*, which basically offered a high-protein diet and that was famous for having you drink eight glasses of water a day. The other was a yoga book. There was a chapter on meditation in the book, and I read it that night around midnight. It suggested a meditation in which you close your eyes and simply say "om" quietly and repetitively for a half-hour. I gave it a try, and to my surprise I slipped effortlessly into the essence-space again and stayed there for about two hours. Finding that I could touch into the space in a friendly way was a happy discovery, and I vowed to do as much of my changing as possible in a gentle manner. A couple of years later, I would learn transcendental meditation and its advanced techniques, which I have practiced on a daily basis now for over twenty years. I now believe that if we can accustom ourselves to experiencing a daily contact with the deep self, we do not have to arrange accidents or other painful ways of getting in touch with it.

I also put the diet book to work immediately and lost something like twenty pounds the first month. In fact, I got sick from losing so much weight so quickly and had to back off a little bit. But I found that if I alternated the high-protein diet with eating only fruits and vegetables, I could stay healthy and lose weight steadily. I dropped about one hundred pounds over the next year, getting down to around two hundred, which is where I am today. (I'm six foot one.) Fruit and vegetables continue to be the mainstay of my diet, which helps me keep my weight down. I still have to watch it pretty carefully, though. When I go off on a workshop or speaking tour for a week, I can put on five or ten pounds eating the rich food my hosts often provide. I also have a thermostat problem working against me: My body temperature runs about two degrees below normal. The only time I get up to 98.6 is when I have a fever. Doctors I have consulted about this problem have tried out a range of thyroid medications on me without much success. One specialist theorized that the prenatal trauma I described earlier may have reset my metabolism lower, causing me to store fat more readily than others.

I will never know whether all these earlier events moved me toward developing a body-centered approach, but my definite beginning as a body-centered therapist had a specific moment in time that I can remember with a vivid clarity of detail. It was one of the most important formative events of my life, and one that informs every moment of my existence. In August 1974 I was living in a beautiful and secluded house that I had rented in Green Mountain Falls, Colorado. This tiny community is a twenty-minute drive from Colorado Springs, where I had moved earlier in the month to take a job as a professor of counseling at the University of Colorado. I had finished work on my Ph.D. at Stanford in 1973, then had gone to work for Stanford as a research psychologist. After a year the grant money for the position was looking shaky, so I looked for a tenure-track position at another university. I was tired of living in the Bay Area, and eager to find a less crowded place with better air. Although I enjoyed my years in California, I knew it wasn't home. The Bay Area is one of the most stimulating places on earth from an intellectual and cultural point of view, but I found the frantic atmosphere better suited to seeking than to finding. I knew somehow that I would not find the serenity and integration I was looking for there. One day in my office at Stanford I circled Montana, Colorado, and Chapel Hill, North Carolina, on a map and sent off letters to the universities there. Although I had never visited Montana or Colorado, there was something about them that drew me. I was contacted by the main branch of the University of Montana and the Colorado Springs branch of the University of Colorado, where I soon landed for an interview. As soon as I stepped off the plane in Colorado Springs, I knew I was home. The dry air, moderate climate, and glorious mountains sold me on it, even though I had some reservations about the university. The facilities were cramped, money was tight, and I sensed a lack of commitment to the kind of innovative research I wanted to conduct. Nevertheless, there were some creative people on the faculty with whom I resonated, and in July 1974 I signed on. It was definitely the right move, and I have been happy there ever since. I still think Colorado Springs is the best place in the world to live.

Although things looked copacetic on the outside, I was experiencing a sense of inner turmoil. As the day grew closer when I would teach my first class to the graduate students in the program, my cognitive dissonance increased to a nearly audible rattle. I knew the counseling and psychother-apy literature inside out, yet there was nothing I knew within myself that gave me an unshakable sense of how people change. The absence of a center of conviction inside me bothered me greatly. When I came to the university I had been treated somewhat like a rock star. They rolled out the red carpet for me, yet I had a hard time accepting the support because I knew that deep inside I did not really know anything worth knowing. One day just before I would begin teaching, I got up early and went for a walk among the towering spruce trees that surrounded my house. The day was sunny and crisp and had a special feel to it. After an hour's hike, I paused under a tree to rest. My mind was a ferment, uncomfortably so. It occurred to me that I might be able to calm my mind down by focusing on the questions I most wanted the answers to. I found myself hatching a unique (to me) question. I asked out loud, to no one but the hillside, the following question: What is the one thing I need to know or experience to bring about change in myself or other people? Another question followed: What is the one thing human beings are doing wrong that if we corrected would bring us happiness instead of conflict? The moment I formulated these questions my mind grew quiet. I realized that I had been seeking the answers to these questions outside myself for years, but it had never occurred to me to ask myself. I turned the question over simultaneously to my own cells and to any higher power that might be able to help me.

Then a remarkable and utterly unique event happened. From somewhere deep inside a benign roar of energy and light poured through my whole body. It came up from my legs and streamed up through my chest, arms, and head. It connected me with the universe from the ground up. I could feel that the energy inside me was identical to the energy that permeated the world outside. It was at once earth, sky, and me.

The energy was so strong that I had to focus all my attention on staying with it. I knew that if I resisted it, it would turn sour, but that if I opened up to it fully, it would feel blissful. I don't know how I knew that, but I tried it, and sure enough, it turned into waves of bliss. The cognitive idea that the energy was expressing was this: The one thing you've been doing wrong is resisting your experience. You resist your feelings, and this resistance puts you in a state of duality. Open up to what's already inside—what actually is—feel it deeply, and learn to love it. That was the message. It seemed so right that I did not hesitate. I opened up to all my feelings, everything I had contained inside me for years. I vibrated with all my fears, I surged with my anger and sobbed with my grief. Wave after wave of feeling washed over me, and I welcomed them all. My breathing changed to full, deep breaths that felt as if they were transporting oxygen to every cell of my body. After a half-hour or so of feeling emotions like fear and anger (although they did not feel unpleasant if I didn't resist them), the nature of the feelings changed. Now I felt radiant waves of pleasure coursing through the cells of my body. I moved around under the trees, doing a kind of slow dance of expressive body movements that the energy seemed to require. After another period of time—perhaps a half-hour—the experience began to fade, and I, a little tired but feeling plugged into the main socket of the universe, walked back home. Always the writer, I sat down to put the experience on paper. It came to fifty-three typed pages.

The very next day, I tried out the new principles on a therapy client. The wife of a faculty member had asked me for help with a problem she was struggling with. It would become my first session of body-centered therapy, although I did not have the words then to call it that. She had been feeling some fears that would not go away, no matter how she tried to talk herself out of them. She had been in several types of therapy over the years, most recently transactional analysis, but nothing she had tried had cleared away her fear. I listened to her story, then pointed out that all her strategies for dealing with the fear were based on resistance.

"You're trying to get away from what you are feeling," I said. "The attempt to distance yourself from it is splitting you in two." Based on what I had learned out under the trees the day before, I urged her to try something different.

"Just be with the fear," I said. "Let's sit with it and feel the sensations." This idea is what we now call "presencing," the first of the nine strategies that we think are fundamental to body-centered therapy. She was puzzled at this new (to her) idea and asked me how to do it. I made up an instruction: "Let your attention rest on the fear. Feel the sensations instead of trying to make them go away." She closed her eyes and turned her attention inward. In a few seconds her expression changed to one of rapt interest. Stress lines disappeared from her face, and her fists unclenched. But then something striking happened. Her breath shifted from high in her chest to deep down in her belly. I remembered how my breathing had changed the day before. I invited her to let her attention include her breathing, letting the breathing change and play as it wished. "Don't resist how your breathing wants to change" is how I put it.

Her breath began to come in deep gulps. After a few breaths it began to accelerate, sounding like a freight-train picking up speed. I was a little scared, but it seemed that some organic and natural process was taking place, so I went with it. Her breathing continued to escalate, and she raised her arms up toward the ceiling. Her eyes opened wide with a faraway look, as if she were in the grip of some larger force. In a moment her breathing peaked and began to slow down. The change in her face was striking. Gone were the worry lines, replaced now with a radiant serenity. "I feel great," she said. "What happened?"

I mumbled some explanation, mainly reassuring her (and me) that this was an entirely natural and good-for-you experience. She spontaneously thought of some creative solutions to the problems she had brought in, and after a little planning on how to implement a few practical changes, she left happily. A phone call a few days later brought the even better news that the fears had disappeared completely. I was pleased and grateful but not really surprised. I knew in every cell of my body that if she opened up and allowed herself to participate fully with what was inside her, she would experience release and freedom. Plus, I could see the change on her face when she made the decision to "be with" rather than resist her fear. That is the best evidence a therapist can have. Even today, after witnessing many thousands of profound and rapid changes, I still feel moved by what happened in that first session.

Over the next two years, I continued to explore the potential of breathing in therapy by noticing my clients' breathing patterns as I worked with them. I discovered the most common basic flaws in the breathing process. I found that some people are breath-holders. When feelings come up, they restrict their breathing in an attempt to control their emotions. Other people are upside-down breathers. Healthy breathing swells the relaxed abdomen on the in-breath. Upside-down breathers tighten their stomach muscles on the in-breath, pushing their breath high up into the chest. This pattern is seen most dramatically in asthma patients, but many people have a milder version of the same thing. Other people are chronic shallow breathers. They never seem to take a full breath, requiring them to catch up with a big sigh now and then.

I soon learned that breathing can accomplish two main things in therapy. If clients were rattled with anxiety and in need of calming, I could reliably help them produce a state of ease in themselves through a specific move. I would show them where to breathe (in the belly, as opposed to the chest), and I would assist them in slowing down their breathing to between eight and twelve breaths a minute. If we could accomplish these two things, it worked every time. This instruction also worked well with clients who were depressed. The slow, deep breathing in the abdomen would lighten depression sometimes in minutes and would give them more energy. I put a great deal of attention in those early years into finding out how to teach people to breathe correctly. This attention to breathing is still a mainstay of our approach.

The second use I found for breathing was in *catharsis*, a word derived from the Greek for "to cleanse." The simple process I developed for cathartic breathing was to invite the client to speed up the breath instead of slowing it down. For example, if the person were holding the breath to control sadness, I would have him or her speed up the breath in order to breathe through the feeling. If I were artful in my application (and blessed with a willing client), the held-in emotion would come to the surface. The client would cry or get angry and resolution of the roiled emotion would occur quite rapidly, bringing about a state of serenity.

Along about this time I saw a film of the late gestalt therapist Fritz Perls. The thing that caught my eye about his work was how he would cut underneath the verbal level of his client's conversation by making observations about body language. He would say, "Look at the way you're picking at your fingernail," or "Tap, tap, tap goes her foot," while his client was talking about something abstract. He often did it in a needling way that got the client angry at him, but at least it got more energy moving in the session. I began to look at body language seriously and was immediately rewarded for doing so. I saw that a client would often signal with his or her body exactly where the issue was being experienced. An eye twitch would signal sadness, for example, even when the client was doing his best to hide it. A hand would stray toward the belly when the client was scared.

At the time there were popular books on body language that made ridiculous generalizations. They said things like if a person crosses his legs a certain way, it means one thing, while if they are crossed at the ankles, it means something else. I had turned my back on the whole subject because of these books, but now I had to modify my opinions considerably. There *was* meaning to movement patterns, and there were even generalizations one could make, but one had to pay close attention to the idiosyncratic nature of the body language. I found myself using body-language observations constantly—always being careful not to interpret them but to use them as ways of bringing clients into touch with their hidden feelings.

After a year or two of experimenting on my own, I began to look around at other systems of body therapy. I had missed out on all the emerging body therapies of the sixties like rolfing and bioenergetics, partly because I was in a traditional graduate program at University of New Hampshire and Stanford. Even had I wanted to experience them, however, it would have been difficult on my bare-bones student budget. After I took my professor job at Colorado, I still had very little money to spend on personal growth, having exited Stanford with some hefty student loans. But reading is free, so I decided to catch up by reading everything I could find on the subject. I amassed some two hundred books, thanks to the good people at the university library who scouted out obscure texts through interlibrary loan from as far away as Scotland. I read the body therapy literature thoroughly, partly to keep from reinventing the wheel and partly to gain support for my own emerging point of view. The first thing I learned was that body-centered therapists are among the world's worst writers. Gifted therapists like Moshe Feldenkrais, Wilhelm Reich, Ida Rolf, and John Pierrakos turned out writings that were tantalizing but sketchy and painful to read. Reich was simultaneously the most brilliant and the worst writer. In one page he could go from a brilliant clinical insight to a rant that sounded like a paranoid streetcorner prophet. After reading the literature, I had to conclude that most of the good stuff in the field had been transmitted through the oral tradition.

So I made a point of going to meet all the pioneers I could track down in order to learn from their oral traditions. Here is where I struck gold. My mind happens to be very good at extracting principles from direct observations. I can watch what somebody is doing and explain the principle readily. As I spent time with a number of body-oriented therapists, I watched them carefully and organized what they were doing into cogent principles. Several times I had the great pleasure of saying to someone like Alexander Lowen, "Let me check this out with you. I looks like the theory behind what you are doing is . . ." and having him reply, "Yes, I never really thought about it like that, but that's exactly what I'm trying to do." I learned this way from films of some of the masters like Fritz Perls, with whom I had only had fleeting "live" contacts, and from living masters such as John Pierrakos, Lowen, and Virginia Satir.

While I was reading the literature and visiting all the gifted therapists I could find, I explored the world of my own body. My main personal practice in those days was to work with my breath. I spent hours on the floor, breathing my way through layers of feelings. I breathed into the living hell of loneliness, anger, and jealousy, and I breathed myself into exalted states of radiant ecstasy. I also watched dozens of babies breathing, so I could find out about breathing from the ground up. I used breathing with my clients in practically every session. My main technique was to have them breathe into the place in their bodies where they could feel the sensations of their feelings. Sometimes this process would last only a few breaths, while at other times it would lead them to long periods of engagement with their breath.

I grew fascinated with the work of Wilhelm Reich. I devoured his opus, which consisted of a dozen or so books, some hard to find. He pioneered the use of breathing in therapy, at least in this century. Amazingly enough, he did it back in the 1920s, in a much more conservative climate. He also made a clinical observation that would change the way therapy is practiced, but he is given little or no credit for it. Basically, he said that we should watch the client's body language carefully, because it is not *what* a person is saying that is important, it is *how* he or she is saying it. For example, if the client says, "Sorry I'm late," with a sheepish grin, it is the sheepish grin that we should note and feed back to the client. Nowadays all therapists worth their salt do this as a matter of course, but few may realize that at one time this move was considered so radical that it provoked a rift between Freud and Reich. Freud's point of view was that if you start messing around with process instead of content, you are playing with fire. Better to keep it safe and slow. This point of view has made orthodox Freudian psychoanalysis into a museum piece today.

To work on my own body, I got rolfed, took yoga classes, joined African dance groups, and did dance therapy work. For several years in the mid 1970s I lived in a tiny apartment and drove a VW bug because all my extra money was going into personal growth activities. Meanwhile I continued to explore my own breathing. After a while I began to feel I could go only so far with working on my breathing by myself, so I asked around and found a Reichian therapist who was supposed to be one of the best. I called her for an appointment and showed up for my first session. It is worth recounting in detail.

Dr. Miller was a woman in her late thirties. At first I was put off by her manner, which alternated between brusqueness and oversolicitude. One moment she would say something like "You poor dear," then the next moment she would switch to "How could you be such a jerk?" I still don't know if that was a technique she used to bring up emotions in her clients, or if it was a character trait in her. I would guess the latter, because her own personal life appeared to be a bit of a disaster.

After I described my goals, she invited me to lie down on a thick foam mat. She told me to take deep breaths through my open mouth. As I breathed, she would tap on various places on my body. She tapped and I breathed. After about twenty minutes I was beginning to feel tingling in my arms and legs from all the breathing. She directed her touch to my solar plexus, stroking it lightly (I had my shirt off) as I breathed. Suddenly I felt a wave of energy similar to the one that precedes an orgasm, though this one did not have a sexual feel to it. It was just pure energy. "Let some sound out," she suggested. I opened my mouth and began to cry out. Suddenly the sound and the breath took me over, and I began to wail uncontrollably. Each wave of energy rolled through my body, bringing with it a scream. I had no idea what I was screaming about because there were no thoughts connected with it. It was definitely a peculiar feeling, because it felt as if my body were doing it on its own, without any conscious participation by me. After a few minutes the wailing and the energy abruptly ceased. I lay on the mat feeling pleasantly spent. She let me rest there for ten minutes or so, then had me stand up. We finished the session face to face, making eye contact.

My work with Dr. Miller was brief because she soon moved to another part of the country. I later heard that she had moved to India to become a devotee of the famed Rolls-Royce-owner and guru Rajneesh. I'll never forget that first session, though, because nothing like it ever happened again. I sought out several other Reichians and bioenergetics practitioners over a year or two in the mid 1970s, taking workshops and trainings from people like John Pierrakos, who had once been in therapy with Reich himself. My experiences with second-generation Reichians convinced me that Reich was one of the great creative pioneers in our field. It is astonishing to me that Reich is so disregarded by the mainstream. Part of this is due to fears of the body on the part of the mainstream, but part must be attributed to Reich himself. He had a knack for offending people, coupled with a paranoid streak that I have seen in other Reichians. It was inevitable that he would come to grief, given his massive blind spots of character. Nowadays, the orthodox Reichian therapy movement is like a cult, full of splits, mutual denunciations, shunnings, and defensive true believers. One year back in the seventies there were only two Reichian therapy books published in this country. One of them consisted mostly of a scathing attack on the other one. If this sounds more like a religion than a therapy approach to you, we agree on our assessment. It is unfortunate that a powerful and potentially useful approach was shackled by adherents who were more committed to squabbling than to bringing out Reich's genius to the profession and the public.

I started out with a naive delusion that someone who is a great therapist will also have a radiantly happy personal life and a high degree of personal integrity. A few visits with living therapy masters soon denuded me of this point of view. I feel sad as I write this, remembering Virginia Satir, surely one of the most loving and gifted of the therapists who practiced in my time. Yet at the same time she never was able to accept love in the same way she gave it, and her death from cancer was lonelier than I wish it had been. It was confusing to see someone like Moshe Feldenkrais do virtual magic on a client, then spend the next few hours in a peevish or even raging tirade at some associate who had asked what Feldenkrais considered a stupid question. The integrity issue was worse. Many if not most of the genius therapists whom I observed in the 1970s had major blind spots of integrity. They perpetrated money scams, slept with their clients and students, and in one case shot an associate in the heat of an argument. When I would question the disciples of a particular therapist about such lapses, I would typically encounter a troublesome point of view: "Sure, he's a thief—or a dirty old man or an alcoholic—"but you have to get beyond all that to see the genius." My question was: Why should we have to get beyond all that? If the system really works, should it not be anchored in integrity? This era is one in which we ought to expect that our leaders walk their talk. That is why in our professional trainings we spend one-third of our time dealing with integrity, making sure our students know that the powerful techniques of body-centered therapy must be grounded in a sense of deep personal responsibility.

I encountered another breathing practice in 1975 that would soon become popular in New Age circles. The Association for Humanistic Psychology had its annual meeting in Colorado that year, and I went up to it to give a lecture and workshop on the approach I was developing. It was a "hot" meeting, full of interesting people doing creative things. Werner Erhard was there, talking about his then-new program, est, along with other innovators such as Ida Rolf, Rollo May, and Virginia Satir. There was a man about my age giving a lecture on something called rebirthing. I had never heard of it before, but somebody told me it involved breathing and came from California, so I would no doubt be interested! I stood in the back of the room and listened to part of Leonard Orr's lecture. He had a strange style of communicating, punctuating his utterances with deep, audible sighs, but what he was saying was of great interest to me. He said he had discovered rebirthing while breathing in his bathtub. His breathing had taken him back through reliving his birth, which had a strong effect on his present life. His background was as a businessman, not a therapist, but his insights were quite resonant with my own.

Shortly thereafter I heard he was staying at the house of a friend of mine near Colorado Springs. I went out to meet him and watch him teach a class on rebirthing. I had one individual session and two sessions in a group setting. The sessions felt good but did not bring up any birth material into my consciousness. That was the only contact I had with rebirthing. While my experiences were pleasant but not profound, others said they had birth experiences and other strong energy experiences that made it worthwhile.

A little later I met another man who was working with breathing. Stanislav Grof, who had administered thousands of therapeutic LSD sessions, had apparently also become interested in the transformative powers of breathing in the 1970s. Several people came to the breath workshops I was then conducting and told me that they had taken workshops from Grof in which he used deep breathing. Stan and I compared notes at several conferences where we were both speaking. It was his opinion that breathing is potentially as powerful as LSD for opening the consciousness. In addition to having people deep-breathe for two hours or so, he used two technologies that he felt made for a deeper experience of the breathwork. One was extremely loud music during the breathing, and the other was paper-and-crayon drawing after sessions. I told him that we didn't use loud music—preferring softer "space" music—and that we used African dance and expressive movement at the end of sessions to help people integrate and get grounded. In addition, I told him that we generally only had people breathe for about an hour because longer sessions, while stimulating, were harder to integrate into daily life. Nowadays, with nearly twenty years of experience in conducting breathwork sessions, we still feel that an hour of breathing is enough. We get calls at our institute from people who have just taken a weekend workshop in rebirthing or other form of breathwork, and who are feeling unsettled as a result. The trouble is usually too much deep breathing. It is easy to get people very high by having them deep-breathe for a few hours straight, but it is not so easy to get them integrated again afterward. I greatly admire Grof's written work, especially his two books on the LSD research, but since I have not experienced or witnessed any of his breathing work, I cannot say anything about it from personal experience.

Next to experimenting in and with my own body, I have learned the most from the thousands of clients with whom I've worked. I learn best through observation and direct practice, so it is to them that I really owe my deepest debt of gratitude. I spent much of the 1980s refining our approach by watching what worked and did not work with my clients. It was not until we had gathered data on several thousand participants in body-centered therapy, both in groups and in individual sessions, that we began to write this book, though the ideas in it have been in formulation for nearly twenty years.

At one time I thought that breathing was the ultimate tool for body-centered therapy, but then I met Kathlyn in 1980. Her nurturing presence, combined with an incredible sensitivity to the meaning of movement, produced remarkable transformations in the people she worked with. I learned by watching her work that movement could be as powerful an agent for change as breathing.

KATHLYN'S STORY

Like Gay, I may have been destined early to become a body-centered therapist. Several years ago my mother gave me my baby book as a keepsake. I laughed when I read the first entry: "Kathy loves to brush her hair and to pull herself up in her crib and dance." I suppose I could have become a hairdresser, but I'm glad my subsequent choices supported the exploration of movement. As a child I was fascinated by people's behavior. The infinite diversity of rhythm and posture, impulse and tension, were a Morse code to a mystery that intrigued me. There seemed to be some key to how life works in the silences between words, the nuances of expression. I often wondered, "Why is his or her expression so different from the words?" I would notice that when the popular kid tossed her head, five or six others followed, almost like dominoes falling. I particularly studied the contrasts between what people said and what they did. I noticed that people were often unaware of their mannerisms, tics, and characteristic responses. In celebration of this rich parade, my younger brother and I used to entertain my mother with elaborate imitations of her friends and sometimes, when we felt particularly bold, her own sighs and exasperated exclamations. I was most interested in what was under the surface, in the meaning of it all. It seems pretty austere for a nine-year-old, but at that age I had decided that

I would be free of the unconscious patterns I could see being passed down through grandmother and mother, from television and schoolmates. Although I didn't use those words, I had decided to become awake to life and the richness of meaning and expression.

I realize now that the games I constructed, especially with my best friend Linda, were often designed to explore other dimensions of awareness. For example, in a game that we played for an entire summer, one of us would sit in the room with eyes closed while the other hid very, very quietly. Then with eyes still closed, we guessed the other's location. Part of the challenge was to see how quickly we could locate each other. We would also call each other on the phone and first ask, "Were you thinking about talking to me?" Often we'd be delighted to find the answer was yes. Linda was a genius mime, and another amusement was to guess what teacher or classmate she was imitating. She would challenge me to stretch beyond my rather shy manner and to be more daring, to take a walk into a strut, to make a whole range of mouth sounds that would send us both rolling on the floor.

Like many little girls, I longed to defy gravity through the medium of ballet. Alas—or fortunately—I was blessed with a sturdy (sometimes "pleasantly plump") body that was very attached to the ground, knock-knees that periodically dislocated and unceremoniously dumped me, and feet that needed special shoes for many years. Since I loved to dance, I began looking for other ways to express that joy of motion. I took tap and folk dance as well as dance classes in school, and I had a wonderful teacher in high school who awakened for me the creative flow between meaning and movement. The height of my school dance career was the piece I called "The Sneeze."

My formal training as a movement therapist began when I met Joan Chodorow (then Smallwood) in the late 1960s through the providential incident I describe in chapter 11. Joan had moved from the world of dance into dance therapy through extensive work with Trudi Schoop and Mary Whitehouse, two of the dance therapy pioneers. Today Joan is also a Jungian analyst. I knew when I saw my first dance therapy session that this was my life work, and I turned my world upside down to accommodate that vision. I veered away from English literature and an imagined future as a professor to create an independent undergraduate major, kinetic emotional communication. Through this major I felt that I could encompass all the areas of my interest: transformation through movement. I structured my days to be absent from my baby son as little as possible while in school, and I got very organized.

When I turned in my senior thesis, an exploration of movement therapy from several psychological viewpoints, Joan showed it to her boss. I was invited to the clinic where Joan worked, a genuine therapeutic community in the experimental style of the 1960s. Patients ran their own halfway house, attended staff meetings where they had access to their charts, and participated in art, dance, and poetry therapy along with more traditional individual and group therapy. This open-door policy reflected the height of the liberal social swing of the time as well as the "create as you go" chaos of breaking through old paradigms. Instead of giving medications, staff members would be with patients twenty-four hours a day during psychotic episodes. New furniture needed to be bought for the dining room of the halfway house once after one patient raged through. Most often, though, patients moved quickly through seemingly intractable conditions in this beautiful and open setting.

Most wonderfully this clinic had an actual movement studio with wooden floors, Orff Shulwerk instruments, and some of the first video equipment. After several weeks at staff meetings I was invited to assist in the day treatment program. Then the weekly dance therapy group, some individual patients, and hospital visits were added. After a month or two I realized with some fear and excitement that I was in an apprenticeship as Joan's first student. This was 1969–70.

At that time no graduate programs offered movement therapy degrees, although the field had been started in the 1940s. Now there are several M.A. programs with accredited curricula and established sequences of learning. There are even competing schools of thought about proper dance therapy behavior and how much the therapist should talk or not talk during a session. Then we were creating the process for transfering this elusive skill from teacher to student.

Verbal therapy requires a complex set of skills but makes few demands on the body. In movement therapy the whole body is the medium of relationship. The therapist communicates and invites exploration from the intelligence and partipation of mind *and* movement. I found that this was much more complicated than the *concept* of healing by moving together. My own unfinished feelings would come up, areas of my body that I hadn't owned and internal conflicts that I tended to get mixed up with patients' issues. Supervision, continued classes in movement skills, and staff meetings helped my own maturation over time, but for several years I would have regular episodes of "I'm going to quit and become a secretary where I'll know what I'm doing."

I learned the alphabet of movement possibility from Joan's example and guidance. This foundation included the shapes and qualities that healthy bodies could express, as well as the developmental sequence that was optimal. Dance therapy group sessions would often be focused on an exploration of some movement dynamic, such as expanding and contracting or making a moving machine together. Sometimes Joan would teach a folk dance step that everyone could do, or hand out simple instruments for us to play while we moved. Sharing these basic rhythms and shapes bonded new patients very quickly and gave some safe structure to the often chaotic inner world that the patients experienced.

Even twenty years ago the influence of the unconscious, the world of dreams and images, had great impact on Joan's therapy style. If a patient brought a dream to the group, we would explore the images and tones in movement, becoming clouds and guns, houses and roaring rivers. Over and over, I would see that a breakthrough in verbal therapy had a movement prelude. I began to be able to predict shifts in patients' progress from their participation in movement. From Joan's colleagues and the months of participation in various movement therapy experiences, I began to discern movement that is therapeutic and socializing from movement that is transformative. Transformative movement has something to do with moving from feeling rather than from form. It has to do with an electric match between inner experience and expression. Healing is made visible in this authenticity. When this kind of movement occurred, everyone recognized its power and was moved by the coherence of the movement.

Patients who connected this way in movement also made connections in their lives very quickly. I began to study the conditions that allowed this movement magic to occur, because it wasn't predictable and didn't seem to follow a recipe. Whenever I would *try* to make it occur, I would fail miserably and publicly. The patients, who had keen antennae for manipulation and insecurity, would immediately mirror and challenge my moves. I used to have recipe cards of various movement games and structures I could use if I ran out of ideas. When I finally let go of having to know what to do and began to participate as another real human being, the patients began to trust this upstart young pipsqueak more and dared to open up their own feelings, needs, and truth. Sessions became more improvisational, more exploratory. From repeated leaps into the unknown I began to see the core dynamic more easily, the important gesture that might open a door to a past wound or memory.

Mary Whitehouse was my mentor and the source of my greatest inspiration in my early development. Although I worked with many fine movement therapists and read the literature thoroughly, Mary's work spoke most deeply to me. She was a legend on the West Coast, and her presence and writings gave voice to the power of moving and inspired a number of therapists. Multiple sclerosis had made it impossible for Mary to practice for several years, so I did not hear much from her until I moved to the Bay Area in 1975. I discovered that not only had Mary moved to San Francisco, she was in remission and teaching again. For three years I met with Mary as student, then as friend, to continue deepening my understanding of transformative movement. In the last years of Mary's life she was very interested in the connection between spirit and movement, in the creative flow toward wholeness built on a lifetime of Jungian theory and movement pioneering. Because her physical movement was often unpredictable, Mary's ability to witness and reflect to the mover was heightened. In our times together I would sometimes bring a topic or dream. Sometimes I would move, and then we would talk.

In my first months of trekking up the steep San Francisco hill and into her intimate and fragrant apartment, I could see the roots of much of my work with Joan. She would sometimes mention the early days of shifting from dance classes to this new phenomenon of movement therapy. In these explorations I found that the authentic movement impulse, the impulse that comes from feeling, needs to be invited anew each session, with each client and in myself. Mary explained once, "I used to go so slowly and so cautiously and a step at a time—for a different reason in the old days than now. In the old days it was so shocking, and so new and people were so afraid of it. . . . Now you have to take them back and do the same thing because they assume they can do it." Mary made a clear distinction from the authentic exploration of self and the traditional medical model. In one of our meetings she said, "The respect for the spiritual meaning which can *never* be turned into medical theory . . . comes down to as simple a thing as my being able to say to them [a college class] 'Look, the world is not made of what's *wrong*. It's made up of what's *right*, and it's the experience of what's available and what's right and what can be let out that's *just* as important as the other half. Because the medical model emphasizes what's wrong and turns it into therapy. There's some other process involved.' "

Respect for the individual's unique journey is a legacy from Mary, who worked in a studio rather than in a hospital and often with individuals in one-on-one sessions. Today I find myself totally convinced that each person has all the resources for healing inside, based on testing out Mary's emphasis on facilitating "what's right."

The learnings I gained from being with Mary form the basis of my work today. The quality of Mary's presence alone was very powerful, unencumbered by expectations and assumptions. In her easy, actively waiting presence I discovered my inner self much more quickly than I had ever imagined. She was always ready to see the truth, just what was happening under the masks. Nothing true offended her. Authenticity delighted her, and she would often clap her hands and exclaim, "Oh! Oh!" or chortle. One of her favorite phrases was "No praise, no blame." Just what's so. She would say, for example, "You don't have to know. You just have to be true to where you are." Mary originated what is known as authentic movement. Many later movement therapists have taken the germ of moving from the internal impulse and built various structures on that base. Mary was most interested in the mover's experience. I think she was increasingly aware toward the end of her life of the power of the witness to create a safe and open structure for the mover to step into the unknown. Like many pioneers, however, she was immersed in doing the work. Others analyzed it and sometimes formed organizations around it. After one of her last public appearances, at the Seattle American Dance Therapy Association conference, she said that given the current standards of practice, she wouldn't qualify as a dance therapist. She was most interested in the mystery of movement. As she said on one occasion in 1978:

> It seems to me that . . . movement is in itself something
> that will help people change. . . . But in addition to finding
> out how and what and why and doing all the moves, there has
> to be some way of including the experience of people
> working. . . . That's what I care about—some shocking
> realization that you will never have control over it. . . . The
> whole point of it is not having control over it. You may be
> comfortable one day and not the next. You may think you
> know what you're doing one day and not the next. You're not
> a good practitioner if you can't carry both sides.

A skilled reflector, Mary could observe a movement sequence exactly and relate it to last session's incomplete gesture and a particular image or quote from Jung. She was not afraid to bring her own inner experience into the session in the form of images or quotes from a recent book. She made little distinction about whose material was emerging, and I think this lack of boundaries, although helpful in therapy, was the source of many projections and relationship issues in her life. And the tremendous value of including everything, letting everything in the session be of service, has empowered my own trust in the *process* to do the work. My skills are not magic, but the process of letting go and following what wants to happen is magic.

Mary gave infinite permission to allow. "Are you willing?" was a phrase she often used. From her example I learned to wait for the impulse to move that came from underneath muscular tension and underneath the cognitive critic's agenda. I learned to invite the voice of my essence and to follow it. I got comfortable with silences as a dynamic gathering process. I found myself asking, as Mary did, What wants to happen here? How does this finger want to move? What is the impulse in my stomach just now? Mary had developed intuition to a high art and knew from her Jungian background that the hunch often comes from the periphery. She taught me to widen my focus to catch the small gesture, the quick glance, the mover's shift at the edge of my vision. That was where the action was, the opening to the unconscious. In almost every session today I rely on the germ of truth in the nuances of movement, knowing that the smallest impulse contains the whole story.

Gay and Kathlyn Hendricks offer professional trainings, tapes, and videos that complement the material in this book. If you would like a catalog and schedule of upcoming trainings, write or call

The Hendricks Institute
P.O. Box 994
Colorado Springs, Colorado 80901

telephone: (719) 632–0772